POCKET ENCYCLOPEDIA

GARDENING

POCKET ENCYCLOPEDIA

GARDENING

JENNY PLUCKNETT

Abbeydale Press

This edition printed in 2009

© 2000 Bookmart Limited

All rights reserved.

ISBN: 978-1-86147-304-2

1 3 5 7 9 10 8 6 4 2

Published by Abbeydale Press,
an imprint of Bookmart Limited,
Registered number 2372865,
Trading as Bookmart Limited,
Blaby Road, Wigston, Leicester,
LE18 4SE, England

Originally published in 1999
by Bookmart Ltd as
The Small Garden

Printed in Thailand

CONTENTS

How to use this book 6

CHAPTER 1
Working out your own design 9
Making a plan to scale 10
Designing the garden 12

CHAPTER 2
Designs for specific shapes and areas 15
Courtyard garden 16
Square garden 20
Short, wide garden 24
Long, narrow garden 28
Split-level garden 32
Paved town garden 36
Small front garden 40
Roof garden 44

CHAPTER 3
Designs for problem positions 49
Garden on a new site 50
Shady spot 54
Windy location 58
Overlooked garden 62
Concrete garden 66
Steeply sloping land 70

CHAPTER 4
Designs with special features in mind 75
Low-maintenance garden 76
Children's garden 80

Garden with a view	84
With the elderly in mind	88
Integrating a swimming pool	92
Wildlife garden	96

CHAPTER 5
Groundwork	101
Identifying your soil	102
Improving soil condition	104
Garden compost	106
Checking acid or alkaline levels	108
Watering	110
Electricity in the garden	112

CHAPTER 6
Form and shape	115
Ground surfaces	116
Paths, steps and edgings	118
Walls and screens	120
Fences	122
Hedges	124

Introducing water	126
Moving water	128
Plant frameworks	130
Arches, pergolas and arbours	132
Containers	134
Ornamental extras	136
Children's play space	138
Garden furniture	140
Barbecues	142
Lighting	144

CHAPTER 7
Key plants	147
Shrubs	148
Deciduous trees	150
Evergreen trees	152
Architectural plants	154
Grey and silver foliage plants	156
Gold and bright green foliage plants	158
Vigorous background climbers	160

CHAPTER 8
Plants for colour and decorative detail	163
Bulbs for all seasons	164
Colourful climbers	166
Winter colour	168
Long-season flowers	170
Temporary colour	172
Ground cover	174
Plants for scent	176
Water plants	178
Herbs and decorative vegetables	180

CHAPTER 9
Plants for problem areas	183
Plants for shade	184
Plants for full sun	186
Plants for wind and poor soil	188
Index	190
Acknowledgements	192

HOW TO USE THIS BOOK

For ease of use this book is divided into two main parts.

CHAPTERS 1–4 (pages 9–99)

This section provides both the inspiration and the know-how to help you design your garden, whatever its shape or situation. Top garden designers show how, with flair and ingenuity, they have dealt with some of the problems you may experience along the way.

Chapter 1 contains the background information to help you measure your garden accurately and draw up a plan. The next three chapters show how garden designers have tackled the designing of small gardens of every shape and in every situation so that you can pick out those that most closely relate to your particular plot. Gardens with a specific theme are also covered.

For each garden there is a problem solver box which shows the main problems that were encountered and how they were solved. In each case there is one plan which shows the basic design used for the garden and a second to highlight the planting. The following pages show photographs of the finished garden and close-ups of some of the plants it contains.

CHAPTERS 5–9 (pages 101–189)

This section supplies the nuts and bolts for turning the design into reality on the ground.

Chapter 5 shows how to identify the type of soil you have and what you can do to improve its condition. There are lots of tips on the best way to water plants so that they develop strong, deep root systems as well as information on installing garden lighting and power.

Chapter 6 shows the choices available for use in creating the ground surfaces and structures that form the garden's main design shapes. It also covers the ornamental extras like water features, arches and pergolas, garden furniture, containers and lighting for both safety and security as well as for decorative effect.

The final three chapters cover some of the huge range of plants available for every situation, with both descriptive information and practical planting details.

Throughout the book there are illustrated tips on both practical garden projects and plant care, and also on decorative effects to delight the eye.

Jenny Plucknett

CHAPTER 1

WORKING OUT YOUR OWN DESIGN

You may be starting a garden from scratch, in which case you have the freedom to arrange the elements you want within it in almost any form, bearing in mind aspect, prevailing wind, views (both pleasing and ugly), and privacy. Alternatively, you may want to replan a garden that you have previously planted and arranged without originally giving a lot of thought to its overall design, or to redesign a garden you have inherited when moving house. If you have just taken over an established garden it would be wise to wait a year before planning it so that you can assess its present design and planting before you decide which factors you want to retain and which you would prefer to change.

Before working on a design it is best to make an accurate scale plan of the garden, even if this seems rather complicated. Also some thought needs to be given to what you want to use the garden for as well as how you want it to look. Once your garden plan has been drawn up you can use it to arrange the various areas that you require and plan the planting, bearing in mind some of the clever tricks that an expert uses to change the space visually, add excitement and deal with the problems encountered in your particular plot.

Making a plan to scale 10–11
Designing the garden 12–13

Making a plan to scale

Information to include

Aspect
The direction your garden faces, together with the position of the house, surrounding walls, trees, and fences, affects the amount of sun or shade it gets. Use a compass to get an accurate position for north and mark this on your plan. Make a note of the sunny and shady areas at different times of the day. This will help you to position both structures and plants in your garden.

Views
You will want to show off a good view. Framing it with trees or shrubs will highlight it. At the same time an ugly view is best hidden. Mark this on your plan so that you remember to design in a concealing barrier.

Overlooked areas
Privacy can be provided by trees, pergolas and frameworks for climbing plants, so show the areas where the garden is overlooked on the plan.

Noise
An area thickly planted with evergreen shrubs or trees will help to deaden noise, so mark in the position of a busy road or other sources of noise.

The first thing you need to do when designing your garden is to measure the area accurately and make a detailed, scale plan of it. Omit anything you do not want to include in the new design but show the position of anything you want to keep, such as an old tree or specimen shrub. You will also need to show the positions of other fixtures, as these can influence your design. Mark the site of manholes, overhead cables (so that you don't plan a tree in their path) and underground drain lines and cables plus their depth (so that you don't cut through them when digging a pond or other excavations).

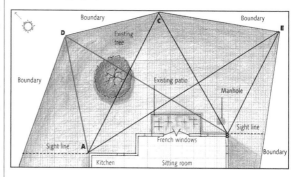

Stages in drawing a plan

1 Do a rough sketch on a large piece of paper first. A long tape, 30 m/100 ft will make measuring easier and more accurate. Start by marking in the area of the house, which should be included in the plan. Mark the positions of doors and windows. To measure the distance of the boundary at each side of the house use a sight line from the house. To do this, stand so that you can look directly along the house wall and with one eye line up a point on the boundary along the same line. Mark this spot with a cane and then take a measurement from the nearest house corner to this point. Then do the same on the opposite side.

2 Now move on to the garden. By using triangulation, positions can be plotted accurately. Measure from one house corner, **A**, to the end of the garden

to a point such as a boundary corner, **C**. Then measure the distance of **C** from the opposite house corner, **B**. Mark these two distances on the plan. Do the same from **A** and **B** to the opposite boundary corner **D** (or any other boundary corners). If the house and garden are wide you may need to measure from a number of points along the house to a range of boundary points – see lines from **A** and **B** to **D**, **C** and **E** on the plan, above.

3 Once the boundary distances are recorded, move on to those items in the garden that cannot be moved, such as manholes, oil tanks, and trees or shrubs that you wish to keep. Use triangulation as described in step 2 to plot the positions of each of these. Heating vents, rainwater barrels and garden tap positions also need to be shown. To avoid confusion you may find it easiest to use a different colour for

lines and measurements to each point. For large trees, you will also need to measure the approximate diameter of the trunk and radius of the canopy and mark these on the plan.

4 Now move on to making a proper scale plan. For this you will need a large piece of graph paper. First work out the scale you need to use to fit the complete garden onto the paper: a scale of 2.5 cm to 3 m or 1 in to 10 ft is a usually a good size. Note the scale used on the plan itself, and also show the north point. To mark each pair of measurements use compasses, set to each recorded scaled-down distance, and draw a short curve (see diagram, above). The point at which the curves from two measurements cross is the accurate position. Draw in the boundary lines by connecting these points. Mark the positions of the items such as manholes, trees, shrubs (see step 3) within the garden in the same way and show a rough circle for a tree or shrub canopy.

5 (See diagram, above right.) Mark on the plan the positions of any views to be accentuated or blocked out (making it clear which is which), any overlooked areas of the garden, any wet areas, slopes, and the main wind direction. All of this information is important in helping you design the garden.

6 When the plan is drawn in outline, arrange the elements you wish to include in the design. Use two sheets of tracing paper; one to show the basic structure and one for the planting. Design the basic structure first, then overlay the second sheet on top and position the planting on this.

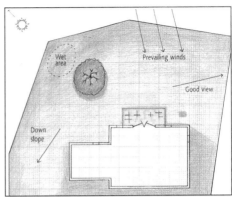

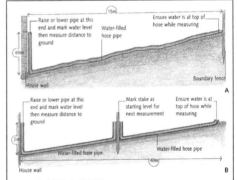

A

B

MEASURING A SLOPE

A simple way to measure a slope is to use the Egyptian method, which uses a garden hose (see diagram **A**). Lay one end of the hose, filled with water, at the top of the slope and run it down the slope, holding the second end in the air to avoid water loss and ensuring that the water remains in the pipe end at the higher level.

Gently lower the second end until you can see the water just reaching the top of the pipe. Measure the distance from this water level to the ground and this will give you the drop on the slope.

On a long slope you may need to take two or more measurements, then add them together (see diagram **B** for how to do this).

Designing the garden

Points to consider

The list below gives some of the factors you may wish to include in your design. Pick out those that you would like to incorporate and make your own check-list, grading it in order of priority. In a small garden you are unlikely to be able to fit in everything you would like to include, so less vital choices may have to disappear.

Lifestyle
- Areas for outdoor living/BBQ
- Children's play areas
- Pets
- Clothes line/airer

Structures and fittings
- Boundary wall, fence or hedge
- Patios and paths
- Lawns
- Gates
- Dustbin
- Coal bunker/wood shed
- Greenhouse/cold frame
- Lighting
- Rainwater tanks
- Compost bins
- Pergola/arbour
- Moving water feature/pond

Ornamental extras
- Pots/statues
- Sundial/bird table
- Decorative natural materials

Planting
- Ornamental plants
- Herbaceous border
- Rock or gravel garden
- Vegetables/ herbs/fruit
- Cutflowers
- Raised beds
- Trees
- Wild area
- Wildlife area to attract birds/mammals/ butterflies/bees

There are several points to consider before you put pencil to paper and plan your design, work out the materials you need to implement it and decide on the planting. First of all consider the style of the house – its period, shape and the materials used in its construction, so that house and garden will blend visually. Then think what style of garden you want to create – the following pages will give you some ideas and help you to decide what you prefer.

Formal gardens, with sides that form mirror images, match well with symmetrical houses, but even here most people opt for an easier, natural-looking informal style.

A wild garden with a naturally shaped pond, areas of long grass, fallen timber and wild flowers, will bring in the wildlife that help to keep pests at bay. This garden style appeals to the organic gardener. A wild garden can also be included as part of an informal garden.

The minimalist design of a Japanese garden, with its raked gravel, and carefully positioned sculptural plants and boulders, works well in a small space and is easily maintained. However, if you enjoy working in the garden, you may prefer the cottage-garden style with intermingled vegetables and flowers and plants spilling over paths.

A strong skeleton

When you look through the gardens that follow you will notice that they are based on a simple, strongly shaped skeleton, which ensures that the garden looks good at all times of the year, both when overflowing with greenery and flowers and when growth is more restricted. The pattern may be based on curves, geometric shapes or a mixture of both. A series of interlocking circles,

or squares and rectangles, both provide a clean, distinctive background. Squares and rectangles can also be used very effectively across the diagonal.

Tricks of the trade

In a small rectangular garden a series of centrally positioned circles that decrease in size away from the house can increase the apparent size of the garden. Lines that run away from you can make an area appear longer.

A long narrow space looks more interesting if the length is broken up into a series of separate 'rooms'. Create a focal point with an eye-catching seat, urn or specimen tree or shrub. Provide interest at a range of levels by fixing structures for plants to grow up, such as trellis, arches, pergolas. A secret corner gives interest. Create privacy with a plant-covered arbour; provide shelter from the wind with trellis screens and climbers; frame a view with an archway or shrubs.

Creating a series of terraces is the best way of dealing with a sloping garden. This will require quite a lot of initial work but the resulting series of levels, held in place by retaining walls or banks and linked by steps or paths, can look very attractive. Use a small slope to make a rock garden.

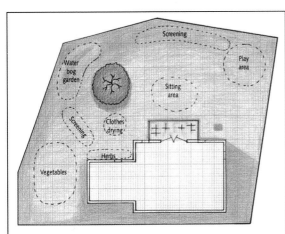

Screening

Water bog garden

Play area

Sitting area

Screening

Clothes drying

Herbs

Vegetables

Time-saving considerations

As well as soil and situation, altitude, rainfall, and wind are contributory factors to what will grow well in your garden. Wherever your garden is situated there will be plants that flourish and others that will be hard to grow. Local garden centres are a good source for plants that thrive locally. Growing these will be much less time consuming than choosing unsuitable alternatives.

Terracing

When terracing it is important to remove the topsoil temporarily during construction, then level the subsoil before replacing the topsoil. If you do not do this the depth of top-soil will vary considerably at different points on each terrace.

THE STAGES OF DESIGN

1 Bearing in mind sunny and shady areas, wind, views, privacy, noise, and practicalities of access, roughly mark in areas for each of the uses you want to include in your design.

2 Now integrate the marked areas, using the basic pattern you have chosen of straight or curved lines or a mixture of both. You can, of course, use a number of overlays to try out a range of patterns. Once you are satisfied with the basic design, go over this in pen.

3 Place the planting sheet over the construction plan and, bearing in mind all the points mentioned in step 1 which will affect your choice of plants, plan the areas to be planted in more detail.

A poorly drained garden shows up in constantly wet or puddled areas. Improving the condition of the soil will greatly improve drainage. Low-lying areas can be used for a pond, or bog garden. However, if the problem is severe, laying drains may be the only answer.

Budgeting

Constructing a garden from scratch can be expensive in terms of materials and hired labour. A loan may be needed if you want to complete the construction and planting in one go. If you can do much of the work yourselves the cost will be considerably reduced.

Alternatively draw up a work time schedule so that you can pay for the work in instalments. Start with the basic construction jobs of installing any electricity, forming the boundary, building a patio and making paths. As a second stage add areas of lawn and some of the key plants plus quick-growing climbers and annuals. The decorative features such as ponds, moving water features, arches, pergolas and arbours can be added later.

See also:
• Form and shape, Chapter 6
• Identifying and improving soil, page 102
• Laying drains, page 103
• Electricity in the garden, page 112

CHAPTER 2

DESIGNS FOR SPECIFIC SHAPES AND AREAS

The shape and situation of a garden have a great bearing on the best type of design to create to ensure that it becomes interesting. Even the plainest and smallest garden is enhanced by a few surprises and a long, narrow strip always benefits from being divided into a series of garden 'rooms'.

In this chapter top garden designers have created innovative solutions to some common problems that arise due to a garden's shape, and factors such as land gradient or situation.

Courtyard garden 16–19
Square garden 20–23
Short, wide garden 24–27
Long, narrow garden 28–31
Split-level garden 32–35
Paved town garden 36–39
Small front garden 40–43
Roof garden 44–47

▲ **Before conversion** the garden had a flowerbed on the left-hand side, a pile of rubble in the centre, a lower area on the right where, possibly, an old shed or greenhouse stood and the space was outlined by a fence and walling.

Courtyard garden

This tiny garden, designed by Jean Goldberry, displays many interesting features. From the house a small pergola creates an arched entrance to the garden and a pathway leads off to the right to a circular terrace with a central statue. Then it turns left up to the main terrace shaded by a wisteria which clothes the pergola with long, falling streamers of lilac-blue flowers in late spring. The path then curves around to join up with the original terrace by the house, passing the central raised circular water feature on the left, where a low fountain splashes a collection of pebbles. Tall grasses echo the shape of the falling water. To the right of the path stepping stones, softened by ground-hugging plants, line up to lead off to the right to a spot that is discreetly hidden by shrubs.

▼ The planting scheme was cleverly arranged to give this tiny area depth, perspective and a lush feel.

THE GARDEN'S PROBLEMS	HOW THEY WERE SOLVED
Rubble in the centre of the garden.	This rubble, utilized for hardcore, created a base for the brick terrace.
The garden was not only small, but also flat and uninteresting.	A design was created to include a range of levels which would give the space more interesting contours.
Wind, mainly from the right-hand side, was a problem in this small space.	Trees were planted to provide shelter for the raised sitting area.
An unattractive view of a huge area of a neighbour's wall to the right.	The pergola over the sitting area was constructed to hide some of the wall and raising the terrace also helped.
The owner was very keen to have a water feature but was concerned about the safety of grandchildren when visiting.	A raised brick-edged water feature with a shallow layer of pebbles and a low geyser was constructed in the centre of the garden. The height makes it safe for small children.

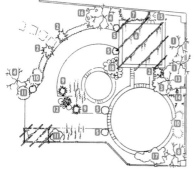

DESIGNER'S PLANTING SCHEME

Key plants
1. Sorbus commixta 'Embley'
2. Rosmarinus officinalis 'Miss Jessup's Upright'
3. Cistus x purpureus
4. Cornus controversa 'Variegata'
5. Box, Buxus sempervirens clipped into a globe
6. Wisteria floribunda 'Macrobotrys'
7. Japanese fatsia, Fatsia japonica 'Variegata'
8. Crab apple, Malus 'Van Eseltine'
9. Juniper, Juniperus communis 'Hibernica'
10. Lavender, Lavandula x intermedia
11. Hebe 'Caledonia'
12. Yucca gloriosa

Decorative detail
13. Geranium psilostemon
14. Globe artichoke, Cynara scolymus
15. Miscanthus tinctoria 'Nanus Variegatus'
16. Geranium pratense 'Mrs Kendall Clark'
17. Penstemon 'Alice Hindley'
18. Astilboides tabularis

Plants for added colour
Morning glory, Ipomoea purpurea
Nemesia strumosa 'KLM'
Lobelia 'Riviera Blue Splash'
Larkspur, Consolida ajacis
Blue daisy, Felicia heterophylla 'Spring Marchen'
Antirrhinum – tall white variety in sunny spaces

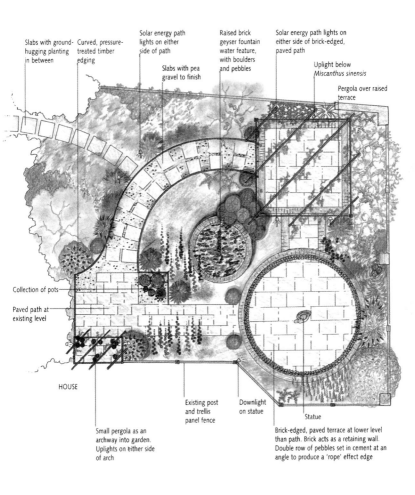

Slabs with ground-hugging planting in between

Curved, pressure-treated timber edging

Solar energy path lights on either side of path

Slabs with pea gravel to finish

Raised brick geyser fountain water feature, with boulders and pebbles

Solar energy path lights on either side of brick-edged, paved path

Uplight below *Miscanthus sinensis*

Pergola over raised terrace

Collection of pots

Paved path at existing level

HOUSE

Small pergola as an archway into garden. Uplights on either side of arch

Existing post and trellis panel fence

Downlight on statue

Statue

Brick-edged, paved terrace at lower level than path. Brick acts as a retaining wall. Double row of pebbles set in cement at an angle to produce a 'rope' effect edge

CONSTRUCTION

There is so much to look at in this tiny garden that it appears much larger than it really is. The clever use of a large variety of hard surface materials, helps to break up the space, as do the subtly changing levels.

Flagstones, of varying sizes, are used for the area next to the house with a step down to the brick-edged circular paved area, where pebbles are used as an edging. The path and square sitting-out area use the same materials but the curved path mixes gravel and paving with an edge of timber to hold the gravel in place. Slabs, edged by creeping plants, form a slightly different-looking walkway that leads away from the initial path and through the area to the left.

▲The view along the side of the house looking towards the circular terrace and statue, with the water feature on the left. The eye is drawn to this central grouping, which gives the courtyard depth and perspective. In summer the garden becomes a haze of pinks, blues and lilacs.

PLANTING

Jean gave the seating area an oriental feel with wisteria on the pergola backed by bamboos and a variegated *Fatsia japonica*. She also used junipers to reflect yet soften the upright pergola posts. Junipers, still small in these pictures but which will grow to over 3 m/10 ft, are also planted to form a frame for the pots by the water feature.

KEY PLANTS

▲The magenta flowers, with their black centre, of this cranesbill, *Geranium psilostemon* form a brilliant area of colour. The leaves are pink tinted in spring, turning a rich red in autumn.

◀The leaves of *Miscanthus tinctoria* 'Nanus Variegatus' add highlights with their cream and bright green stripes. This dwarf clump-forming grass grows to 45 cm/18 in.

The pergola over the sitting area, and the smaller one used to form an archway, persuade the eye upwards and provide an area for climbing plants. The raised water feature introduces yet another level, while the mixed boulders and pebbles provide a contrasting and varied kind of hard surface.

Lighting creates a different look for the garden at night. A down-lighter, is used to pinpoint the statue in the centre of the circular terrace and solar energy path lights, indicate the start of the stepping-stone path and highlights the pergola-covered terrace. This lighting focuses the eye on nearby plants and makes the path safe to use at night.

▲ The curving path that leads back towards the house uses paving edged with gravel to soften the effect and the slightly raised edging prevents soil spilling onto the path. Plants fall over the path's edge to soften the outline. The path can be seen leading off into the background in the centre top of the picture.

Special effects

A raised water feature The type of water feature, (top), with a raised brick edge allows you to sit on the rim of the pool and enjoy the water from close at hand. The low central geyser- like waterfall mimics the sound of a gurgling stream to create a relaxing atmosphere.

In the same way, water spills out of an upside-downpot, (above), to coat the container with a flowing golden glaze. Both these features provide an additional eye-catching focus in winter as well as summer for any area of the garden that lacks other interest.

FOR EXTRA COLOUR

Rock roses display very decorative flowers and *Cistus* x *purpureus* is specially stunning. The decorative tissue-paper thin, magenta pink flowers are highlighted by yellow centres and evenly distributed splashes of dark purple-maroon. Plants of the Mediterranean region, cistus grow well in dry, well-drained soil and this hybrid will grow to about 1–1.2 m/3–4 ft in both height and spread. They also have a long flowering season. Flowers appear in late May and continue well into July.

▲ Forming a background to the circular terrace, a group of tall penstemon 'Alice Hindley' with their bell-shaped pale lilac flowers, frill-edged in a deeper tone, bloom right through from mid-summer to early autumn.

Square garden

A square garden has many advantages over long and short gardens. It does need to be visually shortened with horizontal divisions, nor does it need to be broken up with vertical or diagonal lines in any way. However, a strong defining central shape that brings the eye towards the garden's centre can transform the space, as is clearly shown in this garden designed by Jean Goldberry.

▲ **Before conversion** the garden shed and work-shop provided the main focal point and the plain geometric shape of the garden was clearly emphasized.

▼ **The planting scheme** was kept to two main areas over opposite corners of the garden, with pots on the terraces to provide extra colour.

THE GARDEN'S PROBLEMS

A downward slope from the end of the garden towards the house.

An ugly fence at the end of the garden.

The shape of the rectangular area of paving next to the house is harsh.

A large tree from next door overhangs the bottom of the garden on the left.

A side alley with uninteresting views of neighbouring houses.

HOW THEY WERE SOLVED

A raised patio was formed above the slope.

Raised beds in front of the fence hide it and are easy to maintain.

The terrace was curved to improve the shape, creating a path between the house and the shed.

A summer house was placed in this area as little would grow in this light.

Two wide wire arches were planted with the climbers clematis, sweet pea and a *Trachelospermum* to conceal the view.

DESIGNER'S PLANTING SCHEME

Key plants
1 Bamboo, *Indocalamus latifolius*
2 Box, *Buxus sempervirens* 'Elegantissima'
3 *Choisya ternata* 'Sundance'
4 *Fuchsia* 'Tom Thumb'
5 *Clematis armandii*
6 *Rosa* 'Kathleen Harrop'
7 *Daphne odora* 'Aureomarginata'
8 *Viburnum davidii*
9 *Phlomis italica*
10 *Trachelospermum asiaticum* – over arches
11 *Clematis viticella* 'Alba Luxurians' – over arches
12 *Cistus purpureus*

Decorative detail
13 *Sisyrinchium striatum*
14 *Geranium cinereum* ssp. *subcaulescens* – between slabs

15 *Bergenia ciliata*
16 *Geranium pyrenaicum* 'Bill Wallace'
17 Bronze fennel, *Foeniculum vulgare*
18 *Erysimum* 'Bowles' Mauve'

Plants for added colour
Antirrhinum 'Black Prince'
Osteospermum 'Nairobi Purple'
Maurandya scandens in purple – in spaces on the fence
Petunia – trailing in deep purple, burgundy and red – in pots and baskets
Convolvulus 'Star of Yelta' – on fences and arches
Stock, *Matthiola* 'Giant Excelsior' in mixed colours

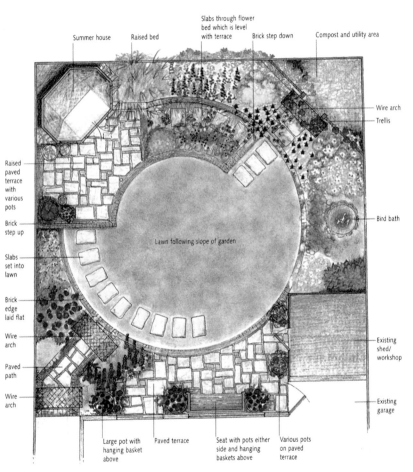

Summer house

Raised bed

Slabs through flower bed which is level with terrace

Brick step down

Compost and utility area

Wire arch

Trellis

Raised paved terrace with various pots

Brick step up

Slabs set into lawn

Brick edge laid flat

Wire arch

Paved path

Wire arch

Bird bath

Lawn following slope of garden

Existing shed/ workshop

Existing garage

Large pot with hanging basket above

Paved terrace

Seat with pots either side and hanging baskets above

Various pots on paved terrace

HOUSE

CONSTRUCTION

The circular central lawn is outlined around its circumference with brick and paving to strengthen the simple, strong shape which is the key to the transformation of this plain square garden. The raised paved terrace at the end of the garden follows the curve and overlaps the lawn and, on the same higher leve, slabs run through the flower bed so that the raised bed behind is reached easily.

Slabs laid in the lawn follow the shape or lead through an archway into the neatly concealed compost area. Square trellis covers the fences to break up the harsh outlines and provide a framework for attaching climbers.

The summer house, positioned diagonally across a corner, is in an

▲ Positioning a summer house underneath the branches of a large tree, extending over the corner from next door, turns an unsuitable spot for plants into a decorative and enjoyable feature.

PLANTING

Jean used a range of grasses, bamboo, a clipped box and shrubs to provide a basic round-the-year evergreen structure. Striking rich pink and purple perennials and annuals provide some summer colour: petunias, the osteospermum 'Nairobi Purple', the fuchsias and the climbing *Maurandya scandens* amongst them.

KEY PLANTS

▲ A trellis and archway mask the compost area, entered through a wrought iron gate. These also provide a framework for honeysuckle and the evergreen *Clematis armandii* which has early, scented white flowers.

◄ A range of gold and cream-splashed ivies, *Hedera helix* cultivars, soften the edge of the raised stone bed, backed by the rich red, pink and purple flowers of the fuchsia 'Tom Thumb'.

◄ From the end of the garden the view includes the plant-covered arches which straddle the path that curves round from the side of the house and help to hide the house next door.

ideal position to view the garden, while the path from the side of the house, edged with bricks to define its route, is angled to reach the slab path around the lawn. With its wire arches covered in climbers, this creates a division between the terrace by the house and the flower bed on the left.

The terraced areas in front of the house and the summer house are broken up with pots of evergreens, for year-round interest, and colourful annuals.

Special effects

Raised flower beds are used almost everywhere in this garden. These both help to contain the soil and are easier to maintain. The lower beds are edged in a framework of neatly laid bricks. The taller bed, at the end of the garden, has large golden-grey rocks laid in the jig-saw-like manner of a country stone wall. The taller stone-edged bed, at 45 cm/18 in, means that little bending is necessary when gardening, and larger, smoother stones provide a seat when a little quiet contemplation is required.

▲ Plants with a range of leaf colours fill the raised bed by the arch. Creamy yellow spikes of *Sisyrinchium striatum* with the golden leaves of *Choisya ternata* 'Sundance' behind. Fuchsia 'Tom Thumb' adds colour at the front and the rose 'Kathleen Harrop' covers the arch.

FOR EXTRA COLOUR

Begonias and fuchsias fill a pot to bursting with their dark purple and green leaves and pink, red and white flowers. This mixture is a good choice for a more shaded area of the terrace. Begonia tubers can be lifted in autumn and dried off then replanted in spring. In frost-prone areas many fuchsias will survive if the stem base is planted 5 cm/2 in below the soil surface and a deep layer of mulch is added. Alternatively bring pots indoors.

See also:
- Raised beds, page 108
- Building a low brick wall, page 120
- Arches, pergolas and arbours, page 132

Short, wide garden

The owners of this garden, attached to a 1930's house, wanted it to be modern, minimalist and different. They turned to sculptor and garden designer Paul Cooper to use his combined creative talents to conceive a garden that was both modern and formal.

The original large garden had been sold off as plots, leaving a piece of land that was both wide and very short, with a line of tall conifer trees along the end. As these were planted in the adjoining garden they could not be removed, so Paul decided to create a strong feature to detract from them.

▲ **Before conversion** the garden was laid out with a central lawn and beds around the edges, emphasising its short length and its width.

Trellis panels

THE GARDEN'S PROBLEMS

A line of 6 m/20 ft conifers at the end of the garden, growing in the adjoining garden.

The owners wanted to be able to look out on the garden from the top window of the house and see precise geometric patterns.

The short length of the garden.

Old basic concrete paving slabs were to be retained.

HOW THEY WERE SOLVED

A bold structure that mimicked a gateway was created, alongwith a pergola. Both were painted white to draw the eye away from the conifers.

Using a wide range of hard surface materials, plus grass, Paul has formed an eyecatching minimalist design.

An impression of length was achieved by narrowing lines as they reached the boundary.

Brick edging and the introduction of other materials leads the paving slabs to become part of a wider scheme of defined shapes.

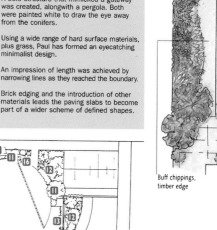

Buff chippings, timber edge

◀ **The planting scheme** was deliberately tidy and compact with most of the shrubs clipped to form neat globes. Low plants are either ground hugging or form tight hummocks.

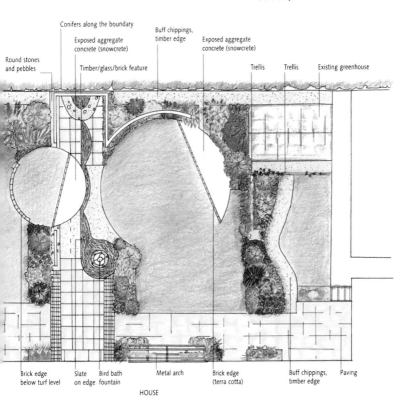

Conifers along the boundary

Exposed aggregate concrete (snowcrete)

Buff chippings, timber edge

Exposed aggregate concrete (snowcrete)

Round stones and pebbles

Timber/glass/brick feature

Trellis

Trellis

Existing greenhouse

Brick edge below turf level

Slate on edge

Bird bath fountain

Metal arch

Brick edge (terra cotta)

Buff chippings, timber edge

Paving

HOUSE

DESIGNER'S PLANTING SCHEME

Key plants
1. Myrtle, *Myrtus communis* 'Variegata'
2. *Mahonia* x *media* 'Charity'
3. Golden Mexican orange blossom, *Choisya ternata* 'Sundance'
4. Privet, *Ligustrum ovalifolium* 'Argenteum'
5. *Rosa xanthina* 'Canary Bird'
6. *Viburnum tinus*
7. *Abelia* x *grandiflora*
8. *Photinia* x *fraseri* 'Red Robin'
9. *Elaeagnus* x *ebbingei*
10. *Viburnum* x *carlcephalum*
11. *Viburnum davidii*
12. *Ceanothus dentatus*

Decorative detail
13. *Agapanthus africanus*
14. Cranesbills, *Geranium macrorrhizum* 'Album' and *G.* 'Johnson's Blue'
15. Foam flower, *Tiarella cordifolia*
16. Iris – tall bearded species and varieties
17. Sage, *Salvia officinalis* 'Icterina'

Plants for added colour
Campanula carpatica – in blue
Coral flower, *Heuchera* 'Palace Purple'
Dianthus 'Doris'
Ceratostigma willmottianum
Red-hot poker, *Kniphofia rooperi*
Eryngium bourgatii

▲ Looking from the house towards the end of the garden. The main structure and water feature, together with the pergola to the right, take the eye off the line of conifers behind.

CONSTRUCTION

Designer Paul Cooper has used white for the main structures, arches, pergola and ground surfaces, to highlight the patterns he has formed with the hard landscaping that mixes curves and straight lines. Structures are kept deliberately clear of climbers which would hide the clean lines and eventually blend in colour with the background, so losing the strong outline they are intended to create.

Where trellis is used, some of the spaces have been blocked in with plywood and then painted to enhance the feel of this garden.

The main giant white structure at the end of the garden is in fact a water feature with water tumbling from the centre top down over glass bricks. Two semi-circles of mirror

PLANTING

This is a garden where man shows his control over nature. Shrubs are kept neatly trimmed in a series of globes, boxes and tidy hummocks. In each space created by the post and rail pergola, a shrub chosen for its colour or leaf shape, forms a simple sculptural silhouette, an unusual alternative to screening the timber with climbing plants.

KEY PLANTS

▲ Long tooth-edged bracts, tinged with pink, create a ruff of silvery spikes that surround the flowers of *Eryngium variifolium*. The strong shape and silvery tints of eryngiums create a perfect foil for the clean lines in this modern garden.

◀ Cranesbill, *Geranium* 'Johnson's Blue', with its bright green leaves and pink-tinged blue flowers, forms good ground cover.

◁ The water feature and central paving seen from the side and looking across a section of lawn. The square arches create strong images against the clipped shrubs and the rest of the planting.

reflect the same-shaped pool below, creating a mirror image of the water that turns it into a full circle. From this pool flow a series of part circles of broken slate used at the edge to mimic water. The line of slate completes its journey near the house as a circle with a bird bath and fountain as a centrepiece.

Ground surfaces are cleverly mixed to create a range of colours and textures that highlight the strong shapes that are such an important part of the design.

Special effects

Mixing ground surfaces Here Paul Cooper has used a wide range of hard surfaces to highlight the shapes that he wanted to bring into focus. There are square paving stones and smaller pavers, which outline the pathway leading to the water feature.

This incorporated the retained areas of paving with those that are new and brings a range of textures and colours that provide further interest.

Brick and timber edgings create clean-cut shapes for the circular lawns, while white-finished concrete, and light buff-coloured chippings highlight the shapes of the main structures. Slates fixed on edge, together with cobbles, provide a rougher finish that contrasts well with the smoother concrete and paving.

See also:
- Trellis, pages 47 and 123
- Moving water, page 128

△ Another sculptural plant that highlights the simple architectural shapes in the garden is the silk-tassel bush, *Garrya elliptica*. In winter the grey-green catkins hang like silvery tree decorations and give the bush its common name.

FOR EXTRA COLOUR

An excellent plant to provide flashes of colour in autumn is the bulbous nerine from South Africa. *Nerine bowdenii* has faintly scented and lily-shaped pink flowers with long drooping stamens. It also comes in white, tinted palest pink, as f. *alba*. *Nerine filifolia* has smaller pink and white flowers with frilled edges.

Long, narrow garden

This garden was bordered by long, narrow beds and had unattractive views. A new conservatory and terrace of hexagonal paving had to be integrated into the scheme, which was to provide a place for entertaining and a place for two small boys to enjoy and use the garden.

Designer Sally Court divided the length into separate sections. The space nearest to the house became an area for family gatherings with a view of a triangular pool. The second section was reserved for the boys' use, and at the end of the garden, which lies in the path of the morning sun, there would be a place for a relaxed breakfast as well as a screened utility area.

Before conversion the garden was lined along both sides with narrow borders which made the space appear even longer and narrower than it actually was.

THE GARDEN'S PROBLEMS

Ugly views of concrete garages at the end of the garden.

The garden's long and narrow shape.

A new conservatory and a terrace with paving need to be considered in the choice of materials.

HOW THEY WERE SOLVED

Raised beds and tall planting hide the views. Climbers act as a decorative screen along the right-hand side.

Each separate section provided a hint of what lay beyond – a trip down the garden was a journey of discovery.

The geometric paving prevented curves being used and so the designer used straight lines for paths and created a triangular pond, which were more in keeping with the overall design.

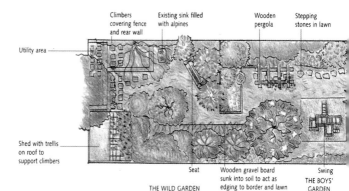

Climbers covering fence and rear wall

Existing sink filled with alpines

Wooden pergola

Stepping stones in lawn

Utility area

Shed with trellis on roof to support climbers

Seat

Wooden gravel board sunk into soil to act as edging to border and lawn

Swing

THE WILD GARDEN

THE BOYS' GARDEN

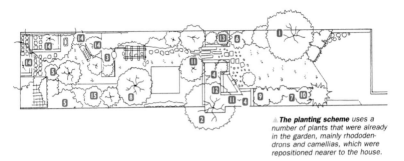

▲ *The planting scheme* uses a number of plants that were already in the garden, mainly rhododendrons and camellias, which were repositioned nearer to the house.

DESIGNER'S PLANTING SCHEME

Key plants
Already existing
1 Tree of heaven, *Ailanthus altissima*
2 Mountain ash, *Sorbus aucuparia*
3 *Pittosporum tenuifolium*
4 Selection of rhododendrons and camellias – relocated
5 Conifers

New
6 *Malus* 'Golden Hornet'
7 *Prunus virginiana*
8 *Magnolia grandiflora*
9 *Pittosporum tobira*
10 *Ceanothus* 'Puget Blue'
11 New Zealand flax, *Phormium tenax* 'Purpureum'
12 *Photinia x fraseri* 'Red Robin'
13 Strawberry tree, *Arbutus unedo*
14 Himalayan birch, *Betula utilis*
15 *Osmanthus delavayi*

Decorative Detail
Clematis macropetala
Japanese maple, *Acer palmatum* var. *dissectum*
Lamium 'White Nancy'
Pulmonaria saccharata
Bergenia silberlicht
Hosta 'Royal Standard'
Romneya hybrid
Ornamental hop, *Humulus lupulus* 'Aurea'
Hydrangea arborescens 'Annabelle'
Paeonia delavayi

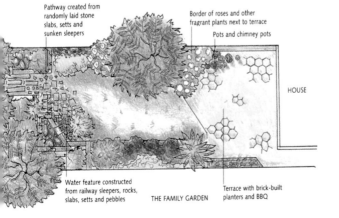

Pathway created from randomly laid stone slabs, setts and sunken sleepers

Border of roses and other fragrant plants next to terrace

Pots and chimney pots

HOUSE

Water feature constructed from railway sleepers, rocks, slabs, setts and pebbles

THE FAMILY GARDEN

Terrace with brick-built planters and BBQ

The conservatory and the paved terrace by the house were the starting point for the garden's design.

CONSTRUCTION

Apart from being long and narrow, the garden was also very flat. Sally added height at the end of the first section by constructing slightly raised beds, edged in railway sleepers, together with a raised pool.

The upper pool, constructed of railway sleepers, has a centrally placed funnel that spills water down into a shallow pool below. The water is recirculated back into the top pond. The raised beds and pond divide off the next section, reached by a gravel path, broken up with stepping stones and partly buried sleepers.

The second section is for the boys with swings, space for football and a bed where they can try out their gardening skills. A pergola and evergreen planting screen the

PLANTING

A number of plants in the garden were retained, some being moved to a new position. A tree of heaven, *Ailanthus altissima* was resited close to the terrace as a backdrop, and a mature *Pittosporum tenuifolium* adds privacy to the end of the garden and has been joined by another specimen tree, a *Magnolia grandiflora*.

KEY PLANTS

As a background to the pond a mountain ash, *Sorbus aucuparia*, provides decoration of clusters of white flowers in spring, followed by bright red berries. In autumn the leaves turn yellow and red before they fall.

Next to the raised bed a bear's breeches, *Acanthus spinosus*, banked on either side by roses, shows off its tall spires of purple-pink and white-throated flowers and attractive large, dark green, spiny, divided leaves.

Looking down the garden from the top terrace. On the left are the triangular pond and raised bed that separate this section from the next.

The unusual triangular raised pool with its overspill into a shallow pebble-lined pond below.

end of the garden, where shrubs create a den for the boys. There are areas of rough grass, mature shrubs and trees, and a seat. The mature planting and trellis covered with climbers give privacy and screen the utility part of the garden.

The bell-shaped white flowers of a *Pittosporum tobira* along the garden path flourish in late spring to early summer. They are scented and gradually turn creamy yellow with age. The leathery dark green shiny leaves are paler on the underside.

FOR EXTRA COLOUR

For colourful early flowers that brighten a shady position the perennial pulmonaria with its blue, pink or white flowers and white- or silver-spotted leaves is a good choice. *Pulmonaria saccharata*, shown, has unusual lilac to pink flowers whereas the variety *P. saccharata* 'Frühlingshimmel' has bright pastel blue flowers with a darker blue centre.

Pulmonaria likes humus-rich and moist soil, as well as full or partial shade.

Special effects

Mixing path materials By mixing the materials used in creating a path, much more interesting effects can be achieved. This also allows you to curve a path made from rigid materials, such as paving, by introducing gravel or stone chippings and then setting the paving with gaps, like stepping-stones, along the length.

With paving for the main walkway other ornate and less resilient materials can also be used, such as bark chippings, broken slate or even shells.

Here Sally has mixed larger paving slabs, smaller setts and sunken sleepers, all laid in gravel. The slabs continue on as stepping-stones through the lawn that the path leads to.

See also:

- *Paths steps and edgings, page 118*
- *Children's play space, page 138*

Split-level garden

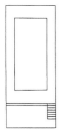

Before conversion the lower rooms of this tall town house were below garden level with a narrow paved strip adjoining the house and a blank wall between this and the garden.

The owners of this garden had differing views of what they required. One wanted a modern, simple and stylish outdoor room, the other preferred a romantic, traditional country-garden look. It was the designer Sally Court's job to bring these two requirements together in a garden that both would like.

The house, on a lower level, was faced from the main downstairs rooms with a blank wall, with the main area of the garden above this. Sally extended the narrow paved areas next to the house outwards so that it became wide enough to use as a sitting and eating area.

The paving and retaining wall were extended in a series of curves, with brick steps echoing this shape up to the top section. The wall was used as a backdrop for a moving water feature to break up the length of the wall and create sound and visual interest on the patio.

Trellis fixed along the boundary fences was stained green (so that it would blend into the background) as was a decoratively designed garden shed at the end of the garden that looks more like a gazebo.

THE GARDEN'S PROBLEMS

The large kitchen and family room set below the main garden and facing a blank wall.

Drainage problems in a garden where the house is on a lower level.

Squirrels constantly dug up the garden to store nuts and seeds collected nearby.

HOW THEY WERE SOLVED

Extending the lower terrace with material similarly coloured to that used in the house, linked the inside with the outdoor space.

A gulley was used to take away rainwater from the house and the terrace in wet weather.

Setting up a special squirrel feeder as well as a birds-only feeder. Soon the squirrels were using the feeder and curtailed their digging.

DESIGNER'S PLANTING SCHEME

Key plants

1　Strawberry tree, *Arbutus* x *andrachnoides*
2　Jelly palm, *Butia capitata*
3　Dwarf fan palm, *Chamaerops humulis*
4　Cabbage palm, *Cordyline australis*
5　Daphne odora 'Aureomarginata'
6　Loquat, *Eriobotrya japonica*
7　Magnolia grandiflora 'Samuel Sommer'
8　New Zealand flax, *Phormium tenax*
9　Black bamboo, *Phyllostachys nigra*

Decorative detail

10　Japanese mock orange, *Pittosporum tobira*
11　*Cistus* x *skanbergii*
12　Cardoon, *Cynara cardunculus*
13　Alexandrian laurel, *Danae racemosa*
14　*Dianella tasmanica*
15　Woodrush, *Luzula sylvatica* 'Marginata'
16　Lilyturf, *Ophiopogon planiscapus* 'Nigrescens'
17　Soft shield fern, *Polystichum setiferum*
18　Prostrate rosemary, *Rosmarinus lavandulaceus*
19　*Parthenocissus henryana*
20　Wisteria 'Snow Showers'

The planting scheme was planned to use plants that are unusual in this area and very architectural in form.

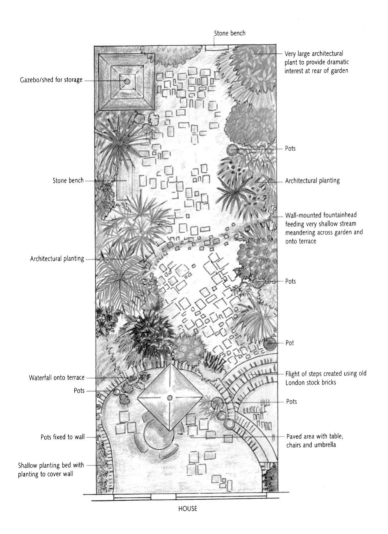

Stone bench

Very large architectural plant to provide dramatic interest at rear of garden

Gazebo/shed for storage

Pots

Stone bench

Architectural planting

Wall-mounted fountainhead feeding very shallow stream meandering across garden and onto terrace

Architectural planting

Pots

Pot

Waterfall onto terrace

Flight of steps created using old London stock bricks

Pots

Pots

Pots fixed to wall

Paved area with table, chairs and umbrella

Shallow planting bed with planting to cover wall

HOUSE

CONSTRUCTION

The major task was to open up the terrace close to the house and to replace the 1 m/39 in retaining wall with a new one that followed a series of decorative curves.

The lower terrace and most of the garden above this were paved in a range of slabs of different sizes with gravel between. Reclaimed honey-coloured bricks were used for the wall and steps.

To create an attractive view from the house, and break up the retaining wall, pots were fixed to the surface around the wall. A fountain was placed on the wall with a stone water-garden trough below it. Three beautiful giant lizards were commissioned, two to act as spouts for the fountain and a third for the top of the wall.

▲ The water feature creates a perfect focal point on the wall of the lower terrace. The giant pots holding evergreen shrubs placed on either side break up the expanse of plain wall.

See also:
• Moving water page 128
• Ornamental extras page 136

PLANTING

A modern theme of structural plants, which provide year-round interest, is used with a range of palms, black-stemmed bamboo, cardoon and New Zealand flax. These blend with verdant climbers to cover the walls, fences and trellis. In frost-prone areas alternative species of these plants may be better suited to winter outside.

KEY PLANTS

▲ In a pot on the terrace an evergreen viburnum, *Viburnum davidii*, provides year-roundy interest. It bears small, white, slim, bell-shaped flowers in late spring followed by sprays of metallic, almost black fruit.

◄ A mat of brilliant yellow is created by the stonecrop, *Sedum acre* which has star-shaped yellow flowers in the summer. It grows to form a low domed shape 5 cm/2 in high by 60 cm/24 in across.

◁ *The view from the upper terrace looking back towards the house. This area is a happy mix of paving and greenery when seen from the house.*

▽ *The panorama from the tower terrace looking towards the garden shed, masked by trellis and climbers and the stone seat set in the sunshine that looks over the garden.*

Other features were introduced into the garden to provide focal points. A second fountain tumbles into a shallow stream that meanders its way across to the terrace, and a stone bench on the opposite side of the garden provides a good view.

▵ An umbrella plant, *Cyperus* species, flourishes in the damp conditions of the water feature and makes a natural home for two of the three basking lizards. Water spouting from the lizards' mouths spatters decoratively onto large pebbles before falling into the stone sink below.

FOR EXTRA COLOUR

Container evergreens may not be very colourful but they provide interest around the year. The bay tree, *Laurus nobles* not only has aromatic leaves but can be clipped into interesting topiary shapes. In an exposed spot or in a frost-prone area it is best taken indoors for the colder months. Grown close to the house, its leaves can easily be picked for use.

Special effects

A garden ornament is a very personal thing. Ornaments can be ornate and classical, fun and frivolous or simple and streamline. They may be mass-produced or, as here, specially designed for their location.

Siting is all-important. Here a giant maroon fish stands on its tail to view passers by, its positioning among the planting at the side of the path creating a surprise.

Paved town garden

Garden designer Sally Court inherited a very small town garden on a slight slope that she considered was overplanted. Laurel, privet and Scots pine, as well as some inappropriately large shrubs, made it dark and unappealing.

Sally decided to remove everything that was there and start again, paving the area throughout and allowing space for wider beds. She took advantage of the slope to create the new garden on slightly different levels: shallow steps take you up to the terrace immediately adjacent to the house and then up again from this section to the terrace with the water feature provided by the fountain and pool.

Changing the garden's design also allowed Sally to move the back gate from the centre of the end fence and position it at one side, making room for a shed. Climbers soon covered the fences on all sides of the garden to provide colour and greenery on a second level, and a groups of pots and a sink garden provide extra space for yet more plants.

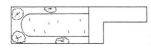

Before conversion there were pathways up both sides, and narrow borders, a small lawn and large trees and bushes.

Shed | Gravel boards | Gravel path

Sink planter

Fountain water feature with trellis panels either side of brick pillars

THE GARDEN'S PROBLEMS	HOW THEY WERE SOLVED
Surrounded by houses in almost every direction the garden had no privacy.	The birch planted at the end of the garden screens it from the houses at the back. Rampant climbers clothe the side fences, which were topped with trellis to add extra privacy.
Straight paths and beds which ran from the house to the end of the garden, making the garden appear even smaller.	The paths, beds and lawn were removed. A water feature placed centrally, part way down the garden, separates the area.
Poor soil condition.	Debris was removed and manure and compost was added to improve the soil.
No birds visited the garden.	Planting was chosen to provide birds with berries and seeds.

The planting scheme was designed around a stunning multistem birch, which gives the impression of a mini woodland, yet takes up little space.

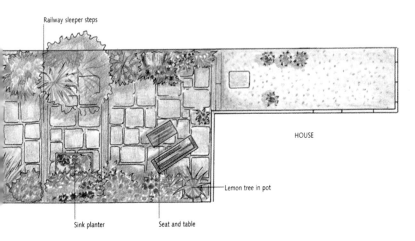

Railway sleeper steps

HOUSE

Lemon tree in pot

Sink planter

Seat and table

DESIGNER'S PLANTING SCHEME

Key plants
1 Birch, *Betula utilis* – multistem
2 *Ceanothus* 'A. T. Johnson'
3 *Pittosporum tobira* – standard
4 *Pittosporum tobira* 'Variegatum' – shrub
5 New Zealand flax, *Phormium tenax*
6 *Pinus mugo* var. *pumilio*
7 *Trachycarpus fortunei*
8 *Elaeagnus ebbingei*
9 *Aucuba japonica* 'Crotonifolia'
10 *Rosa* x *hugonis* – weeping standard

Decorative detail
11 *Astrantia major rubra*, 'Sunningdale'
12 *Hosta fortunei* 'Albopicta', 'Halcyon', *H. sieboldiana*, *H. undulata* and others
13 *Tradescantia* – a mixture of varieties
14 *Trachelospermum jasminoides*
15 *Trachelospermum jasminoides* 'Variegatum'
16 *Rosa* Heritage, Gertrude Jekyll and Tradescant

Plants for added colour
Clematis macropetala, *C. cirrhosa*, *C. armandii*, C. 'Vivyan Pennell', *C. texensis*, *C. viticella*
Cranesbill, *Geranium* – ten species, including *G. renardii* and 'Johnson's Blue'
Paeonia x 'Bowl of Beauty'
Paeonia lutea var. *ludlowsi*

CONSTRUCTION

Sally used reclaimed York stone to pave the major part of the garden, giving it a mature finish. Railway sleepers create wide, shallow steps that take you onto the slightly different levels of the garden.

To increase the garden's privacy and to turn it into a very sheltered spot where she could grow exotics, she added trellis to the top of all the boundary fences.

Two-thirds of the way down the garden she built a centrally positioned low wall from old honey-coloured bricks, with pillars at each end and space at the sides. This is part of the water feature with a lion-head fountain centrally positioned and a deep, semi-circular pool below. This makes an eye-catching centrepiece from the

▲ The stunning white bark of the multi-stemmed birch, Betula utilis, *together with the lion fountain set in the wall in front of it, catch the light and draw the eye to the end of the garden.*

PLANTING

Simplicity is the keynote to Sally's planting in a small space. She uses a theme with plants or colour, then repeats it through the garden to create harmony.

Here she chose the birch as the star of the garden and planned the rest of the planting around this to include a range of textures and round-the-year interest.

KEY PLANTS

▲ A large terracotta jar gives height to a group of containers that hold colourful plants. By replacing pots as the seasons change, Sally can provide round-the-year colour in this small space.

◄ A sink garden comes into its own in a small space, bringing the miniature and very decorative plants it holds up to a higher level and enabling good drainage to be provided.

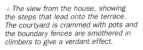
◁ The view from the house, showing the steps that lead onto the terrace. The courtyard is crammed with pots and the boundary fences are smothered in climbers to give a verdant effect.

▽ Looking towards the end of the garden, where the garden shed can only just be seen amongst the greenery.

terrace near to the house and conceals the end of the garden.

The beds are irregular in size, following the staggered edges of the stone paving and together with this groups of pots, create a wide and curving pathway through the entire garden.

▲ A lemon tree, *Citrus limon* 'Meyer', grown in a container provides an exotic touch with its fragrant flowers in early summer followed by fruit. It has been positioned in a corner where it is out of the wind and gets the sunshine throughout the day.

FOR EXTRA COLOUR

Cranesbills, members of the geranium family, are easy to grow and flourish in sun or partial shade and in almost any soil except very wet. The flowers in pink, blue, purple and white appear in summer.

Compact perennial species grow to about 15 cm/6 in tall, and are ideal for use in a sink garden. Taller clump-forming species look effective grown in a flower border or amongst shrubs.

Special effect

Wall fountains can give visual interest and provide the relaxing sound of moving water to the smallest of outdoor spaces and many are suitable for fixing indoors too. They are ideal for use where there are small children.

Many designs are available, from traditional-looking lion or human heads to figures and animals of stone, concrete or lighter metal resin to simple spouts and modern shapes.

Small front garden

Like many front gardens that run alongside busy streets or line the roadside on housing estates, this narrow strip of land lacked any imagination in its design. It was simply made up of a pathway leading along the front of the house, with a bed between this and the house and a strip of grass with some larger shrubs dotted around between the path and the road. By using a zig-zag shape for the path and introducing triangular beds the designer Jean Goldberry transformed the space into an eye-catching and luxuriant seaside garden.

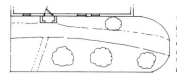

◀ **Before conversion** there was a tarmac path running along the front of the house that continued in front of neighbouring houses, with lawn between the path and road.

Wire beside and above windows

Large pot

HOUSE

Water-washed pebbles on impacted hardcore

Paving slabs

▼ **The planting scheme** As this house is near the sea it was given a coastal planting scheme in strong sea-side colours.

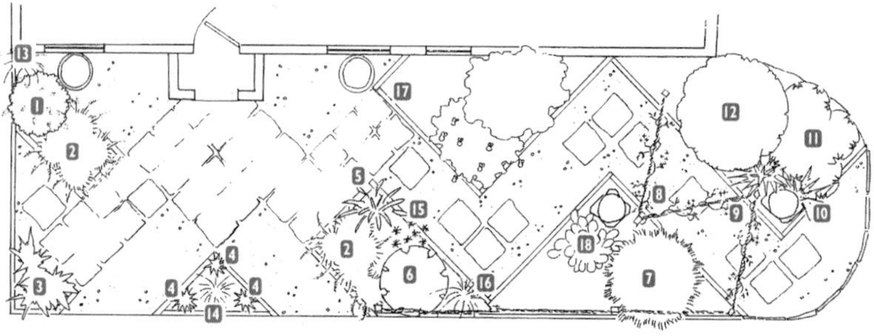

THE GARDEN'S PROBLEMS	HOW THEY WERE SOLVED
The garden was a very long thin strip of land in front of the house.	Strong diagonal shapes were used for beds and paving to break up the length.
The front strip is private but children use the path as a short-cut.	Zig-zag raised beds and uneven surface remove the short cut and ropes divide off the garden from the road.
Visitors took the quick option to the front door, across the grass and through plants.	This route was chosen as the sensible option for the new path to the front door.
Privacy was requested but hedges or fencing were prevented by local regulations.	Tall posts and ropes provide an unusual pergola framework for climbers which will provide privacy.

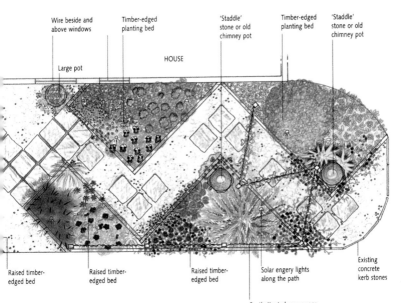

Wire beside and above windows

Timber-edged planting bed

'Staddle' stone or old chimney pot

Timber-edged planting bed

'Staddle' stone or old chimney pot

Large pot

HOUSE

Raised timber-edged bed

Raised timber-edged bed

Raised timber-edged bed

Solar enegry lights along the path

Existing concrete kerb stones

Synthetic sisal rope swags between posts. Rope is coiled around the posts to the top, then zig-zags across from post to post to create a pergola

DESIGNER'S PLANTING SCHEME

Key plants

1 *Hebe* x *andersonii* 'Variegata'
2 Lavender, *Lavandula angustifolia* 'Twickel Purple'
3 Rosemary, *Rosmarinus officinalis* 'Miss Jessup's Upright'
4 Juniper, *Juniperus scopulorum* 'Skyrocket'
5 *Phormium* ssp. *hookeri* 'Cream Delight'
6 *Cistus* x *cyprius*
7 *Fabiana imbricata violacea*
8 Potato vine, *Solanum jasminoides*

9 *Clematis florida* 'Sieboldii'
10 *Yucca filamentosa* 'Variegata'
11 *Skimmia japonica* 'Fructu Albo'
12 *Pittosporum crassifolium* 'Variegatum'

Decorative detail

13 *Pennisetum setaceum* 'Purpureum'
14 *Festuca glauca*
15 *Eryngium variifolium*
16 *Miscanthus sinensis* 'Variegatus'
17 *Viola cornuta*
18 *Bergenia* 'Bressingham White'

Plants for added colour

Pansy, *Viola* x *wittrockiana* 'Cornetto'
Nemophila maculata
Lobelia – in blue and white
Impatiens walleriana Super Elfin Series in violet blue – in shady spots
Cornflower, *Centaurea cyanus* – in blue
Lathyrus 'Snoopea' – trailing over ground

CONSTRUCTION

The cleverly designed zig-zag path of pebbles inset with paving slabs allows the slabs to be laid close together around the front door and main walkway. The pebbles are laid, as are the slabs, on a bed of compacted hardcore to stop weeds from encroaching.

The beds are all outlined with white painted timber. Along the roadside raised beds provide some privacy and a verdant view from the house. Wire and timber trellis to support climbers has been fixed to the house walls around windows and the doorway.

To divide the private land from the public routes beyond it white timber posts 1 m/39 in high with swags of synthetic rope have been introduced.

▲ Tall posts, linked by rope, create a pergola to add interest to the zig-zag pathway and provide a framework for climbing plants.

▲ As a finishing touch the end of the rope is curled around the final post and tied at the bottom.

PLANTING

This garden is designed to be colourful and interesting around the year, with evergreen shrubs, many with variegated foliage, that require a minimum of maintenance. Strong summer colour is provided by annuals such as sweet peas and busy lizzies. The bright blues, purples, reds and white show up well in the clear coastal light.

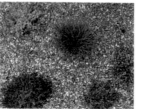

KEY PLANTS

▲ Arching leaves of grasses form fountains of green along the pathway. The blue-green leaves of *Miscanthus sinensis* (in front) balance the cream-streaked leaves of *M. sinensis* 'Variegatus' (behind).

◀ Planting spaces are used to soften the background. Here the grass *Festuca glauca* creates a blue tussock while the golden variegated thyme, *Thymus* 'Aureus' adds sunshine to the surface.

The same idea has been used for the taller posts that make up a pergola at one end. The ropes criss-cross above the pathway and run through large rings fixed to the top or side of each post, winding around the taller posts where they begin and end their run. This leads to a sunny seaside atmosphere to match the location.

Solar-powered lights line the pathway to show the route at night. Using stored energy from sunlight these lights avoid the expense of buying and installing electricity cables beneath the surface of the garden, as well as the upheaval this inevitably involves.

◁ *Looking along the length of this unusual and dramatic front garden, the widening effect of the use of diagonal lines can be clearly seen. Similar gardens to the original appear beyond it.*

△ An Adam's needle, *Yucca filamentosa* stands sentinel beside the pergola and persuades visitors to follow the pathway to the house.

FOR EXTRA COLOUR

The large bright blue summer flowers of cornflowers, *Centaurea cyanus* stand out against the scarlet poppies behind. Colour mix, as well as height, has been taken into consideration here.

Wildflower meadow seeds, grown in a sunny spot, create a colourful wildflower edge or miniature meadow.

Special effects

Swagged rope makes a very effective alternative to horizontal timber rails and a more unusual option than plastic-coated chain link. When using natural hemp rope buy extra length and soak it well first, then leave to dry. If the rope is fixed without this being done it will almost certainly shrink when it dries out after the first rainstorm and the swagged effect will be lost. Once the rope is fixed unwind the ends and comb them out for a tasselled effect. Bind the rope with twine to stop it unravelling further.

Rope also provides an opportunity to use a wide range of fixings and introduce decorative boat knots and curls, an ideal complement to a seaside garden.

See also:
• *Pergolas page 132*
• *Lighting page 144*

Roof garden

The owner of this roof space is a keen gardener with a country garden out of town and when she took over this apartment, with doors leading out onto the roof, her first thought was to turn the roof to good use as a place to enjoy in summer and to look out on through winter. The space was overlooked from almost every direction, providing no privacy, and, furthermore, an unattractive office block was positioned in the prime spot, spoiling what could otherwise have been a stunning view over the city. Another problem was that the roof is also a fire escape route for neighbouring apartments, so gates would have to be inserted and the escape route kept free.

▲ **Before conversion** this was an empty tarmac roof space with double doors from the apartment.

THE GARDEN'S PROBLEMS

The roof was overlooked by windows of adjoining buildings and neighbouring apartments.

An ugly view of an adjacent office block.

Weight is always a problem in gardens that are above ground level.

Wind is a problem at this height.

HOW THEY WERE SOLVED

Trellis was used to provide privacy and a decorative background. Wind tolerant, rampant climbers adorn the trellis for added screening.

A deep bed was created in one corner and trees were planted as a decorative backdrop. A water feature and staggered planting hide the view beyond.

Weight was kept to a minimum. Timber decking was used as it is lighter then paving slabs.

Wind tolerant plants are vital in most roof gardens or balconies. Evergreens provide privacy and colour and regular trimming keeps them small.

▼ **The planting scheme** includes a good evergreen backdrop. Other plants are used for their interesting sculptural shape or their vibrant seasonal colour.

DESIGNER'S PLANTING SCHEME

Key plants
1 *Abelia* x *grandiflora*
2 Himalayan birch, *Betula utilis* var. *jacquemontii*
3 *Camellia* 'Nobilissima'
4 Creeping ceanothus, *Ceanothus thrysiflorus* var. *repens*
5 *Convolvulus cneorum*
6 *Elaeagnus* x *ebbingei* 'Limelight'
7 Myrtle, *Myrtus communis* ssp. *tarentina*
8 Chusan palm, *Trachycarpus fortunei*
9 Juniper, *Juniperus* x *pfitzeriana* 'Mint Julep'
10 Juniper, *Juniperus squamata* 'Blue Carpet'

Decorative details
11 *Acer palmatum* var. *dissectum*
12 *Acer palmatum* 'Crimson Queen'
13 *Buddleia davidii* 'Black Knight'
14 Dogwood, *Cornus* 'Eddie's White Wonder'
15 *Viburnum farreri*
16 *Clematis* 'The President'
17 Climbing hydrangea, *Hydrangea petiolaris*
18 *Jasminum* x *stephanense*
19 *Passiflora caerulea*
20 Star jasmine, *Trachelospermum jasminoides*

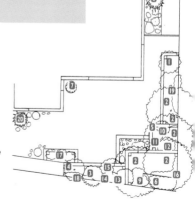

She enlisted the help of garden designer Sally Court, who set to work to produce a design for a high-level haven. As structural information was lacking and the roof was over a block of garages, any weight was positioned along the edges of the roof and over the main structural walls. The roof area was flat and therefore rather uninteresting so Sally decided to use raised beds and form a corner plant grouping so that the tallest shrubs and trees would form the centrepiece and help to mask the office block nearby.

She included a water feature, and fixed trellis along the roof's edges to help to cut down on the force of the wind and provide screening.

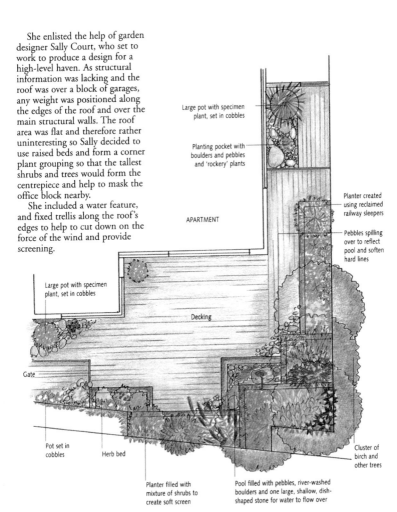

Large pot with specimen plant, set in cobbles

Planting pocket with boulders and pebbles and 'rockery' plants

APARTMENT

Planter created using reclaimed railway sleepers

Pebbles spilling over to reflect pool and soften hard lines

Large pot with specimen plant, set in cobbles

Decking

Gate

Pot set in cobbles

Herb bed

Planter filled with mixture of shrubs to create soft screen

Pool filled with pebbles, river-washed boulders and one large, shallow, dish-shaped stone for water to flow over

Cluster of birch and other trees

▲ View of the corner of the roof garden showing the plants in the raised beds. Containers add colour and pebbles provide natural sculptures.

See also:
• Walls and screens, page 120
• Plants for wind, page 188

CONSTRUCTION

Sally picked natural honey-coloured pressure-treated New Zealand pine for the decking as it is light but tough and has a special grooved non-slip surface. The diamond-shaped trellis used for the screen is of a similar colouring to the flooring and looks decorative.

Raised beds are built of railway sleepers and are set at a range of heights so that a waterfall of planting has been created as viewed from the terrace. Light-weight containers have been chosen in a wide range of sizes and are grouped to complete the lush planting effect.

The pond is sited in the corner of the roof space and backed by the highest planting area. It is deliberately shallow to keep down

PLANTING

Each plant picked for inclusion in this garden had to fulfil many requirements so that a minimum of planting would produce a maximum effect. Those growing in the beds provide a year-round back-drop, while most of the seasonal planting is grown in pots that are easily removed and replaced with the next season's arrangements.

KEY PLANTS

▲ *Passiflora caerulea*, is a fast-growing climber. At the end of summer it produces large white flowers, that have centres of a deep purple-blue. These are followed by edible, yellow fruit.

◀ Grasses and sedges take to life in a container surprisingly well and the leaves stand up to windy conditions. Here, a group of pebbles is an attractive complementary feature.

◄ The pond, created within a framework of railway sleepers and lined with a flexible liner, is fed from above by a simple brass pipe fountain so that the water is always in movement.

▼ A view along the roof terrace shows the step which leads to one of the small gates of the fire escape route.

the weight but pebbles in a range of sizes make it visually interesting at all times of the year.

There is an automatic watering system operated by a timer switch so that the plants are always cared for even if the owner is away.

▲ The highly coloured autumn leaves of Japanese maple, Acer palmatum, are equally attractive when they fall. For a roof garden or balcony it is wise to choose low-growing varieties such as A. palmatum var. dissectum.

FOR EXTRA COLOUR

Petunias are ideal pot plants to add extra summer colour wherever it is needed. They are easy to grow, reward you with a long flowering season, and come in almost every colour imaginable and in both upright and trailing varieties. Grow petunias in light, well-drained soil in full sun. They need some protection from wind and are here placed in pots in positions protected by larger shrubs.

Grandiflora petunias are the ones with very large flowers; multiflora petunias are bushier with smaller flowers and are more tolerant of wet weather.

Special effect

Decorative trellis-work With a wide range of shapes available, trellis need not be used only along the top of a fence to give additional height. A simple design can be created that makes an attractive backdrop, whether clothed in climbers or deliberately left free of foliage.

Pre-constructed arches and arbours are also available and a pergola can be made using a range of shapes and heights. The trellis boundary around the roof space consists of straight panels that have been topped with a stylish scalloped edge, while each post is finished with an ornate finial.

Trellis takes paint and wood stain well and is simple to customize for an original look. In the garden on pages 24–27 designer Paul Cooper filled in some of the spaces in square trellis with plywood and painted these with a chequerboard effect to produce a modern alternative.

CHAPTER 3

DESIGNS FOR PROBLEM POSITIONS

Many gardens have a specific and over-riding problem which has to be addressed as a major part of the design. With careful planning and the right planting, however, most problems can be considerably reduced or even eliminated.

Here our designers tackled six gardens, each with a commonly found but troublesome difficulty. The following pages show how the gardens were transformed into exciting and highly original outdoor spaces.

Garden on a new site 50–53
Shady spot 54–57
Windy location 58–61
Overlooked garden 62–65
Concrete yard 66–69
Steeply sloping land 70–73

Garden on a new site

This garden, built on the site of what was previously a hotel car park, is long, narrow and sloping. The builders had produced long, thin beds along either side, and paths that followed the line of the beds with a further path crossing on the diagonal to join up the two independent routes. The result was an already long and thin area of ground which had been made to appear even longer and thinner. The owner, a keen gardener, wanted space to grow a wide range of plants and

wished to concentrate on those with scent. She also wanted the length to be divided up so that the end of the garden was not immediately visible from the house at the top, and to end up with a design that would make the garden appear shorter and wider.

She turned to designer Antony Henn to solve the garden's problems. He started by shaping the lawn, already there, to form a long, curved outline that narrowed about one-third of the way down. This meant that, with

◀ Before conversion the garden comprised lawn with a narrow bed and paths running along either side.

THE GARDEN'S PROBLEMS

A downward slope away from the house.

The narrowness of the garden, which was emphasized by the shape and position of the present beds and lawn.

The flower bed was built over a previous car park and had a very shallow layer of topsoil so that nothing grew well.

HOW THEY WERE SOLVED

The lawn still slopes but the terrace and arbour on the left were built on top of a flat platform and some beds were built up.

Curving the lawn and beds brings immediate interest. The length is broken up by trellis on one side and the arbour on the other side, at the point where the lawn narrows part way down the garden.

Raising the bed by 60cm/24in and adding more topsoil with well-rotted manure, provides the depth of soil that larger plants require.

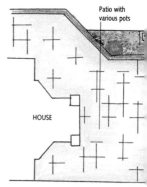

Patio with various pots

HOUSE

▲ The planting scheme introduces a number of trees and shrubs for round-the-year interest, herbs and a range of scented plants.

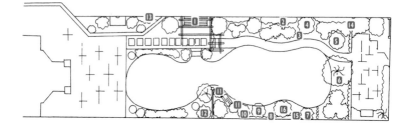

the addition of strategically placed trellis and climbers, parts of the lower section of the garden would be out of view from the top end. However, a hint of what followed would appear through the narrow width of lawn in the centre.

On the left-hand side, which receives sun for most of the day where the lawn narrows, he introduced an arbour so that from here both the top and lower ends of the garden could be viewed simultaneously.

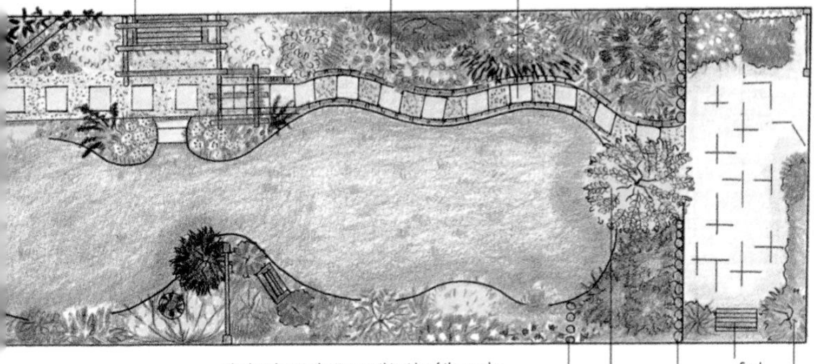

Arbour created by pergola above a seat

Scented roses

Downward-sloping, winding path, brick-edged, with paving slabs and gravel infill

GARAGE

Shade-tolerant planting on this side of the garden

Log retainer

Log retainer

Seat

Existing acer

Specimen tree, *Robinia psuedoacacia* 'Frisia'

DESIGNER'S PLANTING SCHEME

Key plants
1 *Wisteria sinensis* – over arbour
2 *Ceanothus* 'Concha'
3 French lavender, *Lavandula stoechas*
4 *Pittosporum tenuifolium* 'Silver Queen'
5 *Photinia* x *fraseri* 'Red Robin'
6 False acacia, *Robinia pseudoacacia* 'Frisia'
7 *Potentilla* 'Princess'
8 Climbing hydrangea, *Hydrangea Detiolaris* – on fence
9 *Cotoneaster lacteus*

10 Sweet box, *Sarcococca confusa*
11 *Skimmia japonica* 'Rubella'
12 *Kerria japonica*

Decorative detail
13 *Clematis* 'Jackmanii'
14 Winter-flowering jasmine, *Jasminum nudiflorum*
15 Scarlet trumpet Honeysuckle, *Lonicera* x *brownii* 'Dropmore Scarlet'
16 Spanish broom, *Spartium junceum*

Plants for fragrance
Daphne x *burkwoodii* 'Somerset'
Lonicera fragrantissima
Mock orange, *Philadelphus coronarius* 'Aureus'
Jasmine, *Jasminum* x *stephanense*
Scented roses including, climbers, *Rosa* 'New Dawn' and Compassion' plus 'Octavia Hill', Graham Thomas, and patio rose 'Rosy Future'

Looking up the garden towards the house, showing the curving path on the right leading to the arbour.

See also:
- *Long, narrow garden, page 28*
- *Arches, pergolas and arbours, page 132*
- *Plants for shade, page 184*
- *Plants for full sun, page 186*

CONSTRUCTION

The lawn was reshaped with an undulating edge and the main area of construction was on the left-hand side. Part way down the length, a pergola was constructed over a seat to form the arbour. Edged in bricks a curving path of gravel has paving stepping-stones set into it and runs down the side of the lawn.

At the end of the garden a narrow paved path has been widened creating a larger terrace and working area, screened by trellis. In front of the lower terrace, upended logs form a retaining wall for a flat bed which is built up above the paving. The planting, which helps to hide the wall of the garage from the house and to provide privacy for the terrace itself.

PLANTING

The scented flowers introduced into this garden include *Lonicera fragrantissima*, with its creamy white flowers in winter and early spring and *Daphne* x *burkwoodii* 'Somerset' with its purple-pink flowers and heady fragrance. *Philadelphus* 'Manteau d'Hermine' flowers in early summer, then roses and herbs take over.

KEY PLANTS

*For winter interest evergreen shrubs with variegated foliage come into their own. The leaves of *Pittosporum tenuifolium* 'Silver Queen' have silvery white marbling.*

*Shrubs with coloured berries add autumn and winter colour. *Cotoneaster lacteus* has evergreen leaves and produces clumps of brilliant orange-red berries which remain through winter.*

◀ The view from upstairs shows the soft shape of the lawn and path.

The garden originally contained very poor soil. It also has extremes of temperature, one side being very sunny and the other cold and shady. The condition of the soil has been improved with the addition of plenty of well-rotted horse manure and this also helps to retain moisture in the soil on the sunny side and improve drainage on the cold and shady side of the garden.

▲ The seat in the arbour, with a white-flowered cistus in the foreground. Steps lead onto the lawn in one direction while others follow the downward path.

▲ Ceanothus can be grown as a tree or shrub, or used to clothe a fence. Ceanothus 'Dark Star', (above), forms an arching shape and has scented, dark purple flowers. Ceanothus 'Concha' is denser, with deep blue flowers.

FOR EXTRA COLOUR

Wildlife can introduce colour as well as flowers. Here Lavandula angustifolia 'Bowles' Early' is shown with painted lady butterflies. Many of the herbs grown in this garden, amongst which are lovage, angelica, marjoram, mints, lemon balm, fennel, rosemary, borage, thyme and sage, will also attract butterflies.

To attract a particular species of butterfly include plants the larvae need, as well as those that attract the adult.

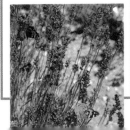

Special effect

Grouping pots is an ideal way of providing a bank of colour at any point in the garden where it is temporarily lacking. In most cases pots in a range of sizes and shapes, but all of the same material, look most effective. Natural materials like pebbles, driftwood, shells and cones provide interesting detail.

Shady spot

The existing small front garden in this shady spot had been destroyed when the house, suffering from subsidence, had to be underpinned so designer Sally Court had an almost free hand in its design.

Tall fences on either side, as well as trees that line the roadside, add to the shady aspect of this small space, so this was an important factor that had to be considered in the new design. The owners also wanted to keep a snake-bark maple, *Acer capillipes*, that was already there and to retain the crazy-paving car parking space at the side of the house. This meant that the ground surface chosen for the garden had to blend with this. Sally opted for bricks, in tones to complement those of the house as well as the crazy paving, and used them to create a hexagonal terrace featuring an ornamental urn as its centrepoint.

▲ **Before conversion** the garden had been all but removed while essential remedial work was done on the house.

▼ **The planting scheme** was designed to provide interest around the year and to create a colourful spring garden.

THE GARDEN'S PROBLEMS

The owners are away from home a lot of the time so they require a low-maintenance garden.

The garden is shady and dry because nearby large trees draw up almost all the moisture.

The design needed to blend in with the present car-parking area.

The area is tiny, with a very narrow planting space.

HOW THEY WERE SOLVED

Sally used paving instead of grass, with shrubs and bulbs for the planting. An automatic watering system was suggested. Bark mulch on beds helps to retain moisture.

Plants were chosen which were suited to the dry shady conditions. The watering system and the mulch alleviate this problem.

Bricks were laid in a herringbone pattern, in a colour to blend with the crazy-paving, linking house and garden.

Using a hexagon shape creates space for deeper beds close to the house and opposite. The use of small-sized blocks also create a spacious feel in the area.

DESIGNER'S PLANTING SCHEME

Key plants
1   Rhododendron 'Everest'
2   Acer palmatum var. dissectum
3   Rhododendron 'Golden Sunset'
4   Rhododendron luteum
5   Cornus kousa var. chinensis
6   Rhododendron 'Gibraltar'
7   Euonymus fortunei 'Emerald Gaiety'
8   Scarlet trumpet honeysuckle, Lonicera x brownii 'Dropmore Scarlet'
9   Hydrangea petiolaris
10 Rhododendron 'Bluebird Group'

11 Rhododendron 'Narcissiflorum'
12 Yew, Taxus baccata 'Fastigiata'

Decorative detail
13 Saxifraga paniculata var. baldensis – in urn
14 Sedum spathulifolium 'Purpureum' in urn
15 Houseleeks, Sempervivums – in urn
16 Hosta 'Royal Standard'
17 Evergreen fern, Polypodium vulgare

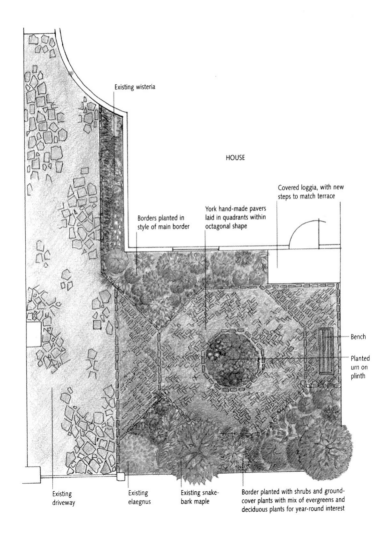

Existing wisteria

HOUSE

Covered loggia, with new
steps to match terrace

Borders planted in
style of main border

York hand-made pavers
laid in quadrants within
octagonal shape

Bench

Planted
urn on
plinth

Existing
driveway

Existing
elaegnus

Existing snake-
bark maple

Border planted with shrubs and ground-
cover plants with mix of evergreens and
deciduous plants for year-round interest

CONSTRUCTION

As this is a very small plot bricks were chosen for the main area of ground surface, the small-sized units being in scale with the setting. At the centre of the design stands an ornamental stone urn which is placed in the centre of a brick hexagon, that is divided into four separate sections of herring-bone laid bricks, each section outlined with a line of bricks laid straight.

A bench looks into the garden and is positioned outside the front door where it captures the small amount of sun that reaches this garden. On the opposite side of the hexagon the bricks continue as part of a further hexagon to meet the crazy paving of the car-parking area.

▲ The centrepoint of the garden is a stone urn that also marks the centre of the hexagonal brick terrace. Planting in the urn is deliberately kept low so that the container itself forms the highlight.

See also:
• Paved town garden, page 36
• Plants for shade, page 185

PLANTING

There are two main planting areas, and the plants Sally has chosen reflect a woodland feel, with azaleas, rhododendrons, ferns and hostas. Both evergreen and deciduous azaleas are included with good autumn colour provided by the deciduous species. Bulbs add a strong splash of extra colour for the spring.

KEY PLANTS

▲ An area of low planting was created for the large urn. *Sempervivum arachnoideum*, the cobweb houseleek, was included with its rosettes of green and red leaves covered in fine white hairs.

◀ The hosta, 'Frosted Jade' is a good choice for a shady spot with its white-edged, strongly veined leaves. The almost white flowers appear in early summer.

Special effect

Patterns with pavers and bricks This paving has many uses, from a patterned area in the centre of a terrace of larger paving, to a country look for a patio or car-parking area. By using different colours or laying the bricks in a range of patterns more effects can be created. Five alternative ways of using small-sized paving units show some of the patterns possible.

◁ Brick-like pavers divide up a large area of paving, adding extra interest to the expanse.

1 Wavy-edge paving is used here and forms an alternative to bricks laid side-by-side. The blocks are laid in a simple side-by-side pattern so that each block fits snugly into the next.

2 Herring-bone is the traditional method of laying bricks, in this case pavers with an antiqued finish.

3 This is an unusually shaped paver that mixes colours and tones and offers the chance to form a wide range of patterns.

4 By mixing gravel and pavers a far wider range of patterns can be created, as here where a series of swirling circles is formed out of wedge-shaped pavers interspersed with gravel.

5 This tinted concrete material, impressed when wet with rubber mats to simulate cobbles, setts or paving, is tough enough to be used for a driveway and comes in a wide range of colours.

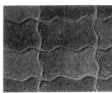

1

2

3

4

5

△ This deciduous azalea, *Rhododendron luteum* has yellow funnel-shaped flowers that open in late spring to early summer and are strongly scented. Many deciduous azaleas provide colourful autumn hues before the leaves fall.

FOR EXTRA COLOUR

For good ground cover include *Persicaria campanulata* which can grow to around 90 cm/36 in with a similar spread and tolerates light shade. This is a clump-forming semi-evergreen perennial that has hairy mid-green leaves which are lighter underneath. On the tall stems bell-shaped fragrant pink or white flowers (the variety 'Southcombe White' has white flowers) appear in clusters from mid-summer through to early autumn.

Windy location

This garden, on the side of a hill and not far from the sea, has good views of hills beyond but has two major disadvantages. It is exposed (and windy) and it is overlooked by a number of neighbouring houses.

Designer Jean Goldberry, whose garden it is, used an ingenious method of dealing with both these problems. By extending the fence with an uneven, undulating top edge she could hide views that were unattractive and highlight those she wanted to enjoy. Because the fence is not solid in its composition it also reduces the strength of the wind.

▲ **Before conversion** the garden had as a boundary a picket fence and a row of Leylandii which had grown to 12 m/40 ft. Although these hid neighbouring houses the hedge in particular also obscured the attractive views.

THE GARDEN'S PROBLEMS	HOW THEY WERE SOLVED
A view of a derelict garage on one side of the garden.	A mirror was positioned at the end of the water feature to hide the wall and to apparently double the size of the pool.
The garden was overlooked but had beautiful views of hills beyond the houses.	A wavy edge was added to the top of the fence, allowing hill views to be seen while maintaining privacy.
The garden had no surface of topsoil so was unsuitable for growing a wide range of plants.	To improve the soil quality, manure and compost were added in large quantities.

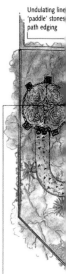

Undulating line 'paddle' stones path edging

N, S, E and W symbols in Celtic script on metal plates screwed to tree sections. Circle of 'paddle' stones (water-worn flat rocks or slates) and timber block seats, each quarter section inlaid with a spiral of pebbles, marbles and glass 'dragon drops'

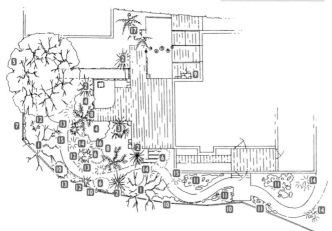

◀ **The planting scheme** was based on small-leaved plants that could withstand the wind and also provide winter interest.

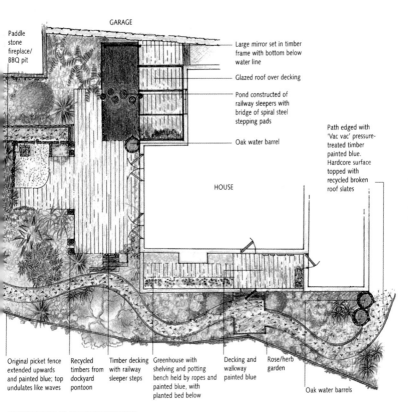

Paddle stone fireplace/ BBQ pit

GARAGE

Large mirror set in timber frame with bottom below water line

Glazed roof over decking

Pond constructed of railway sleepers with bridge of spiral steel stepping pads

Oak water barrel

Path edged with 'Vac vac' pressure-treated timber painted blue. Hardcore surface topped with recycled broken roof slates

HOUSE

Original picket fence extended upwards and painted blue; top undulates like waves

Recycled timbers from dockyard pontoon

Timber decking with railway sleeper steps

Greenhouse with shelving and potting bench held by ropes and painted blue, with planted bed below

Decking and walkway painted blue

Rose/herb garden

Oak water barrels

DESIGNER'S PLANTING SCHEME

Key plants
1   *Eucalyptus kybeanensis*
2   New Zealand Flax, *Phormium tenax*
3   Cabbage palm, *Cordyline australis*
4   Rock rose, *Cistus x corbariensis*
5   *Acer campestre* 'Schwerinii'
6   Cotton lavender, *Santolina chamaecyparissus*
7   Italian buckthorn, *Rhamnus alatemus* 'Argenteovariegata'
8   *Pinus mugo* var. *pumilio*

9   *Clematis* 'Venosa Violacea'
10 *Rosa* Molineux
11 Daisy bush, *Olearia traversii*
12 *Yucca filamentosa*

Decorative detail
13 Sedge, *Carex* 'Frosted Curls'
14 Sedge, *Carex flagellifera*
15 Pheasant's tail grass, *Stipa arundinacea*
16 Sundrops, *Oenothera fruticosa*
17 Soft tree fern, *Dicksonia antarctica*

Plants for added colour
California poppy, *Eschscholtzia*
Poppy, *Papaver rhoeas* Shirley Series
Mignonette, *Reseda odorata*
Livingstone daisy, *Dorotheanthus* 'Lunette' *syn.* 'Yellow Ice'
Alyssum 'Apricot Tapestry'
Statice, *Limonium* 'Pastel Mixed'

▼ Brightly coloured barnacled buoys create a group sculpture on the veranda and help to give this garden a strong nautical theme.

▲ Slipped in behind the steps that lead off the decking platform are slits containing broken roof slates randomly spattered with mussel shells and dotted with a range of magenta pink flowers.

See also:
- Narrow front garden, page 40
- Introducing water, page 126
- Plants for wind and poor soil, page 188

CONSTRUCTION

Jean chose to have a large area of decking in the centre of her garden with plenty of room to dance. She used southern yellow pine which had been 'Vac vac' pressure treated – a clear preservative, harmless to wildlife. The decking is non-slip when wet. Paths are edged with timber, painted blue to match the fence, or water-shaped flat stones. Steps are constructed of railway sleepers covered with chicken wire to stop them from becoming slippery in wet weather.

A rectangular pool leads off a decking-floored veranda with a glazed roof. This is a box made of railway sleepers with a rubber liner. A mirror, cleverly positioned at one end from ceiling to below water level, doubles the apparent

PLANTING

The scheme was based on orange, brown and silver to complement the blues of the fence and pergola. Jean wanted a Mediterranean seaside look and a good winter structure. *Acer campestre* 'Schwerinii', with red-purple young leaves, were chosen to surround the Celtic circle; sedges and pheasant's tail grass provide the exotic effect.

KEY PLANTS

▲ In late spring and early summer the decorative single creamy yellow flowers of X *Halimiocistus wintonensis* 'Merrist Wood Cream' display their beautiful yellow and maroon throat markings.

◀ The pale yellow-green evergreen leaves of the sedge *Carex* 'Frosted Curls' tumble over the blue-painted timber-edged path. The sedge, *Carex flagellifera* has rusty orange leaves.

◀ Steel spirals form stepping stones for the pond.

▼ An undulating top to the fence obscures neighbouring houses and helps to break the wind.

size. It is fixed to a backing of ply to protect the silvering and the glass is made water resistant by painting with glass fibre. The picket fence, with its wavy top edge, reduces the speed of the wind, unlike a solid wall or fence.

▲ Pontoon timbers, rope and anchor continue the strong nautical theme.

▲ The strong, structural shape of this Adam's needle, *Yucca filamentosa*, provides a round-the-year view from the house.

FOR EXTRA COLOUR

Packets of seeds can provide a wonderful splash of colour when sown as a group display. Sow the seeds of poppies in spring in full sun and in fertile, well-drained soil and they will be in flower by summer. Flowers of many poppies then produce decorative large seed pods, allowing you to save the seeds for another year. This is the field poppy, *Papaver rhoeas* from the Shirley Series, the flowers of which come in single, semi-double and double flowers in yellow. Pink, and orange, as well as red.

Special effect

Stepping across water For walking across the water stepping-stones create a less obvious alternative to bridges. Spirals of steel form the stepping-stones, shown before being lowered into place. Paving slabs are another option. Using granite setts, with spaces between for the water to flow around them can create a similar effect.

Overlooked garden

Jean Goldberry uses a range of heights and divisions along the garden's length to break up the space in an interesting way, creating the privacy that the owners longed for. She used a mature *Amelanchier canadensis* at the end of the garden to create a miniature woodland area with tree-trunk stepping stones and a seat of timber planks. Paved terraces breaks up the garden's length and groups of larger pebbles add a sculptural effect. There are raised timber-edged beds and two ponds.

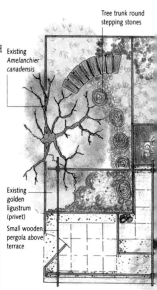

Tree trunk round stepping stones

Existing *Amelanchier canadensis*

Existing golden ligustrum (privet)

Small wooden pergola above terrace

▲ **Before conversion** the garden comprised very overgrown shrubs on either side with grass down the centre, over which a worn-away path led to the back gate.

THE GARDEN'S PROBLEMS

The original garden seemed very long and narrow.

Little privacy, with buildings on the right-hand side looking directly into the garden.

A rectangular space, all on one level, lacking any interest.

HOW THEY WERE SOLVED

Garden 'rooms' created by laying paving in squares and rectangles, breaking up the length.

Pergolas hide the garden from the overlooking windows, creating interest and views from the house.

The level was dropped in the centre, with steps down. Raised beds of different heights add interest.

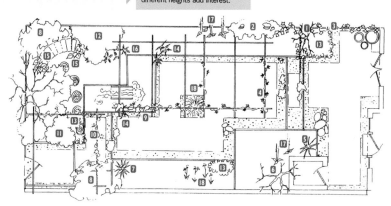

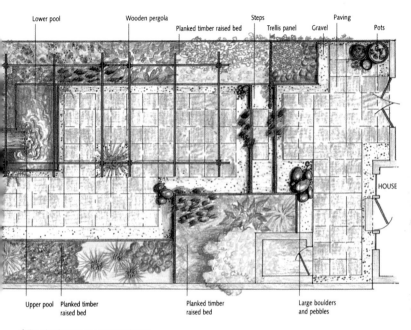

Lower pool Wooden pergola Steps Paving Pots
Planked timber raised bed Trellis panel Gravel

HOUSE

Upper pool Planked timber
raised bed

Planked timber
raised bed

Large boulders
and pebbles

◀ *The planting scheme* uses cool blues
and white in the main, with some rose pink
to provide definition and some golden and
cream-variegated foliage.

DESIGNER'S PLANTING SCHEME

Key plants
1 *Eucryphia milliganii*
2 *Rhamnus alaternus*
   'Argenteovariegata'
3 Vine, *Vitis coignetiae*
4 Golden hop, *Humulus lupulus*
   'Aureus'
5 Mountain flax, *Phormium
   cookianum* ssp. *hookeri*
   'Cream Delight'
6 *Cytisus battandieri*
7 *Yucca gloriosa*
8 *Phyllostachys aureosulcata*
   'Aureocaulis'

9 *Clematis armandii*
10 *Jasminum officinalis*
   'Aureomarginata'
11 *Daphne odora* 'Aureomarginata'
12 *Rhododendron* 'Cilpinense'

Decorative detail
13 *Bergenia cordifolia*
14 Lady fern, *Athyrium filix-femina*
15 *Hosta* 'Sum and Substance'
16 *Euphorbia robbiae*
17 Foxglove, *Digitalis grandiflora*
18 *Iris sibinca* 'Flight of Blue
   Butterflies'

Plants for added colour
Morning Glory, *Ipomoea tricolor*
   'Heavenly Blue'
Busy lizzies and balsams, *Impatiens*
   – in white where spaces available
Wishbone flower, *Torenia fournieri*
Bells of Ireland, *Molluccella laevis*
Tobacco plant, *Nicotiana* Nicki Series
   – in white in sunny patches

CONSTRUCTION

Some initial work was needed to transform this garden and produce the privacy required by the owners. Firstly a range of levels was created along the length of the garden. Paving was then laid, with shallow steps edged in timber leading from one level to the next. The change of levels is only slight, dividing the garden into three separate sections but immediately makes it appear much more interesting.

Matching timber was used to make the raised beds. Those in the central sunken area are three planks high and the one nearest to the house, on the left, slightly higher.

The pools are on different levels so that water from the back pool cascades into the lower front pool then recirculates. Positioned directly

▲The view from the central section of the garden, looking up the steps towards the back gate with the pergola posts just in the picture and the water feature out of sight on the right.

See also:
• Introducing water, page 126

PLANTING

Summer colour abounds in this garden but winter interest is not ignored. This appears in variegated foliage and in the exotic golden stemmed bamboo, *Phyllostachys aureosculcata* 'Aureocaulis'. Pink is introduced in late winter with the pale pink rhododendron 'Cilpinense' and in spring with the variegated *Daphne odora* 'Aureomarginata'.

KEY PLANTS

▲A The lemon yellow and pineapple-scented flowers of pineapple broom, *Cytisus battandieri*, appear in mid- and late summer. Silvery green leaves contrast against the cone-shaped flowers.

◄*Euonymus fortunei* provides winter colour in both its gold- and silver-variegated leaf varieties. *E. fortunei* 'Silver Queen' has bold white margins to the leaves and can be grown as a climber.

▲ Looking from the terrace near to the house down the steps into the sunken garden. A vine (deciduous) and evergreen plants cover the roof of the larger pergola and create a green and private space

▶ Together with the fountain in the front pond the cascading water from the higher pool adds the soothing sound of moving water

opposite the steps that lead down from the terrace, the water feature creates a decorative picture from indoors, all year round. The long pergola also provides interest from the house.

At the end of the garden a soft path of wood chippings is interspersed with stepping-stones made of sliced tree-trunks. These have been covered with wire netting to ensure they remain nonslip, an important consideration.

▲ The water feature has a channel that takes the water down from the higher pool into the larger, lower one.

▲ The large leaves of this vine, *Vitas coignetiae* 'Incana' soon cover the expanse of pergola and provide dappled green shade and privacy during the months of summer.

FOR EXTRA COLOUR

Flowering plants in pots add colour to any area in the garden where it is temporarily lacking. The plants can remain in a secluded spot until they reach their peak, and can then be moved into position when they can take pride of place. Most plants will cope with less than ideal conditions for a short time.

Conservatories can be too hot and dry for many plants in summer, but at this time the plants flourish outdoors to be brought back indoors when the cooler weather returns. In most areas this hydrangea could be wintered outside.

Special effects

Natural sculpture In this garden groups of pebbles form simple but striking natural sculptures very much in keeping with the gravel edging that divides one area of paving from the next. Many other natural materials can be used successfully in this way. Shells and driftwood can be used to add character to a seaside garden. Tree stumps, cones and logs enhance a woodland area.

Concrete garden

Few outdoor areas are less inspiring to look at, and more daunting to transform, than a concrete backyard. Rather than removing the surface designer Jean Goldberry has built on top of it, using a series of beds stepped up away from the house. A pergola and trellis allow for vertical planting and a raised pond adds a calming influence.

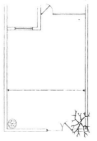

◀ **Before conversion** the yard contained little more than its solid grey base, with a narrow bed down one side and a lilac tree at the end.

▼ **The planting scheme** includes evergreens with leaves tinted in cream, gold and red, as well as other plants in striking shapes for year-round interest.

THE GARDEN'S PROBLEMS

The small size – just 7.7m/25 ft long by 5 m/ 16.5 ft wide.

A concrete surface would be extremely difficult to remove.

Neighbour's upstairs windows overlook the garden.

An uninteresting view from the kitchen window.

The owner has little time to spend on maintenance.

HOW THEY WERE SOLVED

A pergola, trellis, pond and raised beds were introduced to vary levels.

Raised beds were built after drainage holes were made in the concrete.

The pergola will create privacy once the plants grow over the roof and uprights.

The raised beds and the vertical planting create interest all year round.

Maintenance is simple with the raised beds.

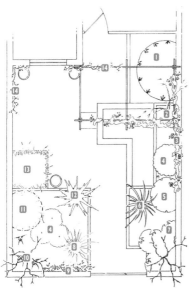

DESIGNER'S PLANTING SCHEME

Key plants
1 *Choisya* 'Aztec Pearl'
2 *Fargesia muneliae* 'Simba'
3 Climbing rose, *Rosa* 'Felicite et Perpetue' – along trellis
4 Rosemary-leaved cotton lavender, *Santolina rosmarinifolia*
5 *Daphne odora* 'Aureomarginata'
6 Flax, *Phormium* 'Cream Delight'
7 *Helleborus argutifolius*
8 Grass, *Cortaderia* 'Gold Band'
9 Ivy, *Hedera canariensis* 'Canary Island'
10 June berry, *Amelanchier lamarckii*
11 Veronica, *Hebe* 'Red Edge'
12 *Romarinus prostratus*
13 Lavender, *Lavandula* 'Hidcote'

14 *Trachelospermum asiaticum*

Plants for added colour
Smilacina racemosa
Hosta 'Sum and Substance'
Schisandra grandiflora
Alchemilla mollis
Viola, *Viola cornuta*
Sweet pea, *Lathyrus* 'Old Spice'
Wallflower, *Erysimum linifolium* 'Variegatum'
Trailing petunia in shades of purple, petunias, in shades of deep purple
Nasturtiums, apricot and pale yellow
Fuchsia 'Tom Thumb'
Lady fern, *Athyrium felix-felina*
Lenten rose, *Helleborus orientalis*
Herbs, sage, chives, thyme.
Pink, *Dianthus* 'Mrs Sinkins'
Madonna lily, *Lilium candidum*

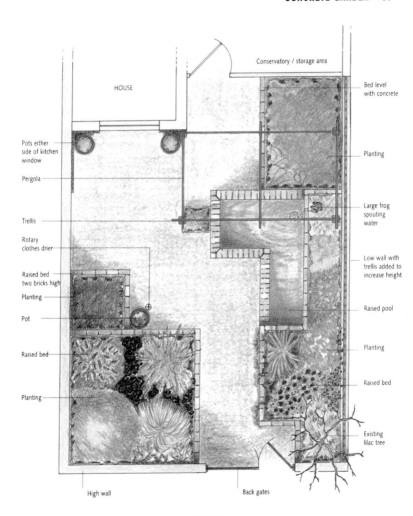

Conservatory / storage area

HOUSE

Bed level
with concrete

Pots either
side of kitchen
window

Planting

Pergola

Trellis

Large frog
spouting
water

Rotary
clothes drier

Low wall with
trellis added to
increase height

Raised bed
two bricks high

Planting

Raised pool

Pot

Raised bed

Planting

Planting

Raised bed

Existing
lilac tree

High wall

Back gates

BACK ALLEY

CONSTRUCTION

The design involved the building of raised beds over the concrete, the erection of a pergola and trellis, and the addition of a pool. Areas of path between the beds are covered with softly shaded slabs.

The raised beds start near the house, gradually increasing in height near the end of the garden. The original bed makes it possible to plant large deep-rooting shrubs like the Mexican orange blossom, Choisya, on the right-hand side.

The pergola and the trellis, on the low wall on the right hand side of the garden, bring support for colourful climbers as well as giving privacy to this small space. More rampant, leafy plants are ideal for areas where shade is required, while those plants with

▲ Looking towards the house through the arch-way of the pergola. Later, the burgeoning plants will turn this into a comfortable and shady sitting-out area.

See also:
- Raised beds, page 108, 120
- Introducing water, page 126
- Arches, pergolas and arbours, page 132

PLANTING

Jean chose the plants for this garden with special care so that they would create a verdant look and maintain privacy around the year. The secret of success was to pick key plants for their stunning shape (ensuring that this is well displayed) and to choose as neighbours those plants that best show off each other's colours and leaf shapes.

KEY PLANTS

▲ For ground cover *Alchemilla mollis*, lady's mantle, was chosen. The leaves spread out to show off the hairy surface that holds the water in place after rain has fallen.

◄ By the house, the scented white flowers of *Choisya* 'Aztec Pearl' can be seen in late spring, followed in late summer to autumn by a second lot of blooms.

▲ The view from the house looking towards the original lilac tree, included in the new design.

▶ The L-shaped bed at the end of the garden echoes the shape of the pond and its plants are on view from the kitchen window.

slimmer, neater growth allow filtered sunlight where this is preferred.

The L-shaped pool creates a soothing, reflective spot and the supporting wall is designed to form a comfortable seat for those enjoying its calming influence.

▲ A dense, low evergreen shrub with bright green aromatic leaves, *Santolina rosmarinifolia* is positioned partway down the garden in full sun. In mid-summer it produces round heads of bright yellow flowers.

FOR EXTRA COLOUR

For a natural effect, in comparison to the bolder pansy cultivars, Jean introduced the smaller, but scented, pale lilac, pink and white flowers of violas, *Viola cornuta*, which appear early, in spring, and flower through to summer.

Grow these, like pansies, in moist, but well-drained soil in sun or partial shade and divide clumps in spring or early autumn to increase plant numbers.

Special effect

Shaped pergolas A pergola can be designed to fit into almost any shape or space in the garden. Once they are covered in climbers, they soon provide a shady spot for relaxing out of the direct sunlight.

For alternative pergola materials and designs to the one shown here, see those on pages 16–27, 40–43, 58–61, 70–73, 76–79, 90, 94–95.

Steeply sloping land

This garden, on the side of a hill, with a high bank at the end of the garden and concrete retaining wall near to the house, was difficult and dangerous to manage. Jean Goldberry terraced it, forming three flat areas, one above the other, linked by wide, shallow steps.

First Jean placed the sitting area at the top of the garden where there were stunning views and positioned a pergola to obscure the view of the town behind it. She next placed a water feature in the centre of the garden, to include a waterfall, where water splashed down from one garden level to the next spreading out into a shallow natural-looking pool. She also added a series of beds of cascading plants to provide colour that could be enjoyed from the house below.

△ **Before conversion** the garden contained a lawn that sloped steeply towards the house, making mowing difficult. There was a narrow slip of concrete near the house from which steps went up to the garden.

▽ **The planting scheme** Part of the brief was to produce a garden which placed special emphasis on autumn colour. Jean also used the steep slope to create a water-fall of blues, reds and oranges.

THE GARDEN'S PROBLEMS

The very steep, sloping land.

The slope made working in the garden difficult. No flat areas were wide enough to work in safety.

Old bank on the top boundary.

The steep slope made it difficult to use the mower.

HOW THEY WERE SOLVED

The sitting area was positioned at the top end of the garden where there were good views over local countryside.

Railway sleepers form an edging for steps and to terrace the space into a series of flat beds and paved areas.

This area was designed to mimic the effect of roadside banks covered in wild flowers.

Grass was deliberately avoided in the design as even after the area was terraced, it would have been difficult to get a mower into position to mow it.

DESIGNER'S PLANTING SCHEME

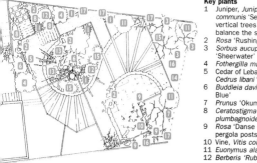

Key plants
1 Juniper, *Juniperus communis* 'Sentinel' – vertical trees to balance the slope
2 *Rosa* 'Rushing Stream'
3 *Sorbus aucuparia* 'Sheerwater'
4 *Fothergilla major*
5 Cedar of Lebanon, *Cedrus libani* 'Sargentii'
6 *Buddleia davidii* 'Nanho Blue'
7 *Prunus* 'Okumiyako'
8 *Ceratostigma plumbaginoides*
9 *Rosa* 'Danse de Feu' up pergola posts
10 Vine, *Vitis coignetiae*
11 *Euonymus alatus*
12 *Berberis* 'Rubrostilla'

Decorative detail
13 *Juncus inflexus* 'Afro'
14 Sweet woodruff, *Galium odoratum*
15 *Nepeta* 'Six Hills Giant'
16 *Farfugium japonicum* 'Argenteum'
17 *Dryopteris filix-mas*

Plants for added colour
Pelargonium 'Lila Mini Cascade'
Lobelia in dark and sky blue to fill spaces
Nasturtium, *Tropaeolum majus*
Zinnia haageana 'Persian Carpet'
Pansy, *Viola* hybrids
Salvia farinacea 'Victoria'

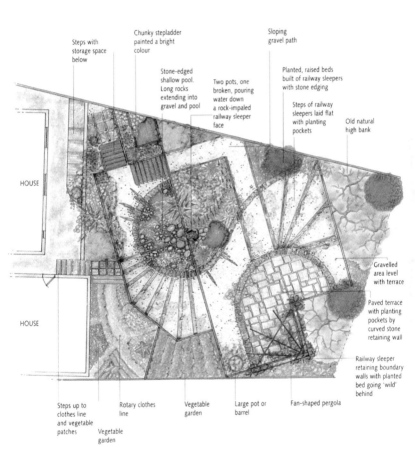

Steps with storage space below

Chunky stepladder painted a bright colour

Stone-edged shallow pool. Long rocks extending into gravel and pool

Two pots, one broken, pouring water down a rock-impaled railway sleeper face

Sloping gravel path

Planted, raised beds built of railway sleepers with stone edging

Steps of railway sleepers laid flat with planting pockets

Old natural high bank

HOUSE

HOUSE

Gravelled area level with terrace

Paved terrace with planting pockets by curved stone retaining wall

Railway sleeper retaining boundary walls with planted bed going 'wild' behind

Steps up to clothes line and vegetable patches

Rotary clothes line

Vegetable garden

Vegetable garden

Large pot or barrel

Fan-shaped pergola

▲ The view of the house looking down from the end of the garden and showing the series of wide and shallow timber-edged steps that are lined with gravel.

See also:
- Windy location, page 58
- Arches, pergolas and arbours, page 132
- Plants for dry soil, page 186

CONSTRUCTION

Terracing involves a lot of initial construction work but it is almost always the best method of dealing with a steep, sloping garden. Being thick, wide and tough, railway sleepers make ideal edging supports for this sort of terraced construction but any treated timber of similar strength would be just as suitable. Stone, a readily available local material, was used to form a low retaining wall alongside the steps and around the top terrace.

The centrally placed water feature uses the same materials. The water tumbles down the height of the retaining wall to end up in a shallow pebble and rock-lined pool on the terrace below.

The sun terrace, at the top of the garden, is made with a surface

PLANTING

This garden has glowing autumn colour with *Fothergilla major*, *Ceratostigma plumbaginoides*, the vine *Vitis coignetiae* and *Euonymus alatus* all showing brilliant orange and scarlet leaves in autumn, highlighted by the coral red fruit of the berberis 'Rubrostilla' and splashes of red, orange and yellow in the flowers of the nasturtiums.

KEY PLANTS

▲ The deep purple flowers of lavender, *Lavandula angustifolia* 'Twickel Purple' edge a raised bed alongside the path joining the terraces to provide scent for passers by on sunny summer days.

◄ Thyme 'Pink Chintz' forms tight mats between the paving slabs and is also used in the free-draining gravel. Mat-forming thymes need cutting back hard if they are to remain compact.

◁ *A view, not long after construction, shows the steep path that leads up to the paved seating area at the top of the garden.*

of paving and retained by a stone wall. Spaces at the edge of the paving provide planting areas for cascading plants and the pergola forms a framework for climbers such as a vine and the scarlet and orange rose 'Danse du Feu'.

▲By using a range of climbing plants growing up a post of the pergola, Jean has rung the changes and provided blooms through much of the year. A large early flowering clematis intermingles with the rose 'Danse du Feu' which has scarlet flowers later in the year.

FOR EXTRA COLOUR

Nasturtiums, *Tropaeolum* hybrids, are easy to grow from seed in moderately fertile, well-drained soil and in full sun. They provide a colourful mass of red, orange and yellow flowers. *T.* 'Alaska' series (shown) have specially decorative leaves speckled and blotched in creamy white. These form good ground cover colour. *T. majus* is a climber, and *T.* 'Peach Melba' has pale creamy yellow flowers with streaked orange-red centres.

▲*A natural effect is achieved by the timber and stone used to form the waterfall and the shallow pond lined with pebbles and rocks below.*

Special effect

Waterfalls provide visual interest and the sound of falling water helps to bring a sense of harmony with nature.

The water appears from between boulders. Vertical sleepers provide the backing to the fall and slivers of stone act as natural breaks to the tumbling water before it enters the pool below. The water is pumped back up to the top of the fall, to follow the same procedure again and again.

This circulating water can be powered by a submersible pump if the height is not more than 1.2 m/4 ft. Otherwise a surface pump would be needed and this requires a separate electricity supply.

CHAPTER 4

DESIGNS WITH SPECIAL FEATURES IN MIND

Agarden that is planned with a central theme, a particular use, or has a distinct advantage or specific requirements, needs special thought in its design and choice of planting.

In this chapter we show how our garden designers have dealt with six gardens, each planned around a specific requirement.

Low-maintenance garden 76–79
Children's garden 80–83
Garden with a view 84–87
With the elderly in mind 88–91
Integrating a swimming pool 92–95
Wildlife garden 96–99

Low-maintenance garden

With a garage and a lane at one end of this very long garden (and the house itself the other side of the lane), it was important to draw people into and through the garden to the opposite end. Jean Goldberry created the main areas of interest at the far end and these include a pond, decked terrace for eating and a pergola above the extended original patio. Along the side of the garage she created a zig-zag pergola to follow the lines of the ground surface of gravel, grass and planting.

▲ Before conversion the garden was surrounded with a conifer hedge on one side, with a high wall and a timber fence on the other and was mainly weed-covered soil.

THE GARDEN'S PROBLEMS

The owners both work full-time and prefer to enjoy the garden rather than spend time working in it.

The space is very long and thin with a garage and the lane at one end.

A flexible space for eating, which could accommodate a range of numbers of people, was required.

HOW THEY WERE SOLVED

Decking, gravel and paving provide hard, easy to care for surfaces. Terracota pots hold geraniums, which need little watering, and the planting is mainly of evergreens with a bark chipping mulch.

Heavy timber railway sleepers set in a diagonal design help to break up the length. Features were added to draw visitors through to the end of the garden.

The eating area is formed of decking. Raised beds and paving around this area create a well. The surrounding surfaces can then be used as seats.

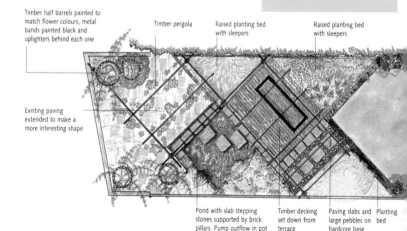

Timber half barrels painted to match flower colours, metal bands painted black and uplighters behind each one

Timber pergola

Raised planting bed with sleepers

Raised planting bed with sleepers

Existing paving extended to make a more interesting shape

Pond with slab stepping stones supported by brick pillars. Pump outflow in pot

Timber decking set down from terrace

Paving slabs and large pebbles on hardcore base

Planting bed

DESIGNER'S PLANTING SCHEME

Key plants
1 Japanese angelica tree, *Aralia elata*
2 Common myrtle, *Myrtus communis*
3 *Sophora tetraptera*
4 *Leptospermum scoparium* 'Red Damask'
5 Spotted laurel, *Aucuba japonica* 'Crotonifolia'
6 Spurge, *Euphorbia characias* ssp. *wulfenii*
7 *Cytisus* 'Killney Red'
8 *Holboellia latifolia* – climbing
9 *Lonicera x tellmanniana* – climbing
10 *Rosa* 'Etoile de Hollande'– climbing
11 *Vitis vinifera* 'Purpurea'
12 Black bamboo, *Phyllostachys nigra*

Decorative Detail
13 Aquatic grass, *Glyceria maxima* 'Variegata'
14 *Rudbeckia fulgida* var. *sullivantii* 'Goldsturm'
15 *Nymphaea tetragona* 'Helvola'
16 *Doronicum carpetanum*
17 Daylily, *Hemerocallis* 'Frans Hals'

Plants for added colour
Pelargonium 'Mme Fournier'
Nasturtium Jewel Series
Pot marigold, *Calendula* 'Geisha Girl'
Antirrhinum majus Coronette Series
California poppy, *Eschscholtzia californica*
Bells of Ireland, *Moluccella laevis*

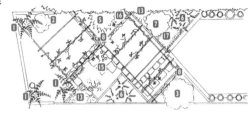

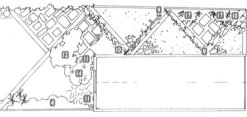

△ **The planting scheme** uses low-maintenance evergreens that need little pruning and bright yellow, orange and red which stand out against the dark blue-green pergola and decking.

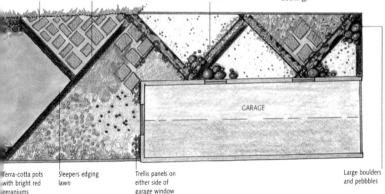

Slabs with herbs between

Sleepers covered in wire netting laid flat over free-draining base

Zig-zag pergola

GARAGE

Terra-cotta pots with bright red geraniums

Sleepers edging lawn

Trellis panels on either side of garage window

Large boulders and pebbbles

CONSTRUCTION

Strong diagonal lines and a range of heights divide this narrow garden into a number of interesting areas. The paved terrace at the far end was extended to form a diamond-edged pattern which allows more space and a pergola was added to create interest at a higher level.

The square pond, set at an angle, is edged with paving. It is set below the level of the terrace but at the same height as the decking. The yellow pine decking is pressure-treated to make the pine rot-proof and non-slip when wet. The higher sides provide seating and a low table completes the eating area.

The lawn that follows is edged with sleepers to retain the neat shape. These are set just below lawn level for easy mowing. Beyond

▲ The strong shape of the paved patio at the far end of the garden is repeated in the decking and pond, and the materials used contrast and complement each other, highlighting the clean design.

PLANTING

Raised beds and potted plants are used highlight the planting and this helps to keep trees and shrubs small. Three triangular raised beds border the sitting areas. The climbers – *Holboellia latifolia*, *Lonicera* x *tellmanniana* – and the crimson rose 'Etoile de Hollande' are grown against the garage and over the pergola.

KEY PLANTS

◀ Runner beans and sweet peas grow up a wigwam of canes in a half barrel container. These provide both height and colour, and the fresh young beans are easy to pick for use in the kitchen.

▶ The aquatic grass, *Glyceria maxima* 'Variegata' grows in a corner of the pond where the striking leaves contrast well with the shorter foliage that surrounds it. This grass can grow to 80 cm/32 in.

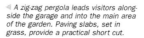
◁ A zig-zag pergola leads visitors along-side the garage and into the main area of the garden. Paving slabs, set in grass, provide a practical short cut.

▽ The square pond, set at an angle, has a raised bed behind it with planting that softens the straight lines. Brick edging contrasts with the other materials used.

See also:
- Raised beds, pages 108, 120
- Introducing water, page 126
- Containers, page 134

this, just before the garage, are slabs set on compacted soil with herbs growing in the spaces.

As running cables for electricity would have been costly, illumination comes from floating candles on the pond and jam jars of night lights hung from the pergola.

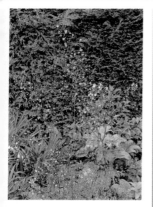

▲ Meadow rue, *Thalictrum* species, are lovers of damp and shady places and are at home in a semi-wild area by a water feature. They thrive in climates where summers are fairly cool.

FOR EXTRA COLOUR

Pelargoniums prefer a situation in full sun but require less regular watering than most container plants, which makes them easier to look after. Flowers continue through most of the summer if they are regularly deadheaded.

Move container-grown pelargoniums indoors in winter, in areas prone to frost, and cut back by about one-third. Repot in spring when the plants begin to grow.

Special effect

Easy-care plants in pots
Evergreens and pelargoniums are a good choice if you are looking for pot plants that need minimum care. Adding water retaining crystals in the potting mix, ensures that soil will retain moisture for longer. Plants grown in containers need regular feeding if they are to flourish but slow-release fertilizers can help.

Pot-grown plants also need repotting, or at least some of the compost replaced, every year or two.

Terracotta dries out quickly in hot weather and so is not always the best material to use in a low-maintenance garden. In areas that are subject to frost check that the terracotta is frostproof as it can flake or crack when the water in the compost expands on freezing.

Lining a wooden container with plastic will help it to retain water and also lengthen the life of the timber.

Children's garden

The children of the house wanted the garden to have a sand-pit, a football pitch with goal posts, a climbing frame, a home for the family tortoise, and some magic and mystery.

Jean designed a whale-shaped lawn which doubles as a football pitch, space was found for the frame and sandpit near the house and the tortoise was given its own house by the bicycle shed. A secret area was created within a ring of Amelanchiers, and adults were not forgotten with seats and a hammock to relax on and a paved area for outdoor meals.

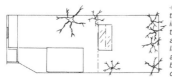

◀ **Before conversion**
the area was divided into two by a wire netting fence. There was a bare, weed-infested lawn, a flower border and a beautiful copper beech and lime trees on the boundary.

Timber steps with boulders and pebbles — Wall painted Tuscan yellow ochre — Trellis with uplight

Paving

Log store — Toy store with shelves

Basement level, with decking and timber painted yellow ochre — Sandpit with light — Trellis around paved area with arch over gap

▼ **The planting scheme**
uses very bright colours and includes plants that are easy to grow such as sunflowers and nasturtiums, as well as trees picked for autumn colour.

THE GARDEN'S PROBLEMS

The boys wish for a football pitch was very important.

The tortoise needed a home and this had to be included in the plan.

Space was needed for the climbing frame already in existence.

A strip of paving outside the basement kitchen and main living area which was too narrow to use.

HOW THEY WERE SOLVED

A long whale-shaped lawn provides the pitch at an angle to prevent balls being aimed at the house.

An area beside the bike shed forms night and winter quarters.

Sited behind the circle of trees, the equipment was painted a deep blue. A blue slide and a climbing rope were introduced.

This area was widened, floored with decking and painted yellow to link indoors with outdoors.

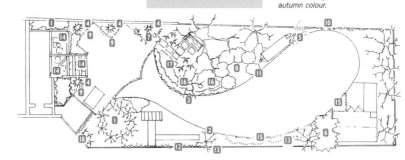

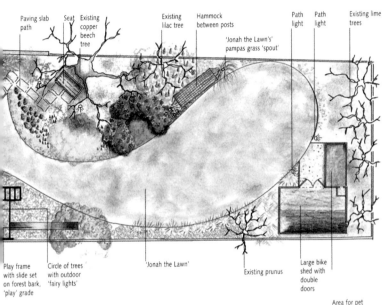

Paving slab path · Seat · Existing copper beech tree · Existing lilac tree · Hammock between posts · 'Jonah the Lawn's' pampas grass 'spout' · Path light · Path light · Existing lime trees

Play frame with slide set on forest bark, 'play' grade · Circle of trees with outdoor 'fairy lights' · 'Jonah the Lawn' · Existing prunus · Large bike shed with double doors · Area for pet hutches

DESIGNER'S PLANTING SCHEME

Key plants
1 *Amelanchier lamarkii* – to create a circle of trees
2 Crab apple, *Malus* 'John Downie'
3 *Sorbus* 'Joseph Rock'
4 Juniper, *Juniperus communis* 'Hibernica'
5 Pampas grass, *Cortaderia selloana* 'Albolineata'
6 Yellow-groove bamboo, *Phyllostachys aureosulcata* var. *aureocaulis*
7 Rosemary, *Rosmarinus* 'Prostratus'
8 Redcurrant, *Ribes rubrum*
9 Lavender, *Lavandula angustifolia* 'Hidcote'

10 Vine, *Vitis coignetiae*
11 *Tropaeolum speciosum* – growing over currant bushes
12 Thornless blackberry, *Rubus lacinatus*

Decorative detail
13 Black-eyed Susan, *Rudbeckia fulgida* var. *sullivantii* 'Goldsturm'
14 Daisy, *Bellis perennis* Roggli Series
15 Sedge, *Carex* 'Frosted Curls'
16 Catmint, *Nepeta* 'Souvenir d'André Chaudron'
17 Male fern, *Dryopteris filix-mas*

Plants for added colour
Sunflower, *Helianthus annus* 'Russian Giant'
Nasturtium, *Tropaeolum majus*
Love-in-the-mist, *Nigella damascena* Persian Jewel Series
Lettuce, green and red 'Salad Bowl', *Lactuca sativa*
Livingstone daisy, *Dorotheanthus bellidiformis*
China aster, *Callistephus* 'Kyoto Pompon'

CONSTRUCTION

Once the area outside the basement had been laid with decking, and painted yellow to match the colour scheme in the house, the timber-edged steps were built up to the terrace. This was laid with an integrated sandpit. The patio paving also extends to a seat beneath the copper beech which looks towards the house and the children's play area.

The giant whale-shaped lawn, created from tough perennial rye grass, extends almost to the end of the garden and the shape allows the goal posts to be positioned at an angle to the house, to avoid accidents with balls.

At the far end of the garden a shed takes the bikes and in front, to one side, is the tortoise pen with

▲The play space has a 'carpet' of a thick layer of bark chippings for a soft landing.

▶The brilliant yellow, dark-centred flowers of the black-eyed Susan, *Rudbeckia fulgida* var. *sullivantii* 'Goldstrum' grow alongside the 'whale' and provide patches of bright colour behind the lettuce border.

PLANTING

Plants were chosen for a range of different reasons. The whale lawn was decoratively edged with cut-and-come-again red and green salad bowl lettuces to provide the tortoise, as well as the family, with a constant supply of food, and a pampas grass provides the whale's water spout.

The circle of amelanchiers makes a magic fairy-ring when hung with lights, and these together with the sorbus 'Joseph Rock' and the vine, *Vitis coignetia*, provide rich highlights of red and gold as winter approaches.

KEY PLANTS

◀ The seat that overlooks the play area and the house is backed by euphorbia. The scented *Choisya ternata* is deliberately allowed to grow over it on one side.

◀ *Looking down the curving 'whale' lawn towards the bicycle shed and tortoise house. The patio provides ample space for eating outdoors.*

▽ *The sandpit, which is set into the patio, can be watched over from the seat under the beech tree opposite and the sand is kept clean by the use of a cover, (below).*

sleeping quarters in the shed itself. The climbing frame and slide are tucked away behind the circle of Amelanchiers and the hammock provides a viewing point for games and football.

▲ The timber-sided paved steps that lead from the basement are lined with pebbles and overhung with evergreen shrubs, including a bushy hebe, the silver-grey lavender, *Lavandula* 'Hidcote' and an artemisia, all benefiting from the good drainage and sunny position.

FOR EXTRA COLOUR

Brilliant orange French marigolds, *Tagetes* 'Safari Tangerine' can be easily grown from seed by young-sters. The large seeds are easy to handle and can be sown *in situ*. They provide a patch of long-lasting bright colour.

Another great favourite with children is the sunflower, *Helianthus annuus* 'Russian Giant' which grows to a towering height.

Special effect

A sandpit soon falls out of use as the family grow up and take up new interests. However, it is not difficult to turn the dug-out area to new use as an ornamental pond when children stop playing with the sand. Alternatively, with the sand removed and the space filled with good topsoil, a bed can be created for ground-hugging plants.

Garden with a view

The owners of this new house wanted an informal effect to tie in with the countryside behind the garden. The garden was sited on steep land emphasizing the view beyond.

The garden was divided into two, with each area having a different feel. The section nearest the house became a traditional country garden while the lower area was more wild, to blend into the landscape. Small waterfalls, rocky streams, and plants create a jungle-like luxuriance.

◀ **Before conversion** As the house was newly built there was no garden, just a lot of builder's rubble.

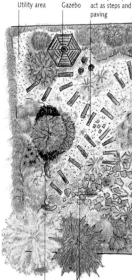

Utility area   Gazebo   Railway sleepers act as steps and paving

'Tree benches'

Sloping terraces with a series of small pools spilling into the bottom pool. Dramatic planting scheme creates a 'jungle' effect

THE GARDEN'S PROBLEMS

A steep slope facing away from the house.

Making the most of wonderful views.

A new house with a garden full of builder's rubble and no topsoil.

A cold garden with very little sun.

HOW THEY WERE SOLVED

The area near the house was flattened and a terrace built to catch the morning sun.

The view was accentuated by planting tall specimens on the sides, leaving the central area low.

Rubble was removed, the land was contoured and topsoil added.

A wet woodland feature with paths and streams running through it was created in the lowest part of the garden.

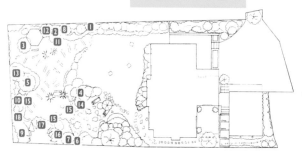

◀ **The planting scheme** The section of the garden nearest the house had a traditional country garden scheme while there was more exotic planting on the lower level.

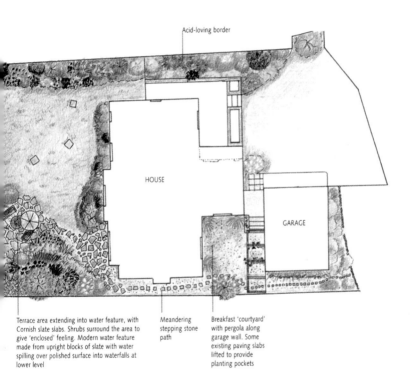

Acid-loving border

HOUSE

GARAGE

Terrace area extending into water feature, with Cornish slate slabs. Shrubs surround the area to give 'enclosed' feeling. Modern water feature made from upright blocks of slate with water spilling over polished surface into waterfalls at lower level

Meandering stepping stone path

Breakfast 'courtyard' with pergola along garage wall. Some existing paving slabs lifted to provide planting pockets

DESIGNER'S PLANTING SCHEME

Key plants
1. Phillyrea latifolia
2. Hawthorn, Crataegus laevigata 'Crimson Cloud'
3. Ornamental cherry, Prunus avium 'Plena'
4. Elaeagnus x ebbingei 'Limelight'
5. Maple, Acer griseum
6. Chusan palm, Trachycarpus fortunei
7. Strawberry tree, Arbutus x andrachnoides

8. Osmanthus decorus
9. Robinia pseudoacacia 'Frisia'
10. Eucryphia x nymansensis

Decorative detail
11. Lenten rose, Helleborus orientalis
12. Spindle tree, Euonymus europaeus 'Red Cascade'
13. Spindle, Euonymus f. albus var. intermedius
14. Maple, Acer griseum

15. Hostas, ferns and Iris sibirica
16. Gunnera manicata
17. Spurge, Euphorbia characias ssp. wulfenii
18. Foxglove tree, Paulownia tomentosa

▲ Steps of railway sleepers in the gravel in the lower section of the garden lead down the slope and link one small flat terrace with another.

CONSTRUCTION

Once the builder's rubble had been removed the garden was land-scaped, with a level section created near to the house which dropped to sloping land below. Seen from the house, the lower section of the garden is not in view until the edge of the top terrace is reached and so forms a secret garden waiting to be discovered.

Small flat terraces were dug out at points on the slope of the lower area as places to sit. Here water forms in small pools before running down the slope again ending up in a larger pool at the bottom end of the garden, where a utility area is kept well out of sight. The terraces are linked by timber steps and gravel pathways that pass close to waterfalls and fast streams

PLANTING

The garden nearest to the house contains a long, wide herbaceous border along one side, and shrubs and trees opposite this provide shelter for the terrace. In the lower section of the garden a jungle-like effect was created with plants such as the foxglove tree, *Paulownia tomentosa* with its fragrant lilac-pink flowers.

KEY PLANTS

▲ *Elaeagnus* x *ebbingei* 'Limelight' planted in the border between the top and lower sections of the garden forms a link between the traditional upper section of the garden and the more exotically planted lower section.

◄ The seat on the lower terrace looks down the timber-edged steps. Cranesbill geraniums provide foreground colour and a newly planted *Robinia pseudoacacia* 'Frisia' adds colour beside the seat.

▲ The top terrace of gravel and sunken railway sleepers, and the timber bench, are enclosed by planting to create a sheltered area and a place from which to enjoy the view of the countryside.

▶ Water tumbles down from the top garden in small waterfalls, along streams lined and edged by large craggy rocks.

of tumbling water, ending up at a gazebo hidden from sight.

The water feature starts from close to the top terrace in a pool, this position is highlighted by giant standing stones (right). The water then runs between rough-edged slabs of slate, some of which act as stepping stones, to spill over from the top terrace. It continues its run through the sloping section of the garden to the end of the garden below.

Special effect

Running water Beautiful effects can be created by moving water. In this garden slabs of slate are used for areas of paving and spaces are left between the slate at intervals to form crevices for running water while other slates form stepping-stones for crossing the water.

A similar effect for a more formal area can be created with granite setts, with spaces left between them for the water to flow around.

▲ Pictured here in summer, the decorative peeling bark of the paper-bark maple, *Acer griseum* creates a focus even in winter.

FOR EXTRA COLOUR

Eucryphia x *nymansensis* bears its cup-shaped white flowers from late summer through to autumn and provides colour at a time of the year when flowers are often in short supply. It is a tall evergreen shrub that can grow to as much as 15 m/50 ft, so is only suitable for a garden like this that backs onto open countryside. Here it acts as a frame to the view behind.

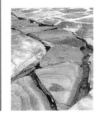

With the elderly in mind

This garden, devised by Barbara Hunt in conjunction with the charity Age Concern, was created for a garden exhibition at Hampton Court, London. It seeks to help to compensate for some of the problems that arrive as we get older, from lack of energy and mobility, to failing eye-sight. With wide, paved areas, the garden uses a range of materials, and has a pergola, raised beds and a raised pool. The pond and many of the beds are edged with seating so that they can be enjoyed from close at hand. A bird bath, bird table and the inclusion of plants to attract bees and butterflies bring nature to the garden.

POINTS TO CONSIDER

Mobility – a problem for some of those for whom the garden was designed.

Eye-sight may be poor for some garden users.

Scent is particularly important for older people.

SOLUTIONS

Wide paths provide access for wheel chairs and for people to walk side-by-side. Gentle slopes rather than steps. Lots of seating in both sun and shade.

Using strong and contrasting colours helps to overcome the problem older eyes have in adjusting to a move from an area of light to one in the shade.

When eye-sight or hearing are reduced, flowers which give off scent provide a lot of pleasure.

▶ **The planting scheme** uses bright colours and positions plants of con-trasting colours side by side. It also includes a number of plants with either aromatic foliage or fragrant flowers and others to attract bees and butterflies.

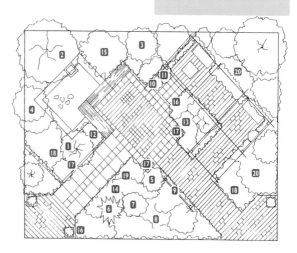

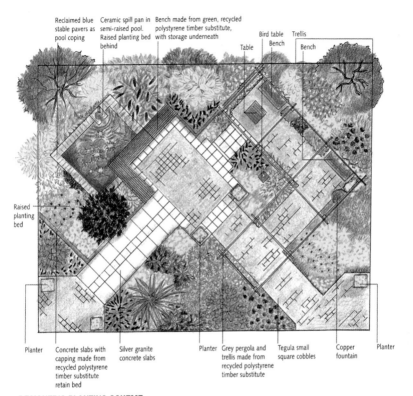

Reclaimed blue stable pavers as pool coping

Ceramic spill pan in semi-raised pool. Raised planting bed behind

Bench made from green, recycled polystyrene timber substitute, with storage underneath

Table   Bench

Bird table   Trellis

Bench

Raised planting bed

Planter

Concrete slabs with capping made from recycled polystyrene timber substitute retain bed

Silver granite concrete slabs

Planter

Grey pergola and trellis made from recycled polystyrene timber substitute

Tegula small square cobbles

Copper fountain

Planter

DESIGNER'S PLANTING SCHEME

Key plants
1 Japanese maple, *Acer palmatum f. atropurpureum*
2 Rock maple, *Acer saccharinum* 'Wieri'
3 Indian bean tree, *Catalpa bignonioides* 'Aurea'
4 Golden bamboo, *Phyllostachys aurea*
5 Dwarf mountain pine, *Pinus mugo*
6 New Zealand flax, *Phormium tenax*

Plants with aromatic foliage
7 *Artemisia* 'Powis Castle'

8 *Eucalyptus gunnii*
9 Mint, *Mentha rotundifolia* 'Variegata'
10 Jerusalem sage, *Phlomis fruticosa*
11 Rosemary, *Rosmarinus officinalis*
12 Salvia *officinalis* 'Icterina'
13 *Santolina virens*

Decorative detail
14 *Achillea* 'Moonshine'
15 *Buddleia fallowiana*
16 Lavender, *Lavandula vera*
17 *Argyranthemum* 'Jamaica Primrose'
18 *Rudbeckia* 'Marmalade'

19 Salvia *officinalis* 'Purpurascens'
20 *Lilium* 'Connecticut King'

Plants with fragrant flowers
Jasmine, *Jasminum officinale*
Lavender, *Lavandula angustifolia* 'Hidcote'
Japanese honeysuckle, *Lonicera japonica* 'Halliana'
Philadelphus 'Virginal'
Rose, *Rosa* 'Dreaming Spires'
Viburnum x *bodnantense* 'Charles Lamont'

▲ The pond has a wide raised edge that provides comfortable seating and a chance to view plants and water close to.

CONSTRUCTION

The paving was picked for its non-slip and non-reflective properties. Changes in colour and materials are used to herald clearly, for the less well-sighted, that they are entering a new area. Seating surfaces in dark green are made from a recycled polystyrene waste material which is warm to the touch and relatively maintenance free. It does not absorb water so can be quickly dried after rain.

The pergola provides a frame for climbers, and shade for the seating area below, from which the scent of the climbers can be enjoyed.

Raised beds and the raised pond bring the pleasures of plants and water up to a more accessible level to those walking, sitting or in wheel-chairs.

PLANTING

Apart from providing a number of specimen plants with decorative leaf-shapes and autumn colour, Barbara picked plants for their aromatic leaves or fragrant flowers. She chose bright colours that could be seen clearly by those with poorer sight. Orange and yellow have been used extensively, often side-by-side for vivid contrast.

KEY PLANTS

▲ A mix of leaf and flower shapes and colours allows each plant to be defined against the other. The silver leaves of a *Eucalyptus gunnii* overhang the pale yellow flowers of Achillea 'Moonshine'.

◄ The bright sunny colours of black-eyed Susan, *Rudbeckia fulgida*, the yellow flowers of the lily 'Connecticut King' and bright orange marigolds show up strongly against a green background.

⊿A bird table is ideally placed if it is close to buildings so that it is possible to view the feeding birds whatever the weather.

▶The water feature tumbles water into the pond below and acts up as a bird bath. The water is recycled from the pond back up to the top saucer again.

FOR EXTRA COLOUR

Flowers in tones of a single colour work well in a container. Here the small, soft pink flowers of *Nemesia* Carnival Series rise above the rim while the pendent deep pink flowers of the climbing *Rhodochiton* appear around the edges and trail down to the ground.

⊿In these raised beds Barbara has used the two colours most easily seen by older eyes. The bright orange flowers of *Rudbeckia* 'Marmalade' are elevated to eye-level creating a strong contrast against the paler yellow daisy-like heads of the *Argyranthemum* 'Jamaica Primrose'.

Special effect

Attracting the birds Bird baths and bird tables not only bring wildlife close to home but they create attractive garden sculptures. Provided the situation is suitable and safe for birds, hidden from circling birds of prey and protected from marauding cats, bird baths and tables can be used as a focal point on a small terrace, at the crossroads of paths or the end of a pathway, and in many other situations.

Here potter and designer, Denis Fairweather has created a bird bath from which water pours into the pond, adding sound to the enjoyment of the other senses.

The table and water spill are made from recycled polystyrene waste material which can be sawn, drilled, nailed, glued and jointed in the same way as timber. He has formed a pair of pecking birds on the rim of each to attract real birds to enjoy the facilities also.

Integrating a swimming pool

The owners of this garden decided to include a swimming pool, but wanted it to be out of sight of the house so that it would be a surprise feature, and when the children invited friends for a swim the noise of their enjoyment would not be too close to the house. The spot had to be free of trees, must not interfere with the line of the house drains, and should be in the sun for most of the day and in a sheltered situation. They chose a spot at the end of the garden with access through the flower garden and a pergola arch. As the garden is on a slope this meant digging out to create a flat terrace for the pool.

Long border with climbing plants on wall

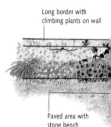

Paved area with stone bench

LAWN AREA

▼ *Before conversion*
the area used for the pool had been a lawn adjacent to the fruit garden.

THE GARDEN'S PROBLEMS

The line of the house drains was an important consideration.

The pool had to receive sun for the longest possible time every day.

A position sheltered from wind was needed but away from trees.

The large expanse of water and the size of the pool had to be considered.

HOW THEY WERE SOLVED

Experts checked the route of the drains before the final position was decided.

The final position was chosen as it would receive sun from first thing in the morning until evening.

A lawned area was chosen with a wall running down one side to provide wind shelter. A pool terrace was created by digging out the sloping land.

Siting the pool out of sight of the house with a sunken terrace surrounding it.

▼ *The planting scheme*
Little extra planting was necessary. A retaining wall on one side backed onto a mature bed and these plants could then be enjoyed from both sides. A second narrow bed, with a low fence behind it, was newly planted and pots were arranged by the pool for additional colour.

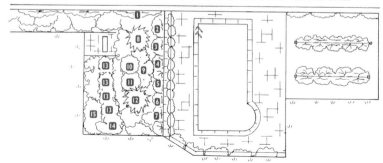

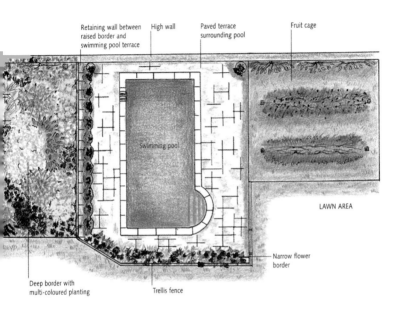

Retaining wall between raised border and swimming pool terrace

High wall

Paved terrace surrounding pool

Fruit cage

LAWN AREA

Narrow flower border

Deep border with multi-coloured planting

Trellis fence

Swimming pool

DESIGNER'S PLANTING SCHEME

Key plants
1   Climbing rose, *Rosa* 'Compassion'
2   Shrub rose, *Rosa* Graham Thomas
3   Shrub rose, *Rosa* Troilus
4   Shrub rose, *Rosa* Fair Bianca – a group of three
5   Shrub rosa *Rosa* The Prince – group of three
6   Shrub rose, *Rosa* Chaucer
7   *Rosa* x *xanthia* 'Canary Bird'
8   *Mahonia* x *media* 'Charity'
9   *Viburnum davidii* – a group of three
10 Mock orange, *Philadelphus* 'Belle Etoile'

11 Mock orange, *Philadelphus* 'Manteau d'Hermine'
12 *Mahonia* x *media* 'Lionel Fortescue'

Decorative detail
13 Peonies, *Paeonia* – mixed species and varieties
14 Lavenders, *Lavandula* species
15 Cranesbill, *Geranium sanguineum* var. *striatum*

Plants for added colour
Cosmos bipinnatus
Lavatera assurgentiflora
Phlox species

▲ The sunken terrace in which the pool has been sited is sheltered from the wind in all directions and has the added advantage of mature planting along one side, with climbing roses that tumble over trellis to add colour to the pool area as well as the flower garden.

CONSTRUCTION

The owners set out to design the surrounding area themselves with some help from the pool construction company. A digger was used to dig out the pool and landscape the surrounding area to form a flat, partially sunken terrace, with the excavated soil being used elsewhere in the garden. Removing the soil is expensive, so it is worth finding an alternative use for it, for example, as a rockery, or in raised beds.

The water is heated by electricity with all the equipment concealed. It is possible to use solar energy in many areas if the panels are sited well. The pool is kept covered when it is not in use to maintain the water temperature, allowing it to be used for long periods throughout the year.

PLANTING

Climbing roses cover trellis that divides off the main flower garden from the sheltered pool terrace. These provide summer colour on one side of the pool. Along an adjoining side a low trellis fence, built to keep out a young puppy, has been made almost instantly colourful with the addition of cosmos and lavatera species.

KEY PLANTS

▲ A vigorous, magenta pink cranesbill, *Geranium* x *oxonianum* forms clumps and flowers right through from spring to early autumn.

◄ The brick-built pergola is surrounded by deep beds with mixed planting giving colour and interest throughout the year. The scarlet flowers of *Crocosmia* 'Lucifer' stand out against the pink of the lavatera in the background and the campanula.

△ A view-point from the flower garden close to the house pinpoints the pool's position on a lower terrace. It also shows the advantage of adding a pool where plants are well established.

▷ A stone seat on the route from the house to the pool shows how well hidden the pool is. It also highlights the garden's mature and colourful summer planting.

△ Surrounding the ground around the trunk of a tree the cranesbill *Geranium nodosum* 'Whiteleaf' adds colour in what is usually a difficult spot to get plants to flower. This is an ideal plant for use in just such a situation as it flourishes in shade and dry conditions.

FOR EXTRA COLOUR

The exotic-looking flowers of clematis species and hybrids come in a range of colours. If carefully selected, it should be possible to have one in flower from spring to autumn.

Clematis armandii, an evergreen with small, scented white flowers, is one of the earliest. *C.* 'Nelly Moser' with its pale pink flowers decorated with a deep pink stripe, appears later, in spring to early summer. In mid-summer the brilliant magenta to scarlet flowers of *C.* 'Ville de Lyon' arrive, followed by the pinky purple flowers *C.* 'Comtesse de Bouchaud' (below) which continue until late summer.

Special effect

Brick structures are expensive to erect but bricks are one of the most durable materials for use in the garden. Here bricks have been used to build a series of pillars to hold up the timber beams for a pergola. The pergola itself extends from one side of the garden to the other and also divides up the garden into a series of 'rooms'. In addition it also helps to screen the pool area from the house itself.

Wildlife garden

Claire and Robin Roper's own garden had many problems. Situated in fairly wild countryside, the house was on an estate, surrounded by other houses, and the site is windy. The garden had returned mainly to weeds and rough grass. More bio-diversity was needed if it was to attract a wide range of local wildlife.

◀ **Before conversion** the site was open, windy and bounded by the gardens of other houses on three sides.

▼ **The planting scheme** uses a wide range of plants to attract wildlife, together with species that are also decorative in shape or colour.

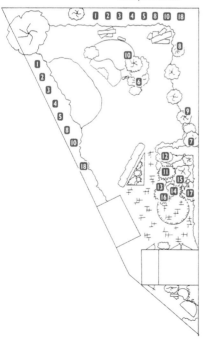

THE GARDEN'S PROBLEMS

The site is very windy.

The garden was open and overlooked. Seclusion was wanted for an eating area near to the house.

Natural drainage from the surrounding gardens ended up in a lower area of this garden.

The soil is poor.

HOW THEY WERE SOLVED

Robin wanted a hedge layer and wanted a wide boundary of mixed native hedge plants. Once they grow, the hedge will provide wind protection and act as a mini-woodland for wildlife.

Bamboo and hazel wattle hurdles provided an instant screen. Trees were planted to create seclusion for the future.

A pond and bog garden was formed here.

An advantage in a wildlife garden as the soil is most suited to delicate species which may otherwise be smothered by tougher plants, which are of less benefit to insects.

DESIGNER'S PLANTING SCHEME

Key plants
1 Hazel, *Corylus avellana*
2 Hawthorn, *Crataegus monogyna*
3 Holly, *Ilex aquifolium*
4 Blackthorn, *Prunus spinosa*
5 Dog rose, *Rosa canina*
6 Elder, *Sambucus nigra*
7 Ornamental crab apple, *Malus* 'Golden Hornet'
8 Guelder rose, *Viburnum opulus*
9 Alder buckthorn, *Rhamnus frangula*
10 Wild privet, *Ligustrum vulgare*
11 Japanese aralia, *Fatsia japonica*

Decorative detail
12 Tall bamboo, *Pseudosasa japonica*
13 Angelica, *Angelica archangelica*
14 Ladies mantle, *Alchemilla mollis*
15 Cardoon, *Cynara cardunculus*
16 Yellow foxglove, *Digitalis grandiflora*
17 Hart's tongue fern, *Asplenium scolopendrium*
18 Honeysuckle, *Lonicera periclymenum*

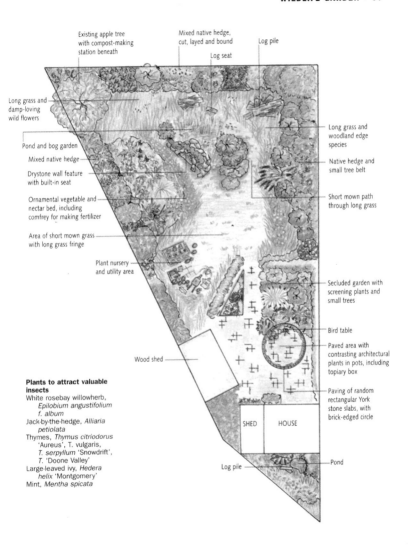

Existing apple tree
with compost-making
station beneath

Mixed native hedge,
cut, layed and bound

Log pile

Log seat

Long grass and
damp-loving
wild flowers

Long grass and
woodland edge
species

Pond and bog garden

Mixed native hedge

Native hedge and
small tree belt

Drystone wall feature
with built-in seat

Ornamental vegetable and
nectar bed, including
comfrey for making fertilizer

Short mown path
through long grass

Area of short mown grass
with long grass fringe

Plant nursery
and utility area

Secluded garden with
screening plants and
small trees

Bird table

Paved area with
contrasting architectural
plants in pots, including
topiary box

Wood shed

Paving of random
rectangular York
stone slabs, with
brick-edged circle

SHED   HOUSE

Log pile

Pond

**Plants to attract valuable
insects**
White rosebay willowherb,
    *Epilobium angustifolium
    f. album*
Jack-by-the-hedge, *Alliaria
    petiolata*
Thymes, *Thymus citriodorus*
    'Aureus', T. vulgaris,
    T. serpyllum 'Snowdrift',
    T. 'Doone Valley'
Large-leaved ivy, *Hedera
    helix* 'Montgomery'
Mint, *Mentha spicata*

The terrace next to the house, backed by bamboos, hurdles and small trees for privacy, has an arrangement of deer antlers and lucky stones found locally, plus a topiary box, *Buxus sempervirens* in a pot.

CONSTRUCTION

Claire and Robin wanted the garden to provide a variety of habitats to attract wildlife. They introduced hedges, two ponds and a marshy area, a meadow, a dry-stone wall, log piles, and long grass and wild-flowers. The pond liner was extended out to one side, creating a small wet meadow. On the pond's cold and windy side a dry-stone wall provides habitats for reptiles, amphibians and invertebrates. It also acts as a suntrap.

At the opposite side of the pond is a log pile which is topped up with extra dead wood. This attracts fungi and a wide range of animals and insects.

The hedge is already a useful shelterbelt and roosting, nesting and foraging site for birds. There

PLANTING

Plants were chosen for both their wildlife value and shape. Dramatically shaped plants are included, such as angelica and cardoon. Most species are natural to the area of southern England where the Ropers live, and so are best suited to attracting local wildlife. It is always important to go for local native plants for this reason.

KEY PLANTS

The herb bed contains an old favourite of England's King Henry VIII, *Chenopodium bonus-henricus*, good King Henry, as well as chives, thymes, bronze fennel, sage, and perennial onion.

Looking across the pond from the 'wet meadow'. Plants include marsh marigold, cowslip, fritiliary, lady's smock, meadowsweet, hemp-agrimony, and water mint.

◁ A pond is an important wildlife attraction. This one looks very natural with large rocks and gravel around the margin and contains locally native plants.

is also a bird feeding station near to the house.

Insecticides, herbicides or fungicides are not allowed in this garden and as much as possible is recycled. A worm bin produces nutrient-rich compost and there is also a compost bin, a bin for making comfrey fertilizer and water-harvesting barrels.

△ One of Robin's newly laid hedges with stakes and binders holding in place the live, laid trees and cut brushwood used to fill it out.

▽ A very architectural plant, angelica, *Angelica archangelica*, has large, divided leaves, bronze stems and greenish yellow flowerheads. Here it grows with an allium (far left) and Jack-by-the-hedge, (upper left), the larvae food plant of the orange tip butterfly.

FOR EXTRA COLOUR

You can sow even a small area of poor soil as a wildflower meadow using a mixture of grass and wild-flower seed recommended for your type of soil and area. In the first year, cut this back at two monthly intervals so that the grass does not smother out the wild flowers. After this, cut only early in the spring and then, in the autumn once the seeds have been shed. Here an area of regularly trimmed grass forms a pathway through the long grass in which oxeye daisies, *Leucanthemum vulgare*, predominate.

Special effect

Woven wigwams are created from supple hazel or willow rods that bend without breaking.

Make a circle with an odd number of evenly spaced holes. Sharpen the end of each upright rod and push one rod into each hole. Weave thinner rods in layers and pull the uprights together, weaving tightly. Pull out the shape and fix by push-ing the rods into the ground.

CHAPTER 5

GROUNDWORK

Recognizing the type of soil you have, and knowing how to improve it and what plants will thrive in it, ensures that the plants you grow will flourish. This chapter describes how to identify your soil type, how to enrich what you have and how to keep it in good condition. It also tells you when and how to water your newly planted plants to give them a good start and a strong and self-reliant root system. How to set about installing power in the garden is also covered, as this allows you to highlight decorative plantings and create wonderful effects with water. Lighting also extends the period you can sit outdoors and enjoy the garden, as well as making it safer to walk around in at night, and more secure from unwanted intruders.

Identifying your soil 102–103
Improving soil condition 104–105
Garden compost 106–107
Checking acid or alkaline levels 108–109
Watering 110–111
Electricity in the garden 112–113

Identifying your soil

Clearing the site

A new garden may appear to be little more than a heap of rubble with little or no topsoil. However, it can be radically improved if you take the following steps:

- Dig out and heap up bricks and larger stones if you think you can use them in the design. Otherwise dispose of them.

- Fork over, or dig the soil to let it in air and water. In the autumn cover with a thick layer of organic matter, then leave until the following spring.

- In the spring dig, then rake the surface smooth. Allow weeds to germinate and remove.

- After planting mulch well to suppress further weed growth.

Soil is rock which over thousands of years has been crushed and mixed with decayed organic matter, known as humus. The three main types of soil are light, sandy soil, which is made up of large particles that do not adhere to each other and through which water and plant food pass easily; medium silt, which is made up of medium-sized, smoother particles; and heavy clay, which is made up of minute particles which pack together, retain moisture and form sticky lumps that dry solid. Most garden soil is a mixture, with one of the above predominating.

Topsoil is the name given to the relatively thin, darker top layer of soil which has built up over the years as it has been enriched with humus through the natural decay of organic matter such as dead leaves, animals and plants, and through cultivation. The subsoil lying below this gives the soil its general character and to a large extent determines whether it is rich or poor in nutrients, and whether it is warm or cold and has good or poor drainage, as well as whether it is acid or alkaline. In a new house and garden there may be no topsoil at all, but subsoil can be converted into topsoil by good cultivation.

Fertile soil, loam, is an approximately equal mix of sand, silt, clay and humus. Humus is a vital, organic, ingredient which introduces a wide range of chemicals and bacteria into the soil. It improves soil texture in its own right, and encourages the activity of earthworms, whose work not only breaks it down and releases its vital ingredients as food for plants, but also aerates the soil.

SOIL TEST

To check what type of soil you have do the following test:

Pick up a handful of damp soil. Rub it between fingers and thumb.

It is sandy if it feels gritty, the grains do not stick together and it is difficult to roll your sample into a ball.

It is a sandy loam if it is gritty but can be rolled into a ball.

It is silt if it feels silky and can be rolled into a ball.

It is a sandy clay loam or a clay loam if it is gritty or sticky and can be rolled into a cylinder.

It is clay if it feels sticky and will form a cylinder which can be curved to form a ring.

See also:
- Mulching, pages 104, 111
- Digging, page 107
- Checking acid or alkaline levels, page 108

SOIL TYPE	ADVANTAGES	DISADVANTAGES
Sandy soil	Light, so easy to work Warms up quickly in spring	Free draining, so quick to dry out Nutrients easily lost
Silty soil	Retains moisture well Often very fertile; improves well	Dries into hard clods
Clay soil	Retains nutrients well Improves well Good for growing a wide range of plants	Hard to work Retains water, so sticky when wet and compacted when dry Slow to warm up in spring

OTHER SOIL TYPES

Chalk soil, which is pale in colour, has many of the disadvantages of clay. It may form only a shallow layer and often contains a lot of stones. It is also usually very alkaline, see page 108.

Peaty soil is dark in colour and spongy in texture. It may be waterlogged and need draining but is often very fertile, being rich in organic matter.

Creating a sump

When installing drainage, you need to provide somewhere for the drained water to collect and disperse from. You may be lucky enough to have a natural drain or ditch that you can use, but you will generally need to dig out a pit into which your water pipes can drain. This is known as a sump or soakaway. The sump should be situated at the lowest part of the garden, and needs to be at least 60 cm/2 ft deep and square. When you have chosen the site and dug the hole, fill it with building rubble or gravel (or a rubble topped with a gravel layer). Then place inverted turf over the drainage material and cover with more turf or soil.

LAYING LAND DRAINS

Poorly drained soils are cold and inhospitable, and their compacted structure deprives the plants' roots of the air they need. Very wet soils cause roots to rot and plants to die. If rain does not drain away but continues to lie in your garden, if only moisture-loving plants thrive, and if the lawn is full of moss, it may be that you need to install drainage.

Dig trenches in the garden for the drains leading into a soakaway (see above, right). Make these at least 30 cm/1 ft deep, with a slight fall towards the soakaway (following any natural slope). Place a layer of coarse grit or fine gravel along the bottom.

Lay the drains (which may be made of clay or perforated plastic) on the bed of gravel. Use a T-shaped connector if you are adding side drains.

To finish off pack more grit or gravel around and over the drains to improve drainage and to help to prevent the holes in the pipes from becoming clogged. Cover with inverted turfs or perforated polythene sheet, then replace the soil or re-lay grass turf.

Improving soil condition

Testing for nutrient deficiency

To check if your soil is deficient in nutrients use a soil-testing kit. However, if you think you have a serious nutrient deficiency it is wise to send off soil samples for a professional laboratory test.

To take soil samples use a trowel and take soil from about 6 cm/2 1/2 in below the surface. Take several samples from around the garden and test individually.

Measure into a jar 1 part soil to 5 parts water. The lid makes a good measure. Shake well then leave to settle and become reasonably clear. This can take from half an hour to a whole day.

(continued opposite)

To improve the structure of the soil dig in lots of bulky organic matter each year (see page 107). In a good loam the soil is made up of crumb-sized pieces that can be seen by the naked eye. The spaces between the crumbs provide channels for aeration and drainage. This structure helps to maintain water and nutrients within the soil. On sandy and silty soil the addition of humus coats the soil particles to form crumbs. On clay soil it works conversely and helps to break down the solid clods into a crumb-like structure.

The benefit of worms to the soil

A good worm population is a sign of a good soil. Worms consume fresh organic matter, breaking it down and release nutrients which are immediately available to plants. At the same time their burrows through the soil create aeration and drainage channels.

▲ Organic mulches improve the soil.

In planted areas

To keep the soil in good condition once you have put in your plants, add compost, manure and other organic matter as a thick layer of surface mulch. It will gradually be worked down to continue to improve the structure. Mulch also helps to prevent the soil from drying out, and suppresses weeds. Mulch when the soil is damp, or the material will draw water out of the soil.

▲ Add coarse grit to improve clay soil.

On heavy, clay soil

Apply lime to improve the structure (not suitable for alkaline clay, or for acid-loving plants, see page 109). Also dig in a good supply of coarse sand or grit as well as plenty of compost and manure. Do not be sparing with quantities, rather deal with one smaller area at a time.

SOURCES OF ORGANIC MATTER

- Horse, cow or pig manure
- Garden compost
- Compost from municipal waste
- Treated sewage sludge
- Spent mushroom compost
- Fresh, dried or composted seaweed
- Composted straw
- Spent hops

Quantities to use annually
- Manure: 5.5 kg per sq m /10 lb per sq yd
- Good compost: 2.5 kg per sq m/ 5 lb per sq yd or 1 barrow load per sq m/sq yd

Checking for nutrients

For healthy growth plants need a wide range of nutrients in the soil. By annually digging in bulky organic matter, the soil should remain fertile. Mulching the soil throughout the growing season helps to improve the soil's fertility. At the start of a soil-improvement plan the soil may be deficient in some nutrients and quantities take some time to build up using this method. In a small garden, planting has to be concentrated, and extra nutrients may be necessary.

The most important nutrients are nitrogen, which aids growth and gives leaves their green colour, phosphorus, for strong root growth, and potassium (potash), which affects the size and quality of flowers and fruit. Nitrogen is likely to be in short supply as it is washed out of the soil and not replenished in cold, wet weather. By digging in bulky organic matter phosphorus and potassium levels should remain high. Potassium deficiency is more likely to occur in light, sandy soil or chalk, and phosphorus deficiency in heavy clay soil or peat.

Trace elements such as iron, zinc, copper manganese and boron are also vital to plant growth. Very alkaline or limy soils can reduce take up of these important elements.

Applying fertilizers

Fertilizers can be powders or granules, or a concentrated liquid to be diluted. Once diluted, the liquid is watered onto the ground around plants. If the soil is dry, water it first. Liquid fertilizer can also be used as a foliar feed, applied in the evening or in dull weather, by spraying the plant's leaves thoroughly.

On bare soil apply dry fertilizer by first dividing the ground into 90 cm/3 ft squares. Spread the fertilizer as evenly as possible.

On established plants scatter the fertilizer around each plant to feed the roots, keeping it away from the stem.

Lightly hoe in the fertilizer and water the area, unless rain is forecast. This makes it available more quickly.

(continued from opposite)

Draw off clear liquid from the top with a pipette and transfer this to the test and reference chambers of the kit container.

Pour the powder from the capsule provided into the test chamber. Shake well until the powder is dispersed.

Allow a short time for the colour to develop then check this against the comparison chart.

FERTILIZERS TO USE

General fertilizers that contain the three main nutrients
Organic Blood, fish and bone, seaweed meal, liquid animal manure
Inorganic Growmore formula and slow-release fertilizers that are released over a period of time, plus controlled-fertilizers that are regulated by the soil's temperature

For nitrogen deficiency
Organic Rock potash, dried blood, liquid seaweed, hoof and horn, fish meal
Inorganic Nitro-chalk, Ammonium sulphate (but makes soil more acid)

For potassium deficiency
Organic Liquid seaweed, wood ash
Inorganic Potassium sulphate

For phosphorus deficiency
Organic Bone meal, fish meal
Inorganic Superphosphate of lime

Trace elements
Organic Seaweed meal
Inorganic Chelated iron compound, proprietary tonics, and trace element granules

See also:
• *Digging page 107*
• *Checking acid or alkaline levels, page 108*

Garden Compost

Compost bins

You can make compost by simply piling the materials up in a corner but using a bin is a neater and more efficient alternative.

Compost bins are readily available. Buy the largest you can fit in. It should be at least 1 m/3–4 ft square to produce more heat and help the contents to rot down quickly. Ideally you need two, one to take fresh material and one for partially broken-down compost, which can be forked over and left covered to go through the final stages of decomposition.

Plastic compost bin with lid, that comes in three slot-in sections.

A timber bin that is simple to construct as it comes as a kit The timber is pre-cut and the bin is sold ready to assemble. Simply slot or nail the sections together, following the instructions.

Homemade compost provides organic matter to improve your soil. Compost is decomposed kitchen and garden waste, including grass clippings. Using a container is neater and speeds up decomposition. The bacteria which break down the vegetable matter need air, warmth, moisture and nitrogen to decompose successfully.

Making compost

It is best to stand the bin on bare soil. Fork over the soil in the base area to aid drainage. Place a layer of twiggy material or straw in the bottom to provide good aeration, 8–10 cm/3–4 in deep. Bulky material soon shrinks down. Continue to fill the bin until you reach the top. Contents should be forked over to even out decomposition. Cover the heap to keep in the warmth. In summer your compost should be ready for use in three to four months. Winter cold slows down decomposition and it may take until the spring for it to be ready.

Pile on kitchen and garden refuse that rots easily. Stems and twigs will need shredding first. It is best to add compost materials in larger, mixed quantities if possible. A good way of doing this is to keep two plastic bags beside the bin, one for kitchen waste and the other for garden waste, then mix together before adding.

Include a layer of manure when a thickness of about 15 cm/6 in has been reached. If this is not available use garden soil and add an activator such as seaweed meal, blood, fish and bonemeal or a proprietary compost activator to introduce more bacteria into the heap. Keep the material in the heap moist you may need to water it in dry weather. Continue to add in layers as above.

Once the bin is full, lift it away and place it by the side of the rotting heap. Cover the heap and start a new one.

◄ With two heaps side by side, one pile can rot down and be used in the garden while the other is being built up.

WHAT TO COMPOST

- Kitchen vegetable waste
- Teabags, tea leaves, coffee grains
- Eggshells
- Vacuum cleaner waste
- Old potting soil
- Lawn mowings
- Thin prunings
- Bonfire ash
- Straw
- Animal manure
- Seaweed
- Autumn leaves. It is best to rot down autumn leaves on their own in a wire basket. These take longer to decompose – up to two years – but the resulting leafmould is ideal for use as potting or seed compost.

WHAT NOT TO COMPOST

- Animal waste such as meat scraps, which could attract rats
- Diseased plant material
- Perennial weeds
- Evergreen leaves like holly or ivy (you can include conifer needles)
- Woody material
- Any man-made waste (plastic etc.)

EXTRA COMPOSTING MATERIALS

You can never have too much compost. For extra supplies visit market stalls and greengrocers' shops at the end of the working day. Use seaweed, straw or green bracken (check first with local regulations if gathering them is legal), or manure from riding stables.

Quick compost tips

- When you use eggshells on your compost heap, crush them before adding them to the waste. This will speed up the rate at which they break down.
- If your garden produces a lot of thick, tough plant material such as woody stems and shrub and tree prunings, consider investing in a shredder.
- The bigger the pile, the more heat builds up inside it and the faster it will break down.
- Forking the heap as it rots, to turn the drier outside material to the middle, helps it to rot evenly.

DIGGING

Digging not only allows you to introduce soil-improving conditioners but also aerates the soil and exposes pests to be gobbled up by enthusiastic predators. To incorporate manure or compost put a layer in the bottom of the trench, then half-fill it with soil. Add more manure and finally fill the trench with soil.

First mark out size and position of the trenches using tough garden string. Dig out a square of soil the width and depth of the spade, starting at the end of the first trench. Pile up the soil at the end of the bed.

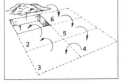

Drive the spade into the soil at right angles to the surface, and a spade's width away from the first opening, then pull back on the handle to lever and loosen the bite of soil.

Lift the spadeful of soil and twist it over, with a flick of your wrist, to invert the clod of soil into the first space. Keep your back straight while doing this, and lift with your knees.

At the end of the row remove the first bite in the next row by driving the spade in at right angles to the first row, then insert the spade between these cuts and parallel to the first trench.

Checking acid or alkaline levels

Growing plants unsuited to your soil

If you long to include plants unsuited to your soil, build a raised bed and import soil to suit the plants you have chosen.

Raised beds

The construction tips on page 120–121 can be used for building a raised bed, but omit mortar from some joints in the first line of bricks. These gaps provide spaces for excess water to escape. When building a raised bed, lay the complete rectangle of bricks that form the bed sides at each level, so that the sides are tied in with the front and back. To fill the bed, first put in rubble to one-third of its depth, then complete by adding soil to the top.

A raised bed or a planting area can be made with wooden boards. Pressure-treated timber should be used.

See also:
• Digging, page 107

Soil fertility and what you can grow, is affected by the pH level, or the amount of lime in the soil. The pH is measured on a scale of 1 to 14. The low numbers denote an acid soil, a neutral soil has a pH of 7 and the higher numbers show that the soil is alkaline or limey. Most soil is slightly acid: a pH of 6.5 is ideal for a wide range of plants, including vegetables. A drop of only one point on the scale shows a soil ten times more acid and a rise of one point shows it to be ten times more alkaline.

When a garden has been cultivated for a long time, the soil tends to become slightly more acid, whereas an alkaline soil is less likely to be affected long-term by the treatment it gets. A soil can be made more alkaline by the application of garden lime, used for improving the soil condition for vegetables.

If the pH falls below 5.0 nutrients are affected. Below this phosphate can become unavailable to plants, the soil becomes more acid and calcium, potassium and magnesium can be washed away. A very alkaline soil is equally hostile to many plants, and can cause nutrients to be 'locked' into the soil. Some plants only survive in acid conditions while others thrive if the soil is alkaline. It helps to know the pH level of your soil and which plants suit it and will thrive – see page 109 for examples.

If your soil is acid you can raise the pH level fairly simply by adding lime. It is important to do this at a different time from using manure, compost or fertilizer. If these are mixed there is a harmful reaction. If you apply manure in the autumn then leave liming until the early spring, about six weeks before planting. Add only a little lime at a time, then test again later and add more if necessary as it can quickly build up.

Measuring the pH level Use a pH kit (right) or a probe meter to check this. Take samples from around the garden. Follow the instructions for whichever method you use.

▲ Adding lime improves acid soil.

Raising the pH on sandy and other acid soils Divide the area to be limed into l m/l yd squares, using pegs and string and weigh out enough lime for each square. Use gloves or a spade to apply the lime one square at a time, sprinkling it as evenly as possible over the surface.

△ Adding garden compost and manure will help to make the soil more acid.

Raising the pH on clay soil Follow the instructions for sandy soil; but thoroughly dig the lime into the soil, (see digging page 107).

Lowering the pH It is hard to make an alkaline soil more acid, although digging in compost and manure helps. Use liquid seaweed foliar spray to provide a quicker method of correcting deficiencies. To create a successful garden choose plants that prefer the natural conditions you have.

LIME

Ground limestone and calcified seaweed are expensive but last longer in the soil. Alternatively use slaked or garden lime. Hydrated or builders' lime can also be used, but in smaller quantities – approximately three-quarters of the quantities given below. It needs to be replaced annually as it is quickly lost.

Use the following quantities of ground limestone to raise pH by 1pH.
• On sandy soil 225 g per sq m/ 8 oz per sq yd
• On loamy soil 450 g per sq m/ 16 oz per sq yd
• On clay soil 680 g per sq m/ 1 lb 8 oz per sq yd

Some plants for acid soil

If you have an acid soil you are lucky, as most garden plants thrive in a fairly acid soil, and over-acidity can be easily corrected by the use of lime. A few plants, including most heathers and lilies, must have acid soil and refuse to grow without it. Camellias (right), azaleas (below, right) and rhododendrons (below) are among the species that will not tolerate lime.

Some plants for alkaline soil

Alkaline soils can demand a more selective approach to choosing your plants. Many species fail to thrive when too much lime in the soil prevents them taking up all the nutrients they require. However, there are also many chalk and lime lovers, including lilacs (right), all the clematis (below, right), and buddleia (below).

Watering

We need to water wisely as this is important for the production of strong, healthy plants. Plants that are watered sparingly but often produce a root system close to the soil surface and these roots soon suffer in dry periods. The healthiest plants are those that develop a strong, deep root system which is able to tap into more reliable reserves well below ground level.

Watering systems

Automatic systems work from a garden tap. A main pipe is laid around the garden then smaller branch tubes are added which lead away to areas where water is needed. Spike fittings are positioned alongside plants to be watered,

▲ Micro-adjustable dripper.

then tiny spray or sprinkler units are screwed into these. The system can be used to water containers and hanging baskets as well as beds and lawns. It is estimated that the system needs to be turned on for ten minutes twice a day, in dry weather to provide sufficient water. A timer is also available which, fitted to the tap, automatically controls the water on and off.

Seep hoses can be part of the above system or laid separately along the ground. Tiny perforations allow the water to seep out slowly and sink well into the soil. Seepage hoses are similar but can also be buried just below the soil's surface. This minimizes water loss through evaporation.

Sprinklers can be difficult to train accurately and are easy to forget, so they can be very water wasteful. Oscillating sprinklers can be adjusted to cover areas of different sizes, static and rotating sprinklers water in a circle, and pulse-jet sprinklers rotate to eject the water in a series of pulses.

Hand watering, using a watering can or a garden hose with a spray attachment, is accurate but time consuming. It does allow you to check the health of your plants as you water each in turn, and is ideal for watering containers and baskets. Allow at least a full can for each large container.

▼ A soaker hose in use.

What and when to water

▲ Adjustable lawn sprinkler in use.

Lawns A lawn of newly sown grass-seed or newly laid turf needs regular watering in dry weather. However an established lawn can survive a period of drought and soon turns greens again when rain arrives. If consistently green grass is particularly important to you give the lawn a good soaking once a week. In dry periods mow frequently but adjust the height of the blades to a longer 4 cm/1½ in. This encourages dense growth and helps to trap any dew.

Large shrubs and trees need regular watering when first planted to

▼ A hose extension can be useful.

create a healthy root system. Once deep roots are established they can find water for themselves and rarely need watering, even in dry conditions.

Small shrubs and hardy perennials start to droop as a sign that they require water. Give the plants a good soaking in the evening when the sun is off the area.

Bedding plants and vegetables need regular watering in dry weather if they are to thrive. Water these plants either first thing in the morning or during the evening (never when they are in strong sun). The closer together plants are the more water they need.

▼ Compost in pots can dry out quickly.

Tubs, window boxes and hanging baskets should be treated as for bedding plants and vegetables. They can dry out very quickly in hot weather, and may need to be watered every morning and evening. Revive hanging baskets by soaking them in a bucket of water.

Saving water

Fix water butts to downpipes to store as much waste rain-water as you can. It is also possible to divert bath and shower water into storage tanks where it can cool prior to being used on the garden.

Watering tips

• Never water plants when the sun is on them. This not only causes leaf burn but wastes water in evaporation. Instead, water in the evening.

• A good layer of mulch, about 8 cm/3 in, spread over the soil surface will prevent evaporation and so help to keep the soil below moist. Mulch when the soil is wet. Never add mulch to dry soil or the mulch will draw water away from the soil instead of holding it in.

• Use ground-cover plants to fill any spaces of bare soil. Once established they look decorative and help to shade the soil and prevent it from drying out.

See also:
• Ground cover, page 174

Electricity in the garden

Safety pointers

The often damp conditions outdoors, and direct contact with the earth, make safety considerations vital. A fault could easily lead to a fatal accident.

- Ensure that installation work is carried out by a fully qualified professional electrician.

- Never service or work on equipment without first switching off and disconnecting from the power.

- Use only fittings and cables designed specifically for outdoor use.

- Check on the condition of cables and equipment and service them regularly.

- Use a residual-current circuit breaker on all sockets used for garden tools so that power is cut off if any thing goes wrong.

If garden lighting or a pump to power a fountain or waterfall is required, it is best to organize this early on, to avoid digging up the garden at a later date. Security lighting, if fixed to the house walls, can be run off the house supply. Some low-voltage garden lighting does not need installing, but uses cables that can be run above the ground. From a safety point of view, consider installing an outdoor socket or fitting one under cover in a garage or porch. This helps to obviate the need for lengths of cable running from within the house.

Hidden power The best way to provide permanent power in the garden is to run it underground. Either special cable must be used or the cable must run through a galvanized steel or rigid plastic conduit. Both run in a channel well below ground level. This type of installation needs to be fitted by a professional electrician as there are strict regulations which must be met and cables and connectors must be weatherproof.

Above-ground cables Low-voltage lighting, which uses a low-voltage transformer sited under cover in an outbuilding, can often be installed with the cables running along the ground. Lay the cable where it is easily seen when you are working in the garden to avoid accidentally cutting through it. Avoid taking the cable over sharp edges like steps or paving which could damage it. If you need to join pieces of cable, use special outdoor cable connectors and for extra protection wrap these in plastic.

▼ Electricity in the garden enables you to install water pumps and garden lighting.

Outdoor socket A weather-proof socket outlet is useful, and safer, for use with power tools (such as those shown below). It must be protected by a residual-current circuit breaker (RCCB). This reacts to break the current circuit when a fault occurs or a cable is accidentally cut.

Where to use power

Garden lighting This falls into two main categories. Lighting which is installed for safety, to help find your way around the garden in the dark, or for security, to highlight and deter interlopers, may be run off the mains supply if the lights are fixed to the house walls. Cable that runs along the wall outdoors must be protected by a length of metal or plastic conduit and all fittings must be weatherproof.

If you wish to highlight the garden's decorative features, such as a shapely or colourful tree or shrub, you have the option of using underground cable or a kit that connects to a low-voltage transformer. Follow the manufacturer's instructions for connecting the light fittings to the flex.

Fountains and waterfalls An electric pump can be sited in a garden pool to provide the power for a waterfall or fountain, both of which continually recycle the same water. Pumps can run from

▲ *Free-standing lantern lights both the path and patio area. Night-time lighting can be activated just when the area is in use and as a security measure.*

the mains supply or use a low-voltage transformer. Hire a qualified electrician to install a mains-supply pump.

▲ *An elaborate and unusual water feature, powered by a simple pump, in which little frogs spurt jets of water into the lowest fountain tier.*

CHAPTER 6

FORM AND SHAPE

With a strong 'skeleton' the garden will look interesting at all times of the year, even if there is the odd planting disaster. This chapter covers the materials that, together with the way they are used, make up the nuts and bolts of a garden's design.

The colour, texture and size of the paving or other materials you choose for paths and sitting areas, the way you define the boundary – whether you outline it with walls, fences or hedges, or a mixture of these – all these choices create quite different final effects. The way the space within the garden is broken up by special water features or given height with arches and pergolas contributes to its form, as does the arrangement of highlights such as containers and ornaments. Children as well as adults need to be able to enjoy the garden. And, finally, once the garden design is in place you will want to be able to sit back on comfortable and complementary furniture, with the addition of a barbecue and garden lighting, to enjoy it in all its moods, both during the day and in the evening.

Ground surfaces	116–117	Arches, pergolas	
Paths, steps and		and arbours	132–133
edgings	118–119	Containers	134–135
Walls and screens	120–121	Ornamental extras	136–137
Fences	122–123	Children's play	
Hedges	124–125	space	138–139
Introducing water	126–127	Garden furniture	140–141
Moving water	128–129	Barbecues	142–143
Plant frameworks	130–131	Lighting	144–145

Ground surfaces

Paving, bricks and timber
Multiply width by length to
work out the number of square
metres/square yards of material
that will be needed.

Gravel or shingle Multiply
width by length, then by depth.
One cu m/35 cu ft will cover
an area of 20 sq m/215 sq ft
to a depth of 5 cm/2 in.

Hard surface choices
• Concrete paving slabs
• Setts and pavers
• Stone and reconstituted
  stone
• Timber
• Bricks
• Cobbles
• Shingle and gravel

Soft surface choices
• Grass seed
• Turf
• Wildflower meadow
• Chamomile
• Creeping thyme
• Clover

Brick is traditional looking
and hard-wearing

Timber decking gives a
warmer, softer look

The materials used for paved or
hard-surfaced areas and lawns,
together with the shape of these
key areas, are extremely important
in forming both the style and the
bold background outline of a garden.
Paving or other hard materials
provide hard surfaces, in the same
way as vinyl, tiles or timber do this
in a house, while the lawn creates
the softer, gentler effect of a carpet.

△ Paving is both durable and pleasing
to the eye.

Planning paved areas

When planning the positions of
areas to sit in, balance the practical
use of the garden with aesthetic
effect. Consider the position of the
sun, the need for shade, shelter
from wind, views, and privacy.

Once you have decided on the
position, size and shape of a paved
area use hosepipe or rope to outline it on the ground. Allow plenty
of space for chairs and tables and
plant containers. Arrange furniture
within the outlined area to check
that it will all fit in the space comfortably. You may need to adjust
the area size to take into account
the paving material you choose so
that you avoid having to cut slabs.

Planting in containers, which
can be moved around, is a flexible
solution in paved areas.

Choosing the materials

Consider both the garden style and
the materials used in the construction
of the house. A paved area next to
the house should have a slight fall
away from the house so that rain
drains away from the building
rather than towards it.

Pre-cast concrete paving slabs are
reasonably priced and easy to lay.
They also come in a wide range of
colours, shapes and finishes. Avoid
a highly textured finish where you
intend to use furniture. Check the
change of colour when slabs are
wet and how slip-resistant they are.

Bricks blend well with a traditional
brick-built house and provide a
natural, country effect. They can
also be laid in a range of patterns.
House bricks are too soft to be
suitable and flake if exposed to
winter weather. Choose frostproof,
hardwearing bricks such as
engineering bricks or brick pavers.

Setts are another small-sized and
decorative alternative. Granite setts

▽ Pebbles or other materials can be
mixed with paving slabs.

are hard-wearing, and look at home in areas where granite is the local building material. Concrete setts give a similar effect, and are cheaper. **Timber decking** is a popular surface, sympathetic to the surroundings in most gardens. Paint or stain can be used to add colour. Old railway sleepers are a very strong, and cheaper, alternative. If timber becomes dangerously slippery when wet, or in frost, staple fine chicken wire over the surface. **Stone** Sandstone, limestone, ironstone, York stone, and slate all blend well with most garden styles but these materials are expensive and difficult to lay. Reconstituted stone is cheaper. Both come as straight-sided slabs or with uneven edges to be laid as crazy paving. Alternatively you can use broken stone or concrete slabs for this. **Cobbles** are uncomfortable to walk on but ideal for forming smaller patterned areas in plain paving. **Gravel and shingle** are both cheap, easy to use and give a softer finish. But they provide some problems too. They are best retained by edging as they tend to 'walk' with you into the house and

▲ Natural stone is perfect next to an old house.

onto the lawn, where they can create a danger when mowing. Some plants can look very effective growing through the surface, but regular weeding will be necessary or the area to be overtaken by seedlings. Laying plastic sheeting underneath the gravel helps to avoid this but holes will need to be made in the plastic for drainage.

Gravel and shingle both provide a measure of security in a front garden as any visitor's arrival is very audible.

SOFT SURFACES

A lawn from turf gives you an instant result, once the ground is prepared, and turf can be laid at most times of the year, but it is cheaper to sow a lawn. The best time to create a lawn, whichever method you use, is spring or early autumn. There are two widely available alternative grass mixes you can use. Those that include rye grass are hard-wearing and easy to care for. Garden owners who want a good-looking finish and are prepared to spend time on looking after a lawn should go for a fine, dense grass.

Alternatives to grasses are clover, camomile and creeping thyme but these are suitable only for small areas. You can also sew an area as a wild-flower meadow using a mixture of recommended grass and wildflower seeds. In the first year this should be cut at two-monthly intervals so that the grass does not smother the wild flowers. After this cut only early in spring and then in the autumn once the seeds have been shed.

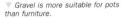
▼ Gravel is more suitable for pots than furniture.

Mixing materials

By combining materials you can create decorative effects. For instance use larger quantities of cheaper paving and provide character, pattern and design detail with small-sized, more expensive alternatives such as granite setts or cobbles to create an uneven surface. This makes a paved area or a path more interesting. Below, pebbles are introduced between areas of paving slabs on a pathway.

Lay the pebbles in spaces left between paving slabs. Fit them as closely together as you can on a bed of mortar.

Lay a stout piece of wood across the pebbles from one slab to the next to check that the pebbles are flush with the paving. If necessary tap the wood with a hammer to bed them in and ensure the surface is completely even.

Paths, steps and edgings

Laying stepping-stones

Stepping-stones that meander across a lawn are less intrusive than a path. They also provide a way of moving across gravelled areas without taking the tiny chippings with you.

Work out the positions of the stones by walking along the route the path will take. Take normal strides and mark the position of each step as you go.

Place the stones in the positions marked and check the effect visually. Walk over the stones to double-check the spacing.

Cut around each stone with a spade, to a depth slightly more than that of the stepping-stone.

Cut beneath the slice to be removed and lift the turf out.

Level the base of the cut-out space with sand Position the stone, check that it is level and just below surrounding grass to avoid damage to the mower.

Path and step choices
- Concrete paving slabs
- Setts and pavers
- Stone and reconstituted stone
- Timber and bark chippings
- Bricks
- Cobbles
- Shingle and gravel
- Grass

Edging choices
- Bricks
- Tiles
- Terracotta strips
- Timber, logs, railway sleepers
- Rocks or giant pebbles
- Low-growing plants
- Low hedges or fences
- Shells

Paths, and paved areas, highlight the design of the garden, providing definition, while the materials you use to create them enhance (or detract from) the character. Steps which lead from one level in a garden to another work in the same way, and can follow the form and materials used for the linking path or add new and interesting textures by introducing different materials. Most of the options covered in Ground surfaces – not forgetting grass, if the area will not get much wear – are also suitable for paths and steps. Edgings add definition and act as a practical divide to keep soil off paths and lawns and to contain softer path materials.

▲ The contrast of bricks with stone can be effective for steps and raised beds.

Providing links

Paths supply a link with each section of the garden from the house, allowing you to wander and admire as well as to work without damaging soil structure. They can be straight or meandering, but need to lead to a specific point of interest, which may be the garage or garden shed, a place to sit and relax, or a closer view of a point of special interest such as a statue, pond or group of pots. Where

paths meet there is an opportunity to create a central pattern using the same or a different material. Pebbles or bricks are ideal for this. This area can then be used to show off a sculpture, or a container holding a topiary bush or a shrub or tree.

The narrowest width advisable for a path is 30 cm/12 in. This will be wide enough for just one person to use the path. If you need to use the path for a wheelbarrow just over twice this width will be more suitable.

If a path will create too hard a line, consider using paving slabs as stepping-stones instead. These can also define a route along a path made of softer materials such as grass or gravel.

Moving from one level to another

Garden steps, both for safety and for aesthetic reasons, are best constructed as wide and shallow as possible. A flight of steps does not have to be straight.

▼ Steps should be broad and shallow.

▲ *Terracotta edging on a brick path.*

▲ *Plants soften the edge of a path.*

Laying timber edging

Timber edging comes as wood strips wired together. You can cut the wire to shorten the strip, or wire two lengths together.

Unwind the roll and use wire-cutters to cut it to length.

Dig out a trench for the edging, having first worked out the height you want the edging top above the ground.

Lay the edging in the trench, checking the height and that it is level along the length. Back-fill with soil and firm well.

For a straight top place a length of timber over the edging strip. Use a club hammer to knock it firmly in place.

Curving steps look good and provide a range of aspects as you pass up or down them. Angle the steps slightly forward to avoid the danger of standing water.

Consider using a different material for the riser and step surfaces – for example bricks topped with stone slabs.

Edging paths, patios and beds
Edging not only defines the shape of a path, patio, flower bed or steps but it is a practical method of containing soft materials such as soil, chippings or gravel. Apart from materials made specially for the role – for example timber

edging, corrugated plastic strip and coiled terracotta – you can use hard materials such as bricks (either flat or set diagonally on edge), paving, tiles or logs, and even railway sleepers. For a purely decorative effect consider the use of large pebbles, shells or other suitable natural material.

Beds can take a softer edging with low hedges or a line of ground-hugging plants, which are ideal for showing off the shape, but to keep the soil and grass in place first fit a lawn edging strip. Make sure that the top of the strip sits just below lawn level to avoid damage to the mower.

▼ *An informal combination of materials.*

▼ *An inventive but formal design.*

See also:
• *Ground surfaces, page 116*

Walls and screens

Building a low brick wall

Even a low wall needs to be built on a firm foundation, or footing, of hardcore and concrete.

Form the footing by excavating a 30 cm/12 in deep trench. Fill it to a 13 cm/5 in depth with consolidated hardcore. Drive in pegs as a guide for the top of the concrete and check that peg tops are level.

Complete the footings by pouring in concrete. Level it off with the peg tops. Use a piece of wood to tamp the concrete level and to remove large pockets of air. Leave to harden for a few days.

Lay the first course of bricks. Form a pier at each end by placing two bricks sideways. On a long wall you will also need to repeat piers at regular intervals.

(continued opposite)

A brick wall is the traditional way of outlining a boundary to a garden and providing it with privacy, and is long lasting and attractive to look at. It can help to keep out intruders and animals, provide shelter, or screen an ugly view. A boundary wall highlights its size and shape. To give the shape less emphasis, to make the space appear larger, or to create more interest, vary the materials used around the perimeter, or vary the wall's height. When mixing walls and fences, construct areas of fence on a low brick or stone wall to create a more integrated look. Where complete privacy is not required pierced concrete or open terracotta blocks provide another visual effect.

Walls are also used as retainers, to hold the soil in a series of stepped terraces in a sloping garden or to create a sunken area. High or retaining walls are not easy to construct and are best erected by a specialist. Materials used may be bricks, stone, reconstituted stone, flint, or concrete blocks, which can be faced

▲ *A dry-stone wall is a haven for plants.*

with stone if preferred. A wall needs capping to protect the construction. Some choices for capping are bricks, set side-by-side across the width, concrete slabs, or some other weatherproof material.

Walls as internal dividers

Within the garden, strategically placed openwork screens can divide the garden into a series of 'rooms' with an enticing view of something interesting beyond. Alternatively, with a covering of plants, they can hide necessary eyesores, like the garden shed or dustbin, or provide privacy for a paved sitting or eating area. Apart

▼ *A low brick wall can make a screen or divider.*

▼ *Raised beds can team with boundary walls.*

(continued from opposite)

Lay subsequent courses after running a ribbon of mortar along the top of the previous row. As shown, 'butter' one end of each brick before you position it.

Frequently use a spirit level to ensure bricks are level. As you work strike off any surplus mortar from the wall sides.

 Trellis-work breaks up an otherwise dull surface and filters the wind.

▲ *Combining painted trellis panels with picket fencing creates an original look.*

from openwork masonry walls, timber trellis, slatted wood, and even openwork wire mesh can be used to form slim dividers. Screens of this type also filter wind and sun very effectively. As they allow some air-flow they do not act as a total barrier creating eddies of wind in the way that a solid wall can do.

Low walls can edge a pond or patio, or act as a decorative divide between different areas and levels in the garden without supplying a feeling of enclosed spaces. To soften

the hard lines of a wall use dry-stone walls with cracks for plants, or create a double-shell wall with a space in the centre to take soil for planting. A higher, flat-faced brick or stone wall can be used as a sheltering background for climbers and a wall that faces the sun makes a home for tender plants. Brick wall piers can act as plinths for containers of flowering plants, and wall baskets and similar containers can add the softness and colour of plants to an otherwise bleak wall.

Firm and adjust the level of each brick as you lay it, using the handle of the bricklaying trowel.

Finally fix coping and pier caps to complete the wall and protect the brickwork from excessive moisture.

Wall materials
- Reconstituted or natural stone
- Bricks
- Flint
- Concrete blocks
- Pierced concrete
- Pierced terracotta

Screen materials
- Timber trellis, stained or painted
- Openwork terracotta or concrete walling
- Slatted wood

GATES

An opening in the garden boundary wall, fence or hedge usually needs a gate to complete it and to keep children or pets inside the garden. Several factors help you decide what type of gate is best suited to your specific situation. The general surroundings, the purpose of the gate, and the materials used for the boundary are all involved in deciding on the best design and materials. High, closeboarded gates provide privacy and security, while low, openwork designs allow a sight of the house or a view from it. Timber or ironwork gates are popular and look best if they match the boundary in height.

See also:
- Fences, page 122
- Hedges, page 124

Fences

Erecting a panel fence

The simplest way to erect a fence is to set the posts in metal spikes.

Position the spike with the protective head inside the top and drive it in with a sledgehammer. Make sure that the spike remains vertical. Check often with a spirit level.

With the post in position in the spike top, check that this is absolutely vertical.

Lay the first panel in position, next to the post, and mark the spot for the next post spike. Drive the spike in as before.

continued opposite)

Fences are a quick and cheap alternative to walls. They act as windbreaks, hide an ugly view and outline a boundary. Height provides privacy but high walls or fences throw long shadows, keeping off sun and rain, which can be a major problem in a small space. While hedges and trellis filter the wind and reduce its strength, wind is only diverted by a solid barrier. A lower fence, topped with trellis and covered in climbing plants, provides a better alternative and still gives privacy.

▲ *A closeboard panelled fence.*

Fences make an instant boundary, take little space and provide instant privacy. They are erected on posts which may be of wood, concrete or metal. These can be fixed into the ground directly, set into concrete, attached to a concrete spur or pushed into the top of a metal spike driven into the ground. In the two latter methods a timber post is not in contact with the soil and so is likely to last longer. Concrete posts are the longest-lasting but are visually less compatible with timber fencing.

Style options

Fences come in a wide range of materials and designs to suit every situation and type of garden.

Panel fencing is the simplest high fence to construct and is cheap to buy. There are two designs, overlapped and interwoven. The overlapped panels provide more privacy. Panels of either design are fixed to posts but are not very strong and are difficult to repair.

Closeboard fencing is tougher and can be made to any height. It is made from overlapped boards held into position on horizontal, triangular-shaped rails. The best method of construction for both types includes a gravel board. This runs along the bottom to protect the board ends from damp, and is easy to replace. The top edge of a closeboard fence can be straight or shaped between posts.

Woven hurdles are used in the classic cottage-garden fence. Hurdles come in a range of heights and are usually made from pliable stems of willow or hazel (which is coarser), which are woven in and out of stouter upright stems. Hurdles are not long-lasting but are easily portable and provide a good temporary barrier while shrubs or a hedge grow.

▼ *Woven hazel hurdles as fencing.*

(continued from opposite)

▲ *Diagonally set timber gives a contemporary look.*

▲ *Picket fencing is a country classic.*

Nail panel brackets to the first post. Nail matching brackets to the second post, then remove the second post temporarily.

Picket fencing, either stained or painted white, provides a good, low boundary for a front garden. It is constructed in a similar way to closeboard fencing but with spaces between the uprights. The top edge of each upright may be rounded, pointed or cut in any design.

Post and rail baffle, or ranch fencing, is simpler in design, constructed from posts linked with two or three horizontal rails. Wire is often fixed between the rails in country areas to keep animals out.

Wire with concrete posts forms the simplest of designs. To hide the basic structure plant fast-growing evergreen climbers along its length. Plastic-coated chain link or chicken wire provides additional plant supports.

Plastic fencing is an easy-maintenance option but is not as strong as most other materials. Available in ranch style or as post and plastic-coated chain.

Trellis fencing comes in a wide range of widths, heights and thicknesses, in both timber and plastic and in square or diamond shapes. Expanding trellis is also available but is not very strong. Trellis makes an excellent internal divider. It can also form attractive open areas in a tall boundary fence and can be fixed to the top of a wall or fence to give extra height for climbing plants.

Position the panel and get someone to hold it while you position the second post. Check the panel is horizontal, then nail into it through the brackets.

Nail a post cap to the top of each post to complete the fence.

Materials choice
• Timber, metal or plastic

Style choices
• Woven panels
• Closeboard
• Wattle hurdles
• Picket fencing
• Post and rail fencing
• Trellis

See also:
• Walls and screens, page 120
• Hedges, page 124

▼ *Post and rail fencing is available in rural or more cultivated style (as shown).*

▼ *Diamond-shaped trellis panels finish off this opening in a plain fence.*

Hedges

Planting a hedge

Before you plant a hedge it is important to prepare the ground well. Dig a trench and, to improve the soil's structure, dig in lots of garden compost or well-rotted manure. The prepared strip needs to be at least 60 cm/2 ft wide. Before planting break down large clumps of earth and sprinkle on a balanced garden fertilizer. If planting in autumn or winter use a slow-acting fertilizer.

Caring for bought plants
Hedging plants are often sold in bundles of bare-rooted plants. Keep the roots moist, for example by placing them in a temporary planting hole. Separate them as you plant.

To ensure a straight hedge use a garden line and insert markers spaced as recommended for each plant. Do not place too close together when there is a risk that individual plants may die. In a windy situation or on a boundary stagger the planting of the trees as shown here.

(continued opposite)

Hedges can mark a boundary, divide the garden into smaller, spaces or form a low, neat outline to formal beds. They can protect plants from adverse weather, deter burglars, help to lower noise levels and attract wildlife. Hedges rarely collapse in a storm in the way that fences, or even walls, can do.

Formal hedges

Clipped, compact evergreen hedges look much the same throughout the year and are ideal for creating a formal outline in or around the garden. They provide a good backdrop for flowers and plants. These hedges need regular clipping to maintain their shape.

The traditionally grown plants for evergreen hedges are privet, yew, laurel, and box. Conifers are also commonly used. Avoid fast-growing Leyland cypress and go for slower-growing alternatives such as *Chamaecyparis lawsoniana* 'Ellwoodii', which will produce a more satisfactory hedge. For neat, low hedges there is the dwarf box, *Buxus sempervirens* 'Suffruticosa'.

Less formal effects

There is a wide range of flowering and fruiting shrubs that can be

▽ *A clipped yew hedge is always attractive.*

trained to form decorative but looser-growing hedges. For spring colour go for forsythia with its sunny yellow flowers that appear before the leaves. For a low hedge *Berberis thunbergii* 'Atropurpurea' has purple-bronze foliage turning a rich red in autumn. Hornbeam, *Carpinos betrays*, has yellow or green catkins in spring and turns a yellow-orange in autumn before the leaves fall. Beech, *Fagus sylvatica*, can provide a formal or informal outline depending on how you trim it. Although it is deciduous, the autumn leaves often remain on the hedge all winter; the copper beech, *F. s. purpurea*, has purple leaves that turn a deep, rich copper colour in autumn.

Plant a mixed hedge for a traditional country look and to attract a wide range of birds who will enjoy the food, protection and

▲ *A box hedge encloses a lavender bed.*

nesting potential. Country hedges may include some of the following: hawthorn and black-thorn, hazel, beech, holly, spindle, privet, dog-wood, dog roses, honeysuckle and guelder rose.

Hedges for security

Thick, prickly hedges form ideal

(continued from opposite)

▲ A country hedge is laid to become thick and impenetrable.

▲ Rosa rugosa is usually still in flower when the first hips ripen.

Dig a large hole for each plant and position it, spreading out the roots. Fill the hole with soil and firm it well.

Finally rake the soil level and water plants thoroughly. Keep well watered for the first season.

deterrents to unwanted visitors if you plant them along road-sides or bordering a front garden. The common holly, *Ilex aquifolium*, is excellent for this. For a variegated form choose 'Ferox Argentea' with cream-edged leaves or 'Golden Queen' with golden margins. *Berberis* x *stenophylla*, also dense and thorny, is a colourful alternative, with its gold flowers in spring and purple-red leaves.

A rose hedge can be both decorative and extremely prickly. Choose *Rosa rugosa* varieties for their closely prickled stems. Many also have flowers with a beautiful scent and large red hips in autumn. The flowers come in white, yellow, and tones of pink through to deep crimson. *Berberis thunbergii* is also

thorny but grows to only about 1 m/3 ft high. Its fresh green leaves below, turn orange in autumn and it has red-tinged, pale yellow flowers and red fruit. Hawthorn, *Crataegus monogyna*, is also suitable and has white or pink-tinged flowers in spring followed by red fruit.

▲ A fuchsia hedge, is an attractive alternative to a formal clipped hedge.

Some hedge plant choices

Evergreen hedges
• Box, *Buxus sempervirens*
• Holly, *Ilex aquifolium*
• Viburnum, *V. tinus*
• Cedar, *Thuja occidentalis*
• Laurel, *Prunus lusitanica*
• Yew, *Taxus baccata*
• Privet, *Ligustrum ovalifolium*

Colourful hedges
• Rose, *Rosa rugosa*
• Hawthorn, *Crataegus monogyna*
• Cotoneaster species
• Hornbeam, *Carpinus betulus*
• Escallonia varieties
• Mexican orange blossom, *Choisya ternata*

Low herbal hedges
• Lavender, *Lavandula* species
• Sage, *Salvia* species
• Cotton lavender, *Santolina chamaecyparissus*
• Rosemary, such as *Rosmarinus officinalis* 'Severn Sea'
• Hyssop, *Hyssopus officinalis*

See also:
• Fertilizers, page 105
• Digging, page 107

FORMING A FEDGE

A fedge is a combination of fence and hedge and is a good way of creating the effect of a hedge in a narrow space. Plant ivies about 2.5–3 m/8–10 ft apart against a fence until they intermingle to form a dense cover over the framework, then clip to control growth. The traditional hedge is made by pushing in and weaving willow stems, which soon root and grow to form a narrow, green barrier.

BEWARE FAST-GROWING HEDGES

The fast-growing Leyland cypress, *Cupressocyparis leylandii*, is not really suitable for a small garden, particularly if you wish to remain on good terms with your neighbours. The advantage of its speedy growth is outweighed by the fact that it does not simply stop when it reaches the required height but continues on apace and so needs topping as well as trimming every year.

Introducing water

Creating a pond

A pre-formed shape enables you to install a pond very quickly, and little skill is required.

Place the pre-formed pond on the ground and mark out its outline with canes. Lay rope around the canes to mark the shape.

Dig out the the pond area, taking into account shelves and changes in depth. Make your hole slightly bigger than the shape.

To check depth measure down from a plank across the hole. Use a spirit level placed on the plank to check that the pond is also level.

(continued opposite)

There is room for a pond or pool in the smallest garden. Although a larger pond creates a light-reflecting focal point, a waterproof tub can hold a miniature pond where space is at a premium.

The pond should be situated in an open, sunny spot. Overhanging trees cast shadows which prevent water plants from flourishing and their falling leaves create problems.

The next decision is whether to go for a formal or informal effect. An informal pond is best sited where a natural pond would occur: that is in a low-lying area of the garden. If you wish to place it elsewhere, build up the background, using the excavated soil, to create a bank or rockery behind. On the other hand, a formal pond sits well in the centre of a paved area, or a lawn. A series of interlocking ponds creates a stunning water garden. Fountains and waterfalls, using a pumped recycling system, will keep the water in good condition, whereas care needs to be taken to balance a still pond if the water is to remain crystal clear.

▽ To get a natural effect, place the pond in the lowest part of the garden.

▲ A tub can be made into a pond.

Formal effect

In a symmetrically planned formal garden simple rectangular, square or round ponds look most in keeping, although a semi-circular pond placed against a wall or fence on the patio can also fit into the design. Formal pools can be raised, with a surrounding wall providing a seat. This is ideal for a pond on a patio. Alternatively the pond can be sunk into the ground.

Use a pond to alter the apparent shape of a garden. A long, narrow pond placed across the width in a long, narrow garden will help to make the space appear wider. Or, equally effective, take the pond almost from one side of the garden to the other at an angle. A walkway across the water can lead you from one area to the next.

The natural look

An informal pond needs to look as natural as possible, in both

MINIATURE PONDS

Wooden tubs, old sinks, plastic plant containers, fish tanks are all suitable. The pond can either be sunk into the ground or placed on top of it. If you add a 15 cm/6 in layer of compost to the base you can plant a small water lily and one – possibly two – aquatics. Cover the soil with a layer of gravel and add a few large pebbles, then fill with water.

▲ For a natural look use a liner.

shape and surroundings. Liners should be black or brown. Natural ponds looks smaller once planted, so allow for this in your choice of size. If you want the water to attract wildlife take grass right up to the edge and provide a shallow beach at one end to make it easy for animals to enter and leave the water. Birds will use this area for drinking and bathing.

Pond-making materials

The simplest way to construct a sunken pond is to use either a pre-formed shape or a flexible liner. Buy the best quality material you can afford as once the pond is installed it becomes a major problem to fix leaks. A flexible liner gives more freedom as you can make the pond any shape you like. If you want to

add fish or larger waterlilies you will need a depth, in part of the pond, of 45–60 cm/18–24 in. Shelves around the edge allow you to include marginal plants which thrive in shallow water.

A sunken formal pond can also be created using these materials. A raised pond is usually constructed using concrete for the base and tough external bricks or reinforced concrete blocks for the sides.

Pond edgings

With lined ponds it is important to cover the pond edge to create a natural finish. If you use paving, tuck the liner underneath the slabs and allow the paving to overlap above the water. If you run grass right up to the pond edge the flap of the liner should be turned down and buried so that the grass has soil to grow in. Allow the grass edge to meet the water and hide the liner. Pebbles also create a natural-looking outline.

POND SAFETY

Avoid ponds while you have small children. It is possible to drown in very shallow water. Instead, consider installing a wall-fixed recycling fountain. A mill-stone or a low basin of pebbles, where water jets out then trickles over the surface, are also suitable.

▼ A stone surround finishes off the pond and keeps the lining anchored.

(continued from opposite)

Place the pool in the hole and check that the edges are completely level from all angles, using the plank and spirit level

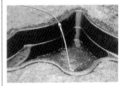

When the pond is snugly in place run water into it, packing fine soil around the edges as the water level rises. Finally push soil firmly under the shelves, ramming it down with a piece of wood.

Material choices
- Pliable plastic or rubber liner
- Pre-formed rigid liner
- Concrete raised pool

Miniature pond containers
- Half-barrel
- Trough
- Saucer-shaped stone or concrete container
- Plastic or other waterproof container

See also:
- Moving water, page 128
- Water plants, page 178

Moving water

Choosing a pump

A pump is needed to provide the power to circulate the water for a waterfall or fountain. Pumps can either be submersible, sited in the water or surface-fixed nearby, in which case they need a housing to protect them.

Submersible pumps are less powerful but deal adequately with most fountains up to about 1.2 m/4 ft high or a small waterfall. They work silently, and low voltage models can be connected to the house electricity supply.

Surface pumps are more powerful, and with a surface pump a range of fountains and waterfalls can be run from one system. The pump and its housing should be positioned as close to the pond as possible so that only short lengths of tube are necessary.

When buying materials for a water feature, discuss with the suppliers exactly what effect you want to create. They will then be in the best position to advise you on the pump most suited to the effect you wish to achieve.

Moving water features

• Fountain
• Waterfall
• Cascade
• Millstone
• Bridges, stepping stones, and walkways

Moving water provides exciting effects and creates a tranquil atmosphere. A fountain, tumbling stream, or waterfall all provide the tinkling sound of moving water. Water-garden centres, television gardening programmes and

⌃ A multi-bowl fountain.

specialist water-garden books, provide inspirational ideas on ways to use moving water. Some novel ideas include vertical falls of water which stream down light-reflecting backdrops, and slow-drip bamboo pipes, as well as the more traditional tumbling streams and gullies. You will need to install a pump for moving water features.

There are innovative fountain heads using almost any shape or material through which a pipe can be threaded, as well as specially produced animals, heads, figures, shells and flowers.

Fountains These are the simplest moving-water structures to fit and usually suit a formal area or formal pond best. A fountain can be an independent feature of single or multi-storey bowls where water falls from a head at the top to ever-larger dishes set one below the other. In this case no extra work is needed except to site the fountain and set up the electricity required to power it and recirculate the water. A fountain added to a garden pond can be positioned centrally in the pond or placed at the edge. Bear in mind that it will look most effective if it is in scale with the pond. A large ornament and wide-spreading jet of water will look incongruous in a small pond and vice versa.

According to the head you choose, water from a fountain can appear in a wide number of shapes from a single spout to multi-tiered sprays, whirls, bells, fishtails and geysers. Fountain kits are available which include a fountain jet, a flow adjuster to alter the speed of the water, and a submersible pump. The pump should be positioned on

▽ Water spilling into a trough over wood in tiers stimulates thinking.

▲ Water cascading over stone ledges needs a natural-looking setting.

a brick or other block to keep it raised above the bottom of the pond. The electricity to power the system can either be taken direct from the mains or make use of a low-voltage connector.

Waterfalls and cascades Waterfalls look best in a natural setting. The soil excavated from the pond can be used to form the base for a rocky outcrop from which the water tumbles in tiers. A waterfall can be built from the same materials used in making a pond. Additional rocks and stones embedded in the

surface give a more natural finish. Pre-formed stream sections are available. The distance from the pond surface to the top step of the waterfall should be no greater than 90 cm/36 in. Get advice on the most suitable pump for the job when planning the design.

Millstone and pebble fountains Water spouting out of the centre of a millstone or falling to over a layer of pebbles creates an effective small-sized feature. These usually come as a kit and are simple to install. Wall-fixed fountains for use indoors or outside can enliven the end of a small terrace or pathway. For a stronger impression use a wall-fixed fountain that sprays the water into a larger semi-circular pond below.

Bridges, walkways and stepping stones A series of interlocking ponds creates a stunning water feature. Ponds can go from one side of the garden to the other, provided a safe method of crossing the water is included in the design.

Ornamental timber bridges are the traditional method used but flatter concrete or timber walkways on a level with the pond edges, or stepping stones of slabs, provide a less obvious route.

▲ A millstone fountain takes very little space. The gurgling sound of the water bubbling up from the centre is soothing and water brings a shine to the surrounding stones.

▲ An arched timber bridge is the traditional way to cross a pond or garden stream although there are plenty of equally attractive alternatives.

POND LIFE AND MOVING WATER

Fish benefit from the introduction of a fountain or waterfall. The splashing increases the oxygen in the water and the rate at which carbon dioxide is released, and helps to stop ponds from freezing over. Waterlilies and surface plants, plus some deep-water aquatics, are best kept away from splashes and turbulent water. Waterlilies need warm, static water, and are damaged by constant splashing which submerges the flowers and rots pads.

Plant frameworks

Some simple plant supports

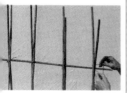

Lines of crossed canes set in pairs in a row give support to runner beans or sweet peas. Tie pairs together near the top, then slide a long horizontal cane into the 'V' and secure.

Wigwams of tall canes arranged in a circle are pulled together at the top and tied in place with string. You can also use a specially produced holder (above) through which the canes are pushed which holds them evenly spaced.

(continued opposite)

In small gardens utilize vertical surfaces as frameworks to grow plants. Walls and fences are obvious choices but free-standing structures covered in plants can enhance the garden's design, providing colour at a higher level and supporting plant stems at the same time. Climbing plants may be trained up timber trellis, wire, plastic or twine to clothe walls or fences, and the use of cane wigwams, ornamental obelisks or metal corkscrews allows you to add extra height wherever you feel it is required, without the need of a wall. Herbaceous plants form the best shapes and remain *in situ* in windy weather if supported by wire frames or twig cages.

Unobtrusive or deliberately decorative

Frameworks may be unobtrusive, simply holding a plant in place, and can be home-made from bamboo canes, plant sticks or stems and twigs cut down in the garden. They can also be very decorative in their own right if they are woven in arched or wigwam shapes. Metal corkscrews, timber obelisks, metal or timber arches and pergolas create strong features as part of a garden's design. Tall and decorative supports such as obelisks, wigwams and corkscrews add height attractively to an area of low growing plants. Arches and pergolas can divide up a garden, forming a number of separate areas, each with a different theme or colour scheme. A strategically placed support densely planted with climbers can also hide an eyesore.

Home-made frames

Supports made from natural plant stems, saplings or twigs are less obtrusive than manufactured alternatives. Willow, hazel, birch or any other supple wood, can be bent and used to create a support as an alternative to more rigid vertical bamboo canes and pea sticks. A circle of canes is easily arranged

▲ *A wooden framework for climbers is a shady sitting area.*

▲ *A climber grows around the front door giving height to this garden.*

(continued from opposite)

The framework for climbing plants can be an ornamental feature in itself.

Twiggy sticks can be pushed well into the ground to support plants. Insert them early on to allow the plants to grow up through them.

the cage is positioned early on in the growing season the plants will happily grow through the support to hide it as it keeps them in shape.

▲ An obelisk makes a pretty focal point.

to form a wigwam with the cane tops tied together. If a string is wound around the poles in a spiral effect, plants are more easily trained and the result can be very decorative. Place the canes in a circle of at least 75 cm/30 in diameter. If extra strength is required for robust climbers add a central stick and use canes of larger diameter. A double line of angled canes, the pairs crossed at the top with a horizontal pole placed in the V forms a straight barrier and support for a row of climbers such as sweet peas or runner beans.

Shorter twiggy stems, pushed well into the soil in a circle or square and intertwined, make a cage shape which is a good support for herbaceous plants. Provided

Supports to buy

A wide range of metal supports is available to suit many plant shapes, heights and arrangements. Most last longer than home-made alternatives. Some are designed to blend into the background as the plants grow. In others, such as obelisks and metal spirals, the frame itself forms an important part of the final effect and looks best if it is not completely obliterated by plant life.

▼ Climbing roses on the verandah posts enhance this timber structure.

Metal supports come in a wide range of sizes and can be linked together to suit individual plants.

A sturdy stake, hammered well into the ground, is needed to support most trees. Use a special tree tie that holds the stem away from the stake, thus avoiding any damage to the stem.

Choice of plant supports
- Walls and fences
- Arches and pergolas
- Wigwams
- Crossed canes
- Herbaceous plant frames
- Metal corkscrews
- Obelisks
- Trellises or wires fixed to fences or walls

QUICK-GROWING COLOURFUL CLIMBERS

Clematis hybrids • Runner beans • Canary creeper • Sweet peas • Nasturtiums • Morning glory • Honeysuckle • Golden hop • Ivy

Arches, pergolas and arbours

Building a rustic arch

These tips on building an arch could also be followed to construct an arbour.

Sketch a design on paper.
To suit your situation and the height and width you require.

When fixing a horizontal section to an upright use this basic joint.

Where two pieces cross, mark the position and cut halving joints in each one, using a saw and chisel.

Use wood glue and a rust-proof nail to hold each joint.

(continued opposite)

Arches, pergolas and arbours add a new dimension to a garden. They also provide a perfect opportunity to grow a wide range of climbing plants.

▲ Tubular metal arches such as this can be bought as ready-made units.

Arches come in a range of shapes which may be round-topped, pointed or square. An arch may be to frame a view or lead the way from the house to the patio, or can highlight the entrance to a path-way or the route beyond a fence or hedge. A row of arches may be lined up along a path.

A pergola is a larger structure made up of a series of joined arches. This may form a single divide between one area of the garden and another but it is commonly made of a double row of uprights held together by roof struts and placed to span a path or form a covering for a patio. A pergola can also be attached along one side to a wall or fence.

Depending on where it is sited, an arbour is a partially enclosed space that may be a garden hide-away, a place in which to sit in private, or a ring-side seat from which the whole garden can be viewed. An arbour or a pergola can be made more rainproof by adding a translucent roofing material to the top.

Construction materials
Arches, pergolas and arbours all form a striking part of a garden's design and look most in keeping if they suit the house and the garden's style. Stained or painted squared-off timber is popular for modern situations, while rustic poles are often used to recreate a country-garden style. These can have the bark removed to help prevent rot and insect infestation or left on to attract small insect-eating birds. Iron or tubular steel with a galvanised, painted or plastic coated finish can also be used. For a longlasting, but more expensive, alternative brick or stone

▼ This timber pergola crowned with roses adds a vertical element.

SCENTED CLIMBERS

Include some of these scented plants amongst those you choose to clothe arches, pergolas and arbours.

Honeysuckle Common honeysuckle, *Lonicera periclymenum*, has white to yellow flowers in mid- to late summer, followed by bright red berries. *L. hildebrandiana* is evergreen or semi-evergreen with fragrant cream-white flowers in summer, also followed by red berries (which are poisonous).

Jasmine Common summer jasmine, *Jasminum officinale* has white flowers in mid- to late summer. *J. beesianum* is evergreen with fragrant pink-red flowers in early and midsummer.

Rambler and climbing roses 'Etoile de Hollande' is a climbing rose with dark crimson, fragrant flowers, 'Sutter's Gold' blooms early with yellow, pink-veined flowers, and 'Compassion' has salmon pink to apricot flowers in summer. 'Felicite et Perpétue' has small, double, pale pink to white flowers.

(continued from opposite)

Bird's mouth joints are useful for connecting horizontal or diagonal pieces to uprights. First mark the position carefully then cut out a V-shape about 2.5 cm/1 in deep in one piece and saw the second piece to fit. Drive a nail diagonally through the joint.

uprights may be built and married up with timber roof struts. Garden seats with a built in arch can be placed against a solid background, forming a simple arbour.

Arches, pergolas and arbours can be made on site or bought in a range of sizes already to be easily erected on site. In most cases you will need to allow for poles which are at least 60 cm/24 in longer than the height required, to provide a fixing into the ground. A span of about 1 m/3–4 ft is about the widest suitable for an arch.

Siting an arbour

An arbour is usually sited in a sunny spot, with the frame and plants providing shade. In a windy situation it is best to site an arbour with its back to a wall, fence or hedge to provide protection. The structure can be positioned parallel with a side or end boundary, run diagonally across a corner, or sited centrally within an open space.

As a seat is the central ingredient of an arbour decide on its size and shape first, then construct around it. The frame material and thickness need to be strong enough to take the span required and also to support vigorous climbers. Draw up a rough sketch of the design you

▲ A white arbour with a built-in seat.

prefer. Include the measurements and take this with you when buying the materials so that you can obtain advice on the thicknesses required. The frame will soon be transformed by clambering plants to make an enclosed space. Scented climbers will make sitting in the arbour a special pleasure.

QUICK COVER-UPS

Your chosen climbers may take some time to get established. While they are growing, sow seeds of annuals such as morning glory, *Ipomoea indica*, which has rich blue flowers; sweet peas, *Lathyrus odoratus*; or the cup-and-saucer plant, *Cobaea scandens*, which has bell-shaped flowers that open creamy green and age to a deep purple, followed by large, decorative seed heads.

Assemble each arch side and the top separately on the ground first. Insert the uprights in already prepared holes, fix temporarily with wooden struts, then drill and screw the top in position. Secure the uprights firmly.

Materials choice
• Sawn timber
• Rustic poles
• Wrought iron
• Tubular steel – galvanized, painted or plastic-coated
• Posts of brick or stone

Containers

Container plant care

Plants grown in containers need a little extra care if they are to flourish and reward you with a constant show of colour. In hot, dry weather water at least once, and if possible twice, a day.

Watering Water retaining granules in the compost can save on watering. A hosepipe makes watering a number of containers relatively quick and easy. For out-of-reach hanging baskets use a lance attachment, compression sprayer or special basket pump. Alternatively, attach a cane to the hose end to lengthen it and keep it rigidly upright.

Feeding To avoid having to feed regularly use a slow-release or controlled-release fertilizer and add it to the compost when you plant the container.

For shrubs and trees sprinkle either of the above fertilizers on the surface in spring, then fork lightly into the compost surface.

(continued opposite)

Plant-filled containers are a must for roof gardens and balconies. They are very versatile, allowing you to clothe a wall in colour or transform an area of the garden.

Containers can lead the eye down a pathway, highlight a paved sitting area, to create a welcoming doorway or line a row of steps. Hanging baskets and window boxes add colour and greenery at a higher level. By grouping different sizes of containers you can create a 'bed' of colour in any area or, conversely, you can use a beautifully shaped container-grown shrub or tree to form a focal point. By under-planting a container-grown tree or shrub you can add a splash of temporary colour when needed.

Plants in smaller pots can be moved about. Tender plants grown in pots can be transferred to a more sheltered spot in colder weather. Pot-grown annuals can be partially immersed in a flower bed when added colour is required, then easily removed and transferred elsewhere.

▲ *A rough-hewn stone trough.*

Choosing containers

Plastic and fibreglass containers are cheap and come in a wide range of shapes and sizes. They are lighter than most of the alternatives and therefore ideal for roof gardens and balconies. Fibreglass, often made to imitate lead, is the stronger and more durable of the two. With careful planting a plastic container can almost disappear behind the contents, or you can use paint to antique or decorate the outside. Check before buying that a plastic container is suitable for use outdoors.

▲ *Terracotta pots come in a range of shapes and sizes.*

▲ *Potted plants can be moved in the winter for frost protection.*

(continued from opposite)

▲ Regular watering and feeding aids growth, which soon hides the container.

▲ Window boxes make a mini garden but must be securely fixed.

Routine care Once a week check containers, dead-head flowers, remove yellowing leaves and those that show signs of pests or disease. Control pests and disease as soon as you find them.

Terracotta pots come in a range of shapes and sizes, from plain clay pots to those with ornate raised patterns, as well as urns with handles and those with side pockets for planting. Earth or compost in terracotta dries out quickly in hot weather so check plants regularly. Ensure the terracotta is frost-proof as it can flake or crack in freezing weather. In winter do not use water-retaining saucers as the water may freeze and crack the pot.

Wooden tubs, half-barrels, and troughs can look rustic or classic depending on the shape and finish. Timber will rot but if treated with paint or a plant-friendly preservative its life can be extended. Lining a wooden container with plastic will also lengthen its life.

Large baskets have become popular because they make unusual and reasonably priced containers. Prolong a basket's short life by oiling it well before planting. Cover the bottom of the basket with cut-down plastic plant-pot bases to keep the soil off the basketware and line it with plastic in which drainage holes have been made.

Glazed pots in bright colours are easily available. Not all are frost-

proof, so check when buying. Choose a colour to complement the intended contents.

Concrete is a cheaper alternative to reconstituted stone. To age a new exterior spread it with yoghurt to encourage algae to grow.

Window boxes come in all the materials mentioned above and look most effective when plants cascade over the sides and conceal the container. Boxes filled with compost are very heavy and need to be securely fixed in position.

Recycled containers Many holders can be transformed into plant containers. They need to be deep enough and should have a base that can take drainage holes. Suitable plant containers are chimney pots, clay land drains, buckets, paint pots with all paint removed, and wheelbarrows.

Hanging baskets and wall troughs may be made of plastic-coated or plain wire, of iron, basketwork or solid plastic. Liners are available in many types of materials. Baskets look best when young plants are inserted in the sides as well as the top so that the plants grow to form a flowering ball.

Container choices
- Plastic
- Fibreglass
- Timber
- Concrete
- Reconstituted stone
- Terracotta
- Glazed pots
- Baskets
- Buckets
- Chimney pots and clay drains

See also:
- Ornamental extras, pages 136–7

▼ A wooden half-barrel can make an ideal container for a small conifer and colourful pansies.

Ornamental extras

Tips on disguising an eyesore

- A carefully positioned upright tree can obscure a power pole. Have someone help you position the tree until the best planting position is found.

- Climbers grown up trellis will soon hide a fixture such as a garden shed, dustbin area or coal bunker.

- Grow climbing roses up a chicken-wire framework to hide a fixture such as the thorns deter burglars and other intruders.

- Stand a low pot containing trailing annuals on a man hole cover to hide it, or buy a specially designed bowl-shaped cover which can be planted but still removed if necessary.

- Use a pergola to hide an ugly overhead view, with a fastgrowing climber forming a roof.

Ornamental choices
- Classic figures
- Birdbaths
- Wildlife and pet sculpture
- Water features
- Beach bounty
- Rocks and pebbles
- Logs and tree stumps

▲ *Stone mushrooms– a fun feature on the lawn.*

A well-positioned ornament or decorative feature will add the final touch to your garden. This kind of feature gives a small garden its final flourish, and can provide extra interest, an element of surprise or even amusement. It may be a

▲ *A classical urn for timeless elegance.*

traditional stone figure, a decorative urn or a modern sculpture or something entirely natural, such as a group of giant stones, a heap of logs or sea-washed driftwood and shells. It may add a touch of humour – plastic decoy ducks on a pond, a concrete cat sitting amongst the catmint or life-sized metal birds pecking at the lawn.

Choosing the right site
Positioning is all-important. Drawing the eye, a focal feature can be placed where it is instantly seen centre stage in the garden or can be placed where it is instantly seen centre stage in the garden. Hidden around a corner, a light-

coloured ornament set on a plinth amongst shrubs provides a surprise and brings life to a dull spot. At the end of a path, forming the view that draws you on, a figure can be set beneath an arch.

An ornament also needs to work with its surroundings. Bear in mind both plants and surface materials used in the spot where you want to place it. Be flexible about the position, moving the object around until you are sure that you have found the best place for it. Groups of pots, natural materials, figures or gnomes will create an interesting focus. Take time to arrange the positions until you are happy with the overall result.

Range of choices
Make sure that the container is suitable for all weather conditions.

Pots and urns Glazed pots are available in rich tones, ideal for providing colour and texture to an overshadowed part of the garden. Classic terracotta urns with handles, or narrow-necked tall, slim jars also make perfect focal points on their own or grouped, perhaps with one lying on its side.

Classic figures in traditional designs are produced in reconstituted stone or concrete, or in fibreglass with a finish that looks like lead.

Animals and birds specially made for outdoor displays come in concrete, metal and plastic. Arrange water birds around or in a pond, animals under a tree or amongst low plants in a bed.

▲ A metal resin lizard wall fountain.

▲ An armillary sphere that is also a sun-dial.

▲ A garden elf water feature adds winsome humour in a green pond-side corner. Water features like this and the one shown top left are relatively simple to install.

Birdbaths, birdtables and sundials combine usefulness and decoration.

Water features A small moving-water feature immediately forms a focal point. Many preformed designs are available or you can construct your own. The only requirements are a drainage hole in the base and matching hole in the top section so that the water can be circulated, and a position for the pump. Use an urn on its side to drip or pour water into a shallow saucer as part of a small water feature.

Garden gnomes Colourful, cheerful and eye-catching, gnomes make a strong and humorous focus wherever they are positioned, alone or in a group.

Natural materials Some of the most effective garden ornaments are designed by nature and available free to be picked up on the beach or in the woods. Smooth, colourful pebbles, big pieces of stone, a group of scallop or spiral shells and driftwood can be used to enhance a water feature. Tree stumps, cones and logs add interest to a woodland area.

▲ These 'stone' birds are made of fibreglass.

▲ This inventive yet realistic bird is made from recycled pieces of metal welded together.

▲ This wooden bird house provides a striking feature whilst taking up little space.

Children's play space

Fine weather draws children, like a magnet, outdoors to enjoy the freedom of space. If you provide a range of exciting play choices to stimulate the imagination they will be happily occupied for hours. In a small garden there is rarely room for a completely separate area for children's play projects. If you don't

bird tables and nesting boxes, as well as feeding the birds. This provides a useful introduction to looking after pets responsibly. Involve the child when choosing an area of the garden specially put aside for him where he can grow his own plants from seed. Quick-result plants such as sunflowers and sweet peas are a

▲ This all-in-one play structure would keep any child happy for hours.

want play structures to overpower a small garden consider position and materials at the design stage, along with the needs of all of the family, so that sandpits, swings, climbing frames or playhouses can be built to blend in, using materials that appear elsewhere in the garden.

Lawns need to be tough if they are to endure energetic play so use a high percentage of perennial rye-grass, which can survive the rigours of pounding feet.

The garden provides a wonderful first insight for small children into the world of nature. Take time to explain how wildlife and plants of the garden live and grow. Involve children in the siting and fixing of

good choice, as are beans, carrots, lettuces and spinach which can be picked, cooked and eaten.

Structures that adapt
Flexibility is important as children's requirements change quickly and play structures soon fall out of use. With some forethought equipment can be erected with the future in mind, so that a play space can take up a new role when the children lose interest in using it.

Swing A well-constructed archway can form a sturdy frame for a swing. Provide a surface of grass or bark chippings for safety. When the swing is no longer in use the arch can form a frame for climbers and soon become a decorative feature.

Sandpit Dig out an area large enough to take sand construction projects of buildings, boats, or whatever catches the imagination. A sturdy surround will help to keep the sand in place, but avoid sharp-edged materials and use sawn logs with the bark removed. If you form the sandpit in an interesting shape the framework can be used to edge a flower bed or pond when the sand is removed.

Climbing frame If you need to fell a tree at any time this could easily become part of an exciting natural frame. Add platform, steps and swings to create extra stimulus. A mature tree in the garden begs to become a climbing frame and will undoubtedly be used, so it pays to add rope ladders and platforms that make it a safer spot to play.

Alternatively construct a climbing frame as part of a pergola or build it with a future use as a pergola in mind. A thick layer of bark chippings, extending well beyond the frame, provides the safest ground surface.

Playhouses Playhouses provide hours of fun and form the inspiration for all sorts of fantasy situations. Adapt a small garden shed by painting it and adding special decorative features inside. Use only unbreakable glass, plastic or PVC for the windows. The house can go on to become a teenagers' retreat or revert to storage space. If you lack the space for a permanent playhouse make an instant one by using a wigwam frame as a base. When required simply cover the frame with blankets or a specially decorated old sheet. Later grow runner beans or peas up it or introduce scent with honeysuckle or roses.

▲ When making a play area for your children, line the ground with a thick layer of bark chippings to soften their inevitable falls. This material also makes the area look more in keeping with a gardener's garden and will help to improve the soil.

Including water

As a small child can quickly drown in water as shallow as 4 cm/1.5 in, it is not wise to include a pond at an early stage in a youngster's life. If you move to a house with a pond, drain it and use it for a sandpit instead. Water does not have to be completely excluded from the garden – instead add a wall fountain or a small running-water feature such as water flowing from an upturned pot into a shallow pebble-filled saucer.

See also:
- Ground surfaces, page 116
- Plant frameworks, page 130
- Arches, pergolas and arbours, page 134

◀ A little raised play house, with its own ladder access, makes a perfect secret hideaway.

Garden Furniture

The ultimate in poolside luxury: loungers with drinks tables attached that can be wheeled back into store.

Caring for garden furniture

Timber needs checking out once a year. Sand down and stain or paint when signs of weathering appear. Some timber needs oiling.

Metal needs regular attention if it is not protected by a plastic coating. As soon as any rust appears, sand to remove, and repaint to seal the surface.

Plastic only needs wiping down with a damp, soapy cloth.

Stone and concrete need a periodic wash down with soapy water and a soft brush. Rinse well to remove all soap traces.

Materials choices
- Timber
- Reconstituted stone or concrete
- Cane and wicker
- Metal
- Plastic
- Canvas
- Metal or plastic frame with padded cover

Well-chosen and well-sited garden furniture extends living into the garden in the most comfortable and relaxing way possible. Garden furniture either needs to be tough enough to stay outdoors all year or be fold-up or stackable so that it is easily stored away when not in use. There are two main types of garden furniture – that used for eating outdoors or that which is for periods when you simply want to lounge in the sun or the shade.

Furniture used for eating outside will usually double up as a temporary resting spot, but garden benches spaced around the garden allow the opportunity of moving from sun to shade at any time. Place a single bench to create a visually attractive element as part of the garden design and where it provides a new and different view of the garden from that of the main sitting area. This type of furniture needs to be robust enough to remain permanently in place.

The most popular chairs for sunbathing, or relaxing in the shade,

Teak furniture suits most areas.

usually have a light, fold-up plastic or plastic-coated metal frame that can be placed at several angles on a ratchet system, and a long, padded, slip over cushion. These chairs can be moved about with ease so that anyone can follow the sun or shade as required.

This well-designed and sturdily built garden furniture comes ready-painted.

Material choices

Furniture can either be chosen to blend with its surroundings or to make a colourful statement. In most cases permanent furniture looks best if it blends with other materials used in the garden, for example natural timber for a brick patio, or a wooden bench to stand below a tree at the end of the garden. For painted furniture, choose colours to blend with those used in nearby rooms of the house or mimic the colours of nearby garden flowers. White furniture works well where white or bright colours are used and green blends attractively into a leafy background.

Timber furniture may be natural in colour, and in tough hardwood such as oak, teak or less robust stained softwood, or it may be painted. Unless wooden furniture

Moulded plastic may not have a long life but it is cheap and light.

is fold-up, it is designed to stay in place around the year. However, wood takes a beating from the wet winters and hot, dry weather in summer, so needs to be regularly maintained with oiling or painting if it is to last when kept outside.

Stone or concrete seats are tough and easy to maintain, requiring no more than a periodic scrub. Curved designs are available, that can be placed around the trunk of a tree.

Cane and wicker, like timber, blend beautifully with the natural surroundings of a garden but they cannot be left outdoors as sun and rain will damage them. Their light weight makes them easy to transport but storage can be a problem. If the patio leads off a conservatory then the furniture can double up for indoor and outdoor use.

Metal furniture may be traditional wrought iron, which is heavy and needs constant maintenance if it is not to rust, or a lighter aluminium copy. Plastic-coated metal is easier to maintain, only needing to be wiped, although a cheaper surface coating can deteriorate.

Moulded plastic furniture, usually in white or green, is now very popular as it is easy to look after, light weight, and weather resistant. Most table tops and legs come apart for storage and chairs stack

to take up a minimum of space over winter. Plastic furniture can be left outdoors throughout the summer. Buy good quality furniture if you want it to last. Cheaper alternatives can crack and discolour on exposure to sunlight.

Canvas-covered director chairs or deck chairs are light to move and fold flat for storage. Director chairs are smart enough to use indoors when required. Canvas rots in time but is easy to replace.

Padded fabric loungers with metal or plastic frames can be used in a lounging or upright position, are light weight and fold up for storage.

Home-made seating adds an individual look to your garden. Concrete paving slabs can be built onto the top of a low wall, a plank screwed to a couple of tree stumps could make a temporary stopover spot in a wild garden or, for something very different, use a special metal chair frame shape and plant it with box to make a topiary seat.

▲ *A marble-topped metal bistro table and co-ordinating folding chair. This type of furniture is decorative and useful for summer drinks, and the table can be left out all year.*

▼ *This wooden lounger seat comes with a well-padded mattress, and with built-in wheels is easy to move around.*

Barbecues

In good weather the garden provides a relaxed place to eat, daytime or evening, and whether it is a family mealtime or you are entertaining friends. If you regularly eat in the garden it is well worth building in a barbecue area as an integral part of the patio design. The best place to site a barbecue is a sheltered spot, well away from trees and large shrubs, and close to the kitchen so that it is easy to transport any food and equipment to and fro.

Choosing a barbecue

Choice of barbecue depends on how often you will use it, how easily and quickly you want results, how many you will cook for, and whether you have easily accessible storage for the barbecue when it is not in use. For those who prefer heat at the turn of a switch there are wheel-around gas barbecues, or if you are only one or two, and like to take the barbecue with you on day trips a small portable barbecue may be more appropriate.

Built-in designs A barbecue that is incorporated in the patio design and uses the same materials is much the least obtrusive, can stay in position around the year and can be made to measure your needs exactly. Barbecue boxes that come in a range of sizes are widely available and these can be slotted into a brick- or stone-built frame allowing you to build the barbecue to your own specification. If you include weatherproof storage space for fuel to one side and a good-sized work-top area for utensils, plates and food, the barbecue will be ready for use whenever you want it.

Wheel-around gas barbecues If you have the space close by to store a barbecue run on bottled gas this is by far the quickest and simplest to use. Heat arrives almost instantly at the turn of a switch and the lava rocks used give food a similar taste to that of a charcoal barbecue. Another feature is that the heat is easy to control, with several types of adjustable flame.

Brick-built patio barbecues are available commercially (as shown here), but if you are good at DIY you can design and build your own custom-made version.

Gas barbecues come in a range of sizes, with a lid that keeps heat in and will also keep the food warm. Many of the designs provide work-tops at either side and storage space below. Weatherproof covers allow you to keep the barbecue outdoors during the summer months, so that it only needs to be stored away during the winter. Gas-powered barbecue woks and griddles are also available, and wheel-around charcoal-burning barbecues are another option.

▲ Gas barbecues, with wheels, and lids that close down over the cooking area, are available in a range of sizes and styles.

▲ A simple portable barbecue is ideal for campers and picnic lovers, and can still be used in the garden.

◀ Portable gas-fired woks and griddles are an alternative to barbecues for outdoor eating.

Portable barbecues These are easy to store and transport if you like taking the barbecue with you on day trips. There is a huge range of sizes and designs available from small, briefcase slim styles to bigger and more robust shapes. If you want to use the barbecue regularly at home it is a good idea to build a platform to bring smaller and flatter portable barbecues up to a working height to avoid bending.

Lighting

Points to bear in mind

- Consider the neighbours when siting garden lighting. Avoid positioning lights that shine directly towards them. Position lights to point downwards.

- Use only lighting fitments designed specifically for outdoor use and use a professional electrician to fit stronger permanent lighting.

- Lights that play on moving water are very effective. Follow any installation instructions very carefully and conceal ground-level fitments among tall water side plants.

- Show off stylishly shaped plants or striking garden features with hidden spotlights.

- Use diffused, softer lights to highlight a specific area of the garden.

- Give a party feel to a special evening event with strings of hired coloured lights, garden flares and protected candles.

Materials choice
- Fixed buried lighting
- Low-voltage lights from a transformer
- Solar-powered lights
- Gas lights
- Lanterns
- Pond lights
- Garden flares
- Garden party lights

See also:
- Electricity in the garden, page 112

Garden lighting greatly increases the enjoyment of the garden. In winter you can view the plants or decorative features in the frost or snow. On a summer night you can eat outdoors or just sit and admire the surroundings. Lights can show off plants, a pond or statue or simply create a romantic ambience. Most important are those lights which allow safe passage through the garden or provide working light for barbecue chefs, and security lights to illuminate unwelcome visitors.

Highlighting plants or special features In a small garden it is usually most effective to pick out only two, or three, features to spotlight. Whether you choose a tree, shrub or special architectural feature, highlighting shape rather than colour usually provides the most effective result. This lighting needs to be professionally installed as there are strict rules governing outdoor cables, which need to be buried, plus the waterproof connectors and fittings that are needed.

Angle the lights to shine away from the viewing position and avoid allowing the source itself to show. The fitting can be concealed

Garden flares are attractive.

behind a low shrub, wall or other fixture or use stones or logs. Before deciding on the final position for a light source move the fitting around, trying different heights for the best effect.

▲ *Outdoor dining area by candle-light.*

For a softer light use low-wattage lights which run off a transformer that brings down the power to a safe level. A lighting set of this type usually includes the transformer and cable (which can be run above the ground), connectors that clip into the cable at any point you choose, and the light fittings, which push into the ground on spikes. This makes it comparatively easy to move the lights about, allowing you to highlight different areas when plants look their best.

Solar-powered lights that draw off energy from the sun in the daytime to give off a soft, diffused light at night conserve energy, cost nothing to run and need no wiring. Gas lighting also provides an attractive, gentle glow.

◁ This garden displays almost every possible form of garden lighting, including underwater pool lights. Lights near the pool not only highlight the planting but make it possible to use the pool at night.

▲ This flat-backed zinc wall lantern can be wired in to a power source.

▼ These post lanterns have reflectors to keep the light focused on the patio and away from the neighbours.

Walking around with safety
Eating and cooking areas need good lighting for safety reasons as well as decorative effect. If the patio is close to the house, undrawn curtains may provide enough light. Alternatively fix lights to the exterior house walls. These are easy to fit as they can be connected to the internal mains power supply. Illuminating house names and numbers is an aid to newcomers to your home, and lighting beside the front door allows identification of callers before you open the door. Paths and routes around the garden also need to be well-lit. Arrange fittings to point out any hazards such as steps or water features.

An aid to security Lights that sense body heat, switching on when they are approached, are an excellent security measure but can double up as safety lighting. The alternative is to use timed lighting which comes on and goes off at a prearranged time every evening.

Temporary party lights Coloured garden party lights can be bought or hired to string around the patio.

If you use oil-filled lamps or candles position them where they cannot be knocked over. Special garden candles and flares add atmosphere, and insect-repellent candles keep the bugs away. Candles need to be placed in open-topped containers, such as jam jars, to keep any breeze from fanning the flame and blowing them out. Safety is important: remember to keep a bucket of water close at hand. In dry weather plants can soon catch fire.

CHAPTER 7

KEY PLANTS

The background plants form the basis for the garden's living framework and create round-the-year interest and form. These are the plants to consider first when designing a garden, as they will look decorative whatever time of the year it is.

Shrubs and trees are the backbone of any garden planting and even the smallest garden can accommodate some of each. Their bold outlines, textures or leaf-shapes bring architectural plants to the fore wherever they are grown. Those plants with variegated leaves of green and silver, white or gold are a wonderful source of colour all year round, especially when flowers are in short supply; while distinctively shaped climbers bring the eye up to a new level, as well as providing privacy, breaking up wind flow and hiding an eyesore.

This chapter provides a taster of the huge and exciting range of these key plants.

Shrubs 148–149
Deciduous trees 150–151
Evergreen trees 152–153
Architectural plants 154–155
Grey and silver foliage plants 156–157
Gold and bright green foliage plants 158–159
Vigorous background climbers 160–161

SHRUBS

Shrubs provide the vital backcloth to the garden's planting. Foliage comes in many tints and there is a huge range of leaf shapes. Some shrubs have variegated leaves, others provide stunning colour, while some keep their leaves throughout the year. Their flowers some wonderfully scented, come in every shape and colour, and many produce decorative fruit. And the huge range of shrubs available means that there will always be some in flower whatever the time of year.

Moving an established shrub

If you decide a shrub has been planted in the wrong position it should be possible to move it to another part of the garden. However, before you start removing the shrub make sure that you have dug a hole large enough to take it and have prepared the soil by digging in well-rotted manure or compost.

Dig out a trench all around the shrub, having first tied up the branches to make it easier. Use a fork and gently loosen the soil around the deeper roots.

To reduce the size of the ball of soil, if it is too large to remove, use the fork carefully so as not to damage the roots – and remove more soil.

(continued opposite)

Arbutus unedo, Strawberry tree
Height and spread up to 8 m/ 26 ft • A. unedo 'Elfin King', is smaller, with height up to 2 m/ 6 ft, spread 1.5 m/5 ft • Full sun • Fertile, well-drained soil; suitable for alkaline soils

Really a tree, but shrubby in growth, the strawberry tree provides lots of winter interest with white flowers in winter to early spring, strawberry-like autumn fruit and a rough, shredding red-brown bark.

Camellia, Camellias
Height and spread up to 4.5 m/ 15 ft, depending on the variety • Good specimen plants • Suitable for containers Partial shade; plant away from early morning sun • Moist, well-drained, acid soil

Camellias, with deep green, glossy, round-the-year leaves, thrive in acid soil, although many will tolerate neutral soil. They provide wonderful winter or early spring colour.

Cornus stolonifera, Dogwood
Height up to 2m/6ft, spread 4m/12ft • Full sun – partial shade • Fertile, well-drained, neutral to acid soil; also tolerates wet soil

A deciduous shrub grown for its decorative, dark red young winter stems. Some dogwoods have bright yellow, orange or green stems. The small, white, late spring flowers are followed by white, often blue-tinged fruit. Variegated forms are available.

▲ Camellia japonica.

Cotinus coggygria, Smoke bush
Height and spread up to 5 m/ 16 ft • Full sun – partial shade • Moderately fertile, moist soil

The fluffy festoons of purple flowers in mid-summer and autumn almost hide the small green leaves to give this decorative shrub its common name. Leaves turn yellow, orange and red in autumn.

Height and spread 60 cm/24 in to 3 m/10 ft, depending on variety • Full sun • Moderately fertile, moist soil

In mid-summer, the pretty pink or white, small, star-shaped flowers, cover this deciduous bush.

Escallonia, Escallonia
Height and spread 2.5 m/8 ft • Full sun, with shelter from wind • Fertile, well-drained soil

A frost-hardy, evergreen shrub, especially good in coastal areas. E. 'Apple Blossom' has early and mid-summer flowers in mixed tints.

Euonymus alatus, Winged spindle
Height 2 m/6 ft, spread 3 m/ 10 ft E. alatus 'Compactus' is smaller, with height and spread 1 m/3 ft • Full sun – partial shade • Well-drained soil

This is a dense, bushy, deciduous shrub with dark green leaves that turn a brilliant scarlet in autumn.

▼ The Dogwood, Cornus alba 'Red Stems'.

△ Catkins of Garrya elliptica.

Garrya elliptica, Silk tassel bush

Height up to 4 m/12 ft, spread 24 m/6–12 ft • Full sun to partial shade, with shelter from wind and frost • Moderately fertile, well-drained soil

An upright, evergreen shrub grown for its long, slim, silvery green catkins that, in the male form, can be up to 20 cm/8 in in length and cover the plant in late winter to look like silver rain. Prune in spring to keep down in size.

Hamamelis x intermedia, Witch hazel

Height and spread up to 4 m/ 12 ft • Sun–partial shade • Moist, well-drained, acid to neutral soil

Witch hazel is grown for the fragrant yellow or dark red winter flowers. Hamamelis x intermedia 'Pallida' has clusters of large yellow flowers. (See also H. x intermedia 'Diane', page 169.)

Mahonia x media, Mahonia

Height up to 5 m/15 ft, spread 4 m/12 ft • Shade • Moderately fertile, well-drained soil

An ornate shrub throughout the year, with sharply toothed, long, dark, evergreen leaves, and long streamers of bright to lemon-yellow, highly fragrant flowers from late autumn to late winter. This makes a good specimen plant.

Philadelphus, Mock orange

Height and spread 1.5 m/5 ft • Full sun – partial shade • Moderately fertile, well-drained soil

The white flowers that appear in mid-summer have a scent similar to orange blossom. Philadelphus x lemoinei has arching branches and fragrant, pure white flowers. Makes a good specimen plant.

Potentilla fruticosa, Potentilla

Height up to 1.5 m/5 ft, spread 1 m/3 ft • Full sun – partial shade, depending on type • Poor, well-drained soil

This compact, bushy, deciduous shrub likes bright sun and produces flowers over a long period from late spring to mid-autumn. Colours vary from white, yellow and pale pink to deep red.

Pyracantha, Firethorn/ Pyracantha

Height up to 3 m/10 ft, spread up to 2.5 m/8 ft • Full sun – partial shade • Fertile soil

A spiny, evergreen shrub pyracantha is usually chosen for its colourful yellow, orange or red autumn berries.

Rhododendron, Rhododendrons

Height up to 3 m/10 ft, spread 4 m/12 ft or more • Mostly shade, where colour is highlighted • Most require moist, well-drained, acid soil

△ Rhododendron 'Cynthia'.

A huge range of species and cultivars provides us with the showy flowers of rhododendron from autumn through winter and, most commonly, in spring, in an enormous range of sizes and shapes. Flower colours can be: white, pink, apricot, red, yellow, purple, lilac; and sizes range from dwarf alpines and small shrubs to large trees. Some shrubs have attractively coloured young growth.

Viburnum plicatum ' Mariesii' Japanese snowball tree

Height up to 3 m/10 ft, spread 4 m/12 ft • Full sun – partial shade • Moderately fertile soil

This deciduous shrub has a spreading, layered shape with white flowers held in swathes above the green leaves in late spring. Leaves turn red In the autumn. Good specimen shrub.

▽ Viburnum plicatum 'Mariesii'.

(continued from opposite)

Use a sharp spade to cut beneath the plant, once the root ball is of a manageable size. Work around the plant from each side.

Have ready a piece of hessian or tough plastic for carrying the shrub. Roll this up, tilt the plant and slip it underneath, then rock the root ball back over it and unroll the hessian around it.

Lift the shrub with assistance, move it to the new planting hole and gently lower it into position. Check that the soil height on shrub and surrounding earth is the same, and remove the wrapping. Fill in the hole, firm the soil, and water thoroughly. In dry weather water well for several months.

DECIDUOUS TREES

Planting a tree

To provide a new tree with the best start in life plant it with care, and in the right position.

First remove the soil to a depth of 30 cm/12 in. Fork over the rest well, working in plenty of garden compost or well-rotted manure.

Insert a stake, placing it on the side of the prevailing wind, leaving plenty of space for the root ball. Hammer it in well.

(continued opposite)

There is room for one or two carefully chosen trees in the smallest garden. Some can be kept small by growing them in a pot. They provide a focus, can hide unattractive structures and create interest at a higher level. A tree may be chosen for its decorative leaf shape or colour, for its flowers or the fruit that follows, or for the colour or texture of its bark – and sometimes you can find all these features in one tree. Dimensions are for maximum growth, often reached only after many years.

Acer griseum,
Paper-bark maple
Height and spread up to 9 m/
30 ft • Full sun – partial shade
• Fertile, well-drained soil
This slow-growing tree has a spreading canopy of dark green, hand-shaped leaves that turn a wonderful orange then crimson in the autumn. Yellow flowers hang from the branch ends in summer. In winter it has beautiful orange-brown peeling bark.

Amelanchier lamarckii,
Shadbush
Height up to 9 m/30 ft, spread up to 12 m/40 ft • Full sun – partial shade • Acid, fertile, moist, well-drained soil
Small tree or shrub which has white hair-covered young shoots and leaves. The new bronze leaves turn green, then orange and red in autumn. Small white flowers, up to 12 cm /5 in long, appear in spring, followed by black fruit.

Betula pendula,
Silver birch
Height up to 25 m/80 ft, spread up to 10 m/33 ft • Full sun – partial shade • Moderately fertile, moist, well-drained soil
Graceful garden tree, well known for its eye-catching silvery bark. Male catkins up to 6 cm/2.5 in long appear in spring and leaves turn from green to yellow in autumn.

Cercis canadensis,
Eastern redbud
Height and spread up to 10 m/33 ft • Full sun – partial shade • Deep, fertile, moist, well-drained soil

Often multi-stemmed, *Cercis canadensis* 'Forest Pansy' has crimson to pink flowers which appear in clusters before the leaves. The heart-shaped leaves are a deep red-purple when new, turning to orange in autumn before falling. In frost-prone areas they will require protection in winter when young.

Cornus mas,
Cornelian cherry
Height and spread 5 m/15 ft
• Full sun – partial shade
• Fertile, well-drained, neutral to acid soil
The dark green leaves of this small, spreading tree turn a wonderful red-purple in autumn. Balls of yellow flowers appear in late winter, followed by the leaves, and bright red fruit are usually produced in late summer.

Betula pendula, Silver birch.

Acer palmatum 'Autumn colours'.

Crataegus monogyna,
Common hawthorn
Height up to 9 m/30 ft, spread up to 8 m/26 ft • Full sun – partial shade • Any soil, except very wet
Thorny tree with small, dark green, glossy leaves and fragrant white flowers with pink central anthers in late spring. Glossy red fruit (haws) appear in autumn. Suitable for a hedge (kept trimmed) or specimen tree, and suitable for towns and coastal areas.

Crataegus monogyna, with haws.

Crataegus laevigata 'Paul's Scarlet', May

Height and spread 8 m/26 ft
• Full sun – partial shade
• Any soil, except very wet

Similar to Crataegus monogyna, above, C. laevigata 'Paul's Scarlet' has abundant clusters of double, deep pink flowers in late spring. Like C. monogyna, it is suitable for towns and coastal areas.

Fagus sylvatica 'Dawyck Good', Dawyck beech

Height 18 m/60 ft, spread 7 m/22 ft • Partial shade
• Almost any well-drained soil, including chalk

This column-shaped but compact beech has bright yellow young foliage, later turning green and finally orange-brown in autumn.

Malus 'Royalty', Crab apple

Height and spread 8 m/26 ft
• Full sun – partial shade
• Fertile, moist, well-drained soil

A small, spreading tree with richly coloured, dark red-purple leaves that mostly remain this colour to turn red in autumn. Almost matching, crimson-purple flowers appear in mid- to late spring, followed by small, brightly coloured dark red fruit in autumn.

Prunus padus, Bird cherry

Height 15 m/50 ft, spread 10 m/33 ft • Full sun •Moderately fertile, moist, well-drained soil

A spreading tree that is more conical in shape when young and produces fragrant white flowers in pendulous streamers in spring, followed by small, glossy black fruit.

Prunus serrula, Cherry

Height and spread 10 m/33 ft
• Full sun • Moderately fertile, moist, well-drained soil

This is a rounded tree with richly coloured, peeling, glossy chestnut-brown bark. As the leaves emerge in spring, white, single flowers appear in small clusters, to be followed by edible, but unpalatable cherries.

Robinia pseudoacacia 'Frisia', Black locust / False acacia

Height 15 m/50 ft, spread 8 m/25 ft • Full sun; needs shelter from strong winds
• Tolerates poor, dry soil but prefers moderately fertile, moist, well-drained soil

A fast-growing tree that is roughly columnar and has golden yellow foliage, which turns a more yellow-green in summer and orange-yellow in autumn.

Satin matsudana 'Tortuosa', Twisted willow

Height 9–25 m/30–80 ft, spread 25 m/80 ft • Full sun • Deep, moist, well-drained soil; not suitable for shallow chalk

A fast-growing upright tree with twisted, contorted stems that are most obvious in winter.

Malus x soulardii ' Red Tip'

when the leaves are off the tree. Bright green leaves and spring catkins are a yellow-green.

Sorbus aria, Whitebeam

Height up to 15m/10ft, spread 7m/22ft • Full sun – partial shade • Moist, well-drained neutral to slightly alkaline soil

With young leaves of a silvery grey in a rounded, cloudy shape, this is a very pretty tree. Older leaves are a dark green with white hairy undersides that show up in a breeze. White flowers appear in late spring, followed by red berries.

Syringa, Lilac

Height and spread up to 4 m/12 ft • Full sun • Fertile, well-drained, neutral to alkaline soil

Lilac has spikes of fragrant white, pink, magenta-red or blue-grey flowers in spring. Syringa vulgaris 'Mme Florent Stepman' has white flowers, 'Paul Thirion' has magenta-red flowers, and 'Charles Joly' has deep purple-blue flowers.

Syringa palibiniana

(continued from opposite)

Tease out some of the thick roots that have run around inside the edge of the pot if planting a container-grown tree.

Place the tree in the hole and put a cane across the hole to check that the soil mark on the tree matches the soil height. Fill the hole with soil, water in, and tread in firmly to ensure that there are no air pockets around the roots.

Water thoroughly and apply a 5 cm/2 in depth of mulch to help conserve moisture. Water in dry weather for some months until the tree is well established.

EVERGREEN TREES

A round-the-year outline to the garden is provided by those trees and hedges that keep their leaves. They can provide a valuable screen as well as a constant form. Those that clip well for example box, holly and privet, make neat, sculptured hedges and can be shaped to form decorative and fun topiary shapes. Evergreens come in a wide range of shapes and colours with many different leaf forms, textures and colours.

Planting a tree in a tub or container

Trees grown in tubs can be used to add interest to a patio and are much less trouble than annuals. This is the only method of successfully growing larger plants on a roof garden or balcony.

Choose a container larger than the pot the tree comes in and at least 30 cm/12 in in diameter. If using a ceramic pot check that it is frostproof. Insert a drainage layer at the bottom before adding a layer of compost. Where weight is not a priority use heavy, loam-based compost for stability.

Remove the tree from its pot and tease out some of the larger roots. Stand it on the new compost and trickle more compost around the sides and up to the original height of the soil on the trunk.

(continued opposite)

Buxus sempervirens, Box
Height up to 5 m/15 ft spread 5–6 m/15–20 ft • Partial shade • Fertile, well-drained soil

This small, bushy tree has glossy, dark green leaves and is ideal for clipping to form a hedge or for topiary, particularly in the forms *Buxus sempervirens* 'Handsworthensis' or *B. sempervirens* 'Suffruticosa'. Variegated varieties are *B. sempervirens* 'Marginata', with a golden edge to the leaves, and *B. sempervirens* 'Elegantissima', which has white leaf margins. Select dwarf box for edging.

Cryptomeria japonica, Japanese cedar
Height up to 25 m/80 ft, spread 6 m/20 ft • Full sun – partial shade • Fertile, moist, well-drained soil but tolerates most well-drained soils, including chalk

A cedar that grows as a tall, cone-shaped column with glossy green leaves that take on a warm russet tint in autumn. The bright orange-brown bark shreds attractively and the female flowers produce small brown cones.

Eucalyptus gunnii, Cider gum
Height 9–25 m/30–80 ft, spread 6–15 m/20–50 ft • Full sun • Fertile, neutral to slightly acid soil

Rounded leaves are silvery grey-green when young, turning lance-shaped and blue-green later. They have an aromatic smell when crushed. *Eucalyptus gunnii* can grow large, so cut it back regularly to encourage

Box tree clipped to spiral shape.

young leaves and maintain a bushy, compact shape in a small garden. Cream flowers appear in summer. The grey bark peels away to reveal yellow-grey new bark below, sometimes flushed with pink.

Ilex aquifolium 'J.C. van Tol', Holly
Height up to 6 m/20 ft, spread 4 m/12 ft • Full sun – partial shade • Moderately fertile, moist, well-drained soil

Hollies are slow-growing, neat and compact. This columnar female holly with shiny, plain green, rounded leaves, is self-fertile, so if only one tree is grown it is still able to produce a mass of bright red berries. 'Golden van Tol' has golden edges to the spineless leaves.

Juniperus scopulorum 'Skyrocket', Rocky mountain juniper
Height up to 6 m/20 ft, spread 50–60 cm/20–24 in • Full sun – lightly dappled shade • Well-drained, sandy, chalky or dry soil

This juniper, as its name suggests, forms a tall, slender spire and provides a strong, sculptural shape that fits neatly into a small garden. It can be used to provide a good contrast with lower-growing plants. Its leaves are grey-green.

Laurus nobilis, Bay
Height up to 12 m/40 ft, spread 9 m/30 ft • Full sun – partial shade • Fertile, moist, well-drained soil

The aromatic, glossy, dark green leaves of bay are commonly used in cooking. Bay can also be clipped into topiary shapes. In spring small balls of tiny creamy yellow flowers appear. Clip well. The plant is suitable for a container.

Cryptomeria japonica.

Laurus nobilis, Bay, in flower.

Ligustrum lucidum 'Excelsum Superbum', Chinese privet

Height and spread up to 9 m/ 30 ft • Full sun – partial shade • Any well-drained soil

A cone-shaped privet with yellow-edged, glossy green leaves, and white flowers in late summer and early autumn. It is suitable as a specimen tree or for hedging.

Ligustrum ovalifolium 'Aureum', Golden privet

Height and spread up to 2 m/ 6 ft • Full sun to partial shade • Any well-drained soil

This bushy privet is grown for its sunny, golden variegated foliage and is suitable as a specimen tree or to grow as hedging.

Magnolia grandiflora, Bull bay

Height up 6–18 m/20–60 ft, spread 15 m/50 ft • Full sun – partial shade; needs shelter from strong winds • Fertile, moist, well-drained, preferably acid to neutral soil

A dense, conical evergreen with decorative, dark glossy green leaves that have a paler green underside, usually with rusty hairs. Large, fragrant flowers appear in late summer.

Photinia x fraseri 'Red Robin'

Height and spread up to 5 m/ 15 ft • Full sun – partial shade;

needs winter shelter in frost-prone areas • Fertile, moist, well-drained soil

A compact, globe-shaped tree with bright red new leaves in spring. Grow it as a specimen tree or grouped with other trees or shrubs.

Prunus laurocerasus, Cherry laurel

Height and spread up to 5 m/ 15 ft • Full sun – partial shade • Moderately fertile, moist, well-drained soil but not shallow chalk

Dense and bushy, the cherry laurel has shiny green leaves and can be cut back to keep its shape. Fragrant white flowers appear in upright spires in mid- and late spring, followed by cherry-like red fruit. Use this shrub as a specimen or for a hedge.

Quercus ilex, Holm oak

Height up to 25 m/80 ft, spread up to 20 m/65 ft • Full sun – partial shade • Deep, fertile, well-drained soil

Slow-growing and rounded in shape, the evergreen holm oak has holly-like, glossy green leaves that are silvery-grey

Taxus baccata, Yew, with berries.

when young. It bears short, oblong acorns.

Taxus baccata, Yew

Height up to 10–20 m/33–65 ft, spread up to 9 m/30 ft • Sun – deep shade • Fertile, well-drained soil, including alkaline and acid soils

A slow-growing, long-lived tree with needle-like, dark green leaves and bright red autumn berries. Yew creates a fine hedge and wonderful topiary shapes but it is very toxic.

A colourful border based on carefully chosen mixed colours.

(continued from opposite)

Work the compost firmly down around the root ball to make sure that the tree will remain stable in wind. Water well, and make sure the plant has adequate moisture, even when it is well established.

ARCHITECTURAL PLANTS

Training a tree to the shape you want

For a multi-stemmed tree or one with branches close to the ground buy a plant with shoots along the length of the trunk. Prune out only those branches that are badly positioned or cross others. Shorten the remaining sideshoots to within 5–10 cm/2–4 in of the trunk. Do this only once.

For a tree with a clear trunk and a spreading top cut back all new shoots on the trunk and above the branching head to about 10–15 cm/4–6 in during the summer. When the tree is dormant, cut the shoots right back to the stem.

(continued opposite)

Where shape is all-important these plants are the stars. They stand out on their own to form a living sculpture and provide a strong focal point Alternatively, you can use the bold shape, texture or stunning colour of one of these plants as a contrasting feature to highlight softer, more muted effects created by other plants positioned around it.

Acer palmatum, Japanese maple
Height up to 8 m/25 ft, spread up to 10 m/33 ft • Sun – partial shade; needs shelter from cold winds and frost • Fertile, moist, well-drained soil

A deciduous tree with beautiful, fringed, fine-fingered green leaves that curl delicately earthwards and turn a wonderful rich red in autumn. Some are variegated, such as *Acer palmatum* 'Filigree', with pale green, cream-mottled leaves that turn golden; *A. palmatum* 'Garnet' has leaves that are very finely fingered and deep crimson in colour.

Cordyline australis 'Torbay Dazzler', New Zealand cabbage palm
Height 3–10 m/10–33 ft, spread 1–4 m/3–12 ft • Sun – partial shade; needs shelter from cold winds and frost • Fertile, well-drained soil

A palm with long, slim, sword-like leaves that arch to form a rosetted head. The green leaves are margined in cream and have cream stripes along their length. *Cordyline australis* 'Atropurpurea' has leaves flushed with purple.

Cornus controversa, 'Variegata'.

Acer palmatum, Japanese maple

Cornus alternifolia 'Argentea', Pagoda dogwood/Green osier
Height and spread up to 15 m/ 50 ft • Sun – partial shade • Fertile, well-drained, neutral to acid soil

This softly layered tree is often described as being shaped like a wedding cake, because of the way it displays its white-margined leaves in clearly defined tiers.

Cornus controversa 'Variegata'
Height and spread up to 15 m/ 50 ft • Sun – partial shade • Fertile, well-drained, neutral to acid soil

A shapely tree with branches that are arranged in tiers. The green leaves are strongly marked with creamy white margins.

Fatsia japonica, Japanese aralia/fatsia
Height and spread 1.5–4 m/ 5–12 ft • Sun – light, dappled shade • Well-drained soil

This is a very striking plant with its large, leathery, toothed,

hand-shaped, dark green leaves, which are up to 40 cm/16 in in size. Fist-like knobs of creamy white flowers appear in autumn, followed by small, round, black fruit. Suitable as a container plant.

Festuca glauca, Blue fescue grass
Height up to 30 cm/12 in, spread up to 25 cm/10 in • Full sun • Poor to moderately fertile, dry, well-drained soil

Grasses, with their tufty, long, slim, arching leaves, provide a stunning contrast to low-growing and earth-hugging plants. This blue-green evergreen perennial grows in cushion-like hummocks and produces violet-flushed, blue-green flowers in summer.

Liquidambar styraciflua, Sweet gum
Height up to 25 m/80 ft, spread up to 12 m/40 ft; 'Golden Treasure' grows to height of 10 m/33 ft, spread 6 m/20 ft • Full sun • Moderately fertile, moist, well-drained, acid to neutral soil

Festuca glauca.

Stipa gigantea, Giant feather grass.

Grow this sweet gum as a specimen where its vibrant autumn colour can be clearly admired. The glossy green, hand-shaped leaves turn a rich red and orange. *Liquidambar styraciflua* 'Golden Treasure' is a slow-growing alternative which has green leaves with yellow margins.

Phormium tenax, New Zealand flax
Height up to 4 m/12 ft, spread up to 2 m/6 ft • Full sun, with protection from frost • Fertile, moist, well-drained soil
The long, slim, sword-shaped leaves of New Zealand flax, folded into a V-shape at the base, grow to form striking, spiky, rosette-shaped plants. The more compact hybrid *P. tenax* 'Dazzler' has stunning red, orange and pink stripes.

Rhus typhina 'Dissecta', Stag's horn sumach
Height up to 2 m/6 ft, spread up to 3 m/10 ft • Full sun • Moderately fertile, moist, well-drained soil
The velvety textured, red shoots of this deciduous shrub look like stag's antlers, giving it its common name. Long, curving fronds of lance-shaped leaves turn a brilliant orange-red in autumn and the furry flower buds turn into red, nobbly flowerheads.

Stipa gigantea, Giant feather grass/golden oats
Height up to 2.5 m/8 ft, spread up to 1.2 m/4 ft • Full sun • Moderately fertile, medium to light, moist, well-drained soil

Dense tufts of tall, arching, blue-green leaves up to 30 cm/12 in long quiver in the breeze on long stems and are highlighted in summer by silver panicles of taller feathery flowers with a hint of purple that go golden as the seeds ripen.

Yucca filamentosa 'Bright Edge', Adam's needle
Height up to 75 cm/30 in, spread up to 1.5 m/5 ft • Sun • Any well-drained soil
Rigid, long, spiky leaves that are dark green with broad golden yellow margins form clump-like rosettes which appears to be bathed in constant sunlight.

Yucca filamentosa 'Variegata'.

BAMBOOS

The delicate, arching stems and curving, feathery leaves of bamboos make these plants a contrast to the bolder and firmer leaf shapes of other architectural plants.

Nandina domestica, Heavenly bamboo
Height up to 2 m/6 ft, spread up to 1.5 m/5 ft • Sun • Moist, well-drained soil
The mid-green leaves of heavenly bamboo curl downwards to show off their striking, serrated shape, which is highlighted by reddish-purple winter colour. Star-shaped white flowers appear in spring, followed by long-lasting clusters of red fruit.

Phyllostachys nigra, Black bamboo
Height 3–5 m/10–15 ft, spread 2–3 m/6–10 ft • Full sun – light, dappled shade; give shelter from frost and cold wind • Fertile, moist, well-drained soil
The arching, slender, green canes of black bamboo grow in clumps and in their second

or third year turn an eye-catching shiny black shown off by the many lance-shaped green leaves.

Pleioblastus pygmaeus var. distichus, Pigmy bamboo
Height up to 1 m/3 ft, spread up to 1.5 m/5 ft • Full sun • Fertile, moist well-drained soil
This low-growing, upright, woody bamboo has mid-green, hollow canes and hairless, long, slim leaves.

Phyllostachys nigra, Black bamboo.

(continued from opposite)

For a tall and upright tree with a dominant central leading shoot, make sure that it has not developed two leaders. If so prune one of them back to its point of origin, leaving the more upright leading shoot to continue growing upward.

GREY AND SILVER FOLIAGE PLANTS

Pruning grey-leaved shrubs

To prevent them becoming unattractively straggly small plants like *Santolina pinnate* cotton lavender, and *Helichrysum italicum serotinum*, curry plant, need to be pruned every spring.

Cut back close to the base, to a point where new shoots can be seen. If plants are pruned regularly this may be only 10 cm/4 in from the ground. A neglected plant will shoot higher up.

The plant will look rather bare immediately after pruning but new shoots will soon begin to grow.

(continued opposite)

Beautiful effects can be created by mixing foliage shape, texture and colour so that a garden never looks dull at any time of the year. Grey-green foliage acts as a highlighter, showing up as a haze of silvery light against the dark-green leaves of its neighbours.

Armoracia rusticana 'Variegata', Variegated horseradish
Height up to 1.2 m/4 ft, spread up to 2 m/6 ft • Full sun
• Fertile, well-drained soil
   This is a perennial closely related to the horseradish with roots which are used for the hot and spicy sauce. It grows in clumps and has long stalks with green, serrated leaves which are splashed with decorative white markings. Clusters of white flowers appear on the plant from spring to late summer.

Astelia chathamica
Height up to 1.2 m/4 ft, spread up to 2 m/6 ft • Sun - partial shade • Moist, fertile, peaty soil
   A clump-forming plant, this perennial produces arching leaves of an interesting silver-green which have a metallic and woolly texture on the upper-side. This plant is not frost-hardy: in frost-prone areas grow it in pots and take indoors during winter.

Ballota pseudodictamnus
Height up to 45 cm/18 in, spread up to 2 m/6 ft • Full sun
• Well-drained soil
   This low-growing, mound-shaped shrub has silvery, egg-shaped leaves that curl upwards on erect, white, woolly stems. In late spring to early summer it has unusual, pink-flushed, white flowers with funnel-shaped green calyces.

Brachyglottis Dunedin hybrids/ Senecio
Height up to 1.5 m/5 ft, spread up to 2 m/6 ft • Full sun
• Fertile, well-drained soil
   This bushy shrub has scalloped green leaves with white hairs that create an overall

silvery effect. Loose clusters of yellow, daisy-like flowers appear from late summer.

Buddleja crispa, Buddleia
Height and spread up to 3 m/10 ft • Full sun • Fertile, well-drained soil
   A deciduous shrub with arching stems and woolly white young shoots and leaves. Mauve, fragrant flowers appear in mid- and late summer. *Buddleia davidii* 'Harlequin' has mid-green leaves with creamy coloured margins.

Dianthus species, Pinks
Height 25–45 cm/10–18 in, spread 30–40 cm/12–16 in
• Full sun • Fertile, well-drained alkaline soil
   Pinks form a decorative edging for the front of a border or alongside a path. They grow to form mounds of slim, silvery foliage topped by a huge range of fragrant flowers, mostly in shades of pink and white, some with petals edged in a second colour, and others with 'eyes' of a different shade.

Buddleia crispa

Elaeagnus angustifolia 'Quicksilver', Oleaster
Height and spread up to 4 m/12 ft • Full sun • Fertile, well-drained soil; tolerates dry soil and coastal winds
   A very decorative deciduous shrub which shows off its silvery shoots and slim, silvery leaves to perfection in spring. Even the flower buds are silvery, opening into small, fragrant, creamy yellow flowers in early summer.

Grey and silver plants generally thrive in dry, sunny places.

Dianthus deltoides, Maiden pink.

Helichrysum italicum serotinum, Curry plant
Height up to 40 cm/16 in, spread up to 75 cm/30 in •Full sun • Moderately fertile, neutral to alkaline soil

An evergreen, low-growing shrub, the curry plant has narrow, silvery leaves and a strong aroma of the mixed spices it is named after. Yellow daisy-like flowers appear from summer through to autumn.

Ilex aquifolium 'Silver Milkmaid', Holly
Height and spread up to 4 m/ 12 ft • Full sun • Fertile, well-drained soil; tolerates dry soil and coastal winds

This holly forms a spreading, open shape, rather than the dense bush usually associated with hollies. It has sharply spined dark green leaves which are strongly marked, with an uneven silvery-white centre.

Lavandula species, Lavender
Height and spread up to 1 m/ 3 ft; Lavandula lanata has height 75 cm/30 in, spread 90 cm/36 in • Full sun • Moderately fertile, well drained soil

The silver-grey foliage of most lavenders forms a complementary background to the strongly aromatic blue-mauve, pink or white flowers, according to species. Flowers are dried to scent linen or pot-pourri and the essential oils are used for both cosmetic and medicinal purposes. *Lavandula lanata* has the lightest coloured foliage. Some lavenders are only half-hardy and need to be grown in a protected spot.

Perovskia atriplicifolia, 'Blue Spire', Perovskia
Height up to 1.2 m/4 ft, spread up to 1 m/3 ft • Full sun • Poor to moderately fertile, well-drained soil; tolerates coastal conditions and dry, alkaline soils

This tall plant with its silvery, furry stems and deeply divided silver-grey leaves is topped by clusters of violet-blue flowers in late summer and early autumn.

Salix exigua, Coyote willow
Height up to 4 m/12 ft, spread up to 5 m/15 ft • Full sun • Deep, moist, well-drained sandy soil; does not tolerate shallow, chalky soil

This beautiful, upright, spherical shrub, with slender shoots bearing long, grey-blue leaves that are covered in silvery grey hairs when young, is ideal for use as a focal point in a small garden.

Lavandula 'Bowles' variety.

Santolina pinnata, Cotton lavender
Height up to 75 cm/30 in spread up to 1 m/3 ft • Full sun • Poor moderately fertile, well-drained soil

Keep this decorative, round to low bushy shrub in a neat shape by pruning hard in spring. It will then provide good ground cover or can be used to form a low hedge. It has deeply indented and slightly aromatic silvery leaves. In summer creamy white to lemon-yellow flowers rise above the leaves.

Border with mixed coloured and and silver foliage planting.

(continued from opposite)

By summer a compact, well-clothed shrub will have been formed. *Santolina pinnata*, cotton lavender, is illustrated.

GOLD AND BRIGHT GREEN FOLIAGE

Taking heel cuttings

This method works well for *Elaeagnus* x *ebbingei* 'Gilt Edge' as well as elders (*Sambucus*), rhododendrons and azaleas.

Pull off the cutting to leave a sliver of bark at the end. Pull downwards so that the sliver of bark comes away at the base. This is the point where the hormones that stimulate rooting are most concentrated.

Using a sharp knife, trim off the long 'tail' close to the base of the cutting and at an angle, then insert the cutting in compost in a pot and cover with a polythene bag or use a cold frame or propagator.

(continued opposite)

In the colder wintertime, or when the weather is dull and uninviting, plants with golden coloured foliage create bright spots in the landscape and give a hint of sunnier days. They also look very effective in a special bed mixed with plants that have sunny flower colours of yellow, rust or orange. Alternatively, mix them with white for a fresh, clean look or blue for a striking contrast.

Carex hachijoensis 'Evergold', Sedge

Height up to 30 cm/12 in, spread up to 35 cm/14 in • Sun – partial shade • Fertile, moist, well-drained soil
    The long, slim, grass-like leaves of this evergreen, clump-forming sedge are decoratively striped in green and yellow. In spring spikes of small brown flowers appear on 15 cm/6 in-long stems.

Catalpa bignonioides 'Aurea', Indian bean tree

Height and spread up to 10 m/ 33 ft • Full sun • Fertile, moist, well-drained soil
    Giant, lime-yellow, pointed, heart-shaped leaves adorn this slow-growing deciduous tree, which appears as a haze of gold when the young leaves first unfold. Very decorative, white, foxglove-shaped flowers with throats of yellow and purple appear in summer, and these are followed by slim, trailing seed pods. Indian bean tree needs shelter from strong winds and young trees should be protected from frost.

Euonymus fortunei.

Choisya ternata 'Sundance', Mexican orange blossom

Height and spread up to 2.5 m/ 8 ft • Full sun • Fertile, well-drained soil
    This dome-shaped evergreen shrub with its attractive divided and slightly aromatic golden yellow leaves provides a sunny feature, even in the gloomiest months of the year. The white orange blossom-scented flowers which appear in spring on other Mexican orange blossoms are rarer and less abundant on 'Sundance'. A sunny position gives the best colour. Provide shelter from frosts.

Elaeagnus x *ebbingei* 'Gilt Edge'

Height and spread up to 4 m/ 12 ft • Full sun – partial shade • Fertile, well-drained soil
    This dense and slow-growing evergreen shrub provides round-the-year brightness with its colourful, pointed leaves, dark green in the centre and surrounded by a wide margin of bright creamy yellow. Slightly smaller, *E.* x *ebbingei* 'Limelight' provides more subtle colour with silvery young leaves that later become marked with yellow and pale green at the centre.

Euonymus fortunei 'Emerald 'n Gold'

Height and spread up to 90 cm/ 36 in • Full sun • Moist, well-drained soil
    This low-growing, bushy ever-green shrub has leaves of bright green edged with a wide margin of sunny yellow that becomes tinged pink in winter.

Elaeagnus x *ebbingei* 'Gilt Edge'.

Hedera colchica 'Sulphur Heart', Persian ivy

Height and spread 5 m/15 ft; *H. helix* 'Buttercup' 2 m/6 ft • Full sun • Fertile, moist, well-drained, preferably alkaline soil
    This is a vigorous climbing ivy with large, elongated, mid-green leaves splashed with yellow. Full sun produces the strongest coloration. An alternative choice is the small-leaved ivy *Hedera helix* 'Buttercup', which needs full sun to bring out its brilliant yellow colouring.

Hedera helix 'Buttercup'.

Hosta fortunei 'Aureo Marginata'.

Hosta 'Gold Standard'
Plantain lily/hosta
Height 65 cm/26 in, spread 1 m/ 3ft; 'Sum and Substance' height 75 cm/30 in, spread 1.2 m/4 ft • Partial shade • Fertile, moist, well-drained soil

Clump-forming hostas are grown for their colourful and shapely leaves. 'Gold Standard' has golden, strongly veined leaves edged with bright green. Funnel-shaped, lavender-blue flowers appear on tall stems in mid-summer. An alternative is 'Sum and Substance', which has heart-shaped, glossy, yellow-green leaves and bell-shaped, pale lilac flowers. Prone to slug and snail damage hostas need good mulching as they will not tolerate drought.

Humulus lupulus
'Aureus', Golden hop
Height up to 6 m/20 ft, spread up to 2 m/6 ft • Bright sun – partial shade • Moderately fertile, moist, well-drained soil

Sambucus racemosa 'Plumosa Aurea'.

This fast-growing and vigorous climber is best trained over a fence, through a tree or up a tall frame, where its golden foliage can be seen to advantage. It dies down in winter, producing fresh growth in spring.

Ilex aquifolium
'Golden Milkboy', Holly
Height up to 6 m/20 ft, spread up to 4 m/12 ft • Sun • Moderately fertile, moist, well-drained soil

The spiny leaves of this holly are mainly a creamy gold, high-lighted by an outer dark green marking. The plant is dense and upright with purple-green stems. A position in full sun produces best colour.

Lonicera nitida
'Baggesen's Gold'
Height and spread up to 1.5 m/5 ft • Full sun – partial shade • Any well-drained soil

The long, arching shoots of this evergreen, bushy shrub produce small, bright yellow leaves and minute, creamy white flowers in spring. Grown in partial shade the plant is less prone to aphids but it needs sun for the best colouring.

Philadelphus coronarius
'Aureus', Mock orange
Height up to 2.5 m/8 ft, spread 1.5 m/5 ft • Partial shade • Moderately fertile, well-drained soil

This deciduous shrub is a shade-happy plant that displays leaves that are golden yellow at first, turning golden green later.

Sambucus nigra
'Aurea', Golden elder
Height and spread of up to 6 m/ 20 ft • Full sun – partial shade • Moderately fertile soil

This deciduous shrub is related to the common elder. Sambucus nigra 'Aurea' is a decorative form of the shrub, with yellow foliage developing from bronze new leaves on pink-flushed leafstalks.

Ilex aquifolium 'Argentea Pendula'.

Choisya ternata 'Sundance' (below, middle right), mixed with other foliage plants.

VIGOROUS BACKGROUND CLIMBERS

Pruning a rambler rose

After flowering and in late summer cut out very old, dead and diseased shoots right to the base. Leave all the young and healthy shoots.

On the remaining main shoots go along the length and prune all sideshoots, cutting them down to between two and four pairs of leaves from the main stem.

These vigorous climbers have a wide range of uses. They will quickly clothe a pergola or archway or cover an arbour. Alternatively use one to hide an unsightly building or train up trellis to screen a coal bunker, bin or garden shed. Grown up a wigwam or obelisk they can soon obscure an upright eyesore. Some of these climbers rely on leaf colour for decorative effect, others form a fine curtain of flowers for part of the year, and a number provide fragrance too. All spread generously.

Actinidia kolomikta
Height to around 5 m/15 ft
• *Sun, with shelter from strong wind* • *Fertile, well-drained soil*
    The green leaves of this twining climber have tips strongly splashed in pink and white to give a colourful cover to walls, fences or the branches of a tree, until the leaves fall in autumn. Full sun gives the best colour variegation.

Ampelopsis brevipedunculata 'Elegans'
Height to around 5 m/15 ft
• *Sun – partial shade, in a sheltered position* • *Fertile, moist, well-drained soil*
    Divided leaves of dark green mottled with pink and white decorate this deciduous climber. Small, inconspicuous green flowers appear in summer, and these are followed by decorative, marbled, pink and purple fruit that turns blue in late autumn. It makes an ideal plant for clothing a wall, fence, pergola or tree.

Hedera colchica 'Dentata', Persian ivy
Height to around 10 m/33 ft; Hedera helix 'Goldheart' grows to around 5 m/15 ft • *Sun – full shade* • *Fertile, moist, well-drained soil*
    This ivy has dark green, elongated, heart-shaped leaves with stems and leafstalks flushed purple. Excellent for ground cover or can be used to conceal a wall or fence in the shade. Its blue-black winter berries are poisonous. *Hedera helix* 'Goldheart' is another ivy that also grows well up a shady wall.

▲ *Actinidia kolomikta.*

▼ *Parthenocissus quinquefolia,* Virginia creeper.

Hydrangea petiolaris, Climbing hydrangea
Height to around 15 m/50 ft
• *Shade, in a sheltered position*
• *Moderately fertile, moist, well drained soil*
    This hydrangea is a vigorous climber, clinging to its support by aerial roots. It will grow over a shady wall or structure, and in summer it produces small, creamy white flowers with flower heads similar to those of a lace-cap type.

Jasminum humile 'Revolutum', Yellow jasmine
Height to 2.5 m/8 ft, spread to

Vitis coignetia.

3 m/10 ft • Sun – partial shade, in a sheltered position in cold areas • Fertile, well-drained soil

Grow this bushy shrub to hide an unattractive view. The delicate, pointed, slim, dark green leaves are semi-evergreen. Masses of fragrant, buttercup-yellow flowers add colour from late spring to early autumn.

Parthenoncissus quinquefolia, Virginia creeper
Height to 15 m/50 ft • Sun – partial shade as • Fertile, well-drained soil

To provide quick cover for a wall, fence, or even a large tree, use this creeper with its serrated green leaves that turn a glorious warm, golden russet in autumn.

Schizophragma integrifolium
Height to 12 m/40 ft • Sun – partial shade • Moderately fertile, well-drained soil

The large, dark green leaves of this plant, which climbs by aerial roots, are almost obscured in mid-summer by the unusual, creamy white, fragrant flowers which have long creamy bracts around the edges.

Vitis coignetiae, Crimson glory vine
Height to 15 m/50 ft • Sun – partial shade • Well-drained, neutral to alkaline soil

Climbing by tendrils, this hardy vine has large, heart-shaped green and strongly veined leaves that turn brilliant yellow, orange and scarlet red in autumn. The small, blue-black grapes are inedible.

Wisteria sinensis, Chinese wisteria
Height to around 8.5 m/28 ft • Sun – partial shade • Fertile, moist, well-drained soil

This twining climber needs a firm support for its vigorous growth. In late spring to early summer it is covered by trailing, pendent streamers of scented lilac or white flowers.

Wisteria sinensis is grown over a pergola showing its lilac flowers.

RAMBLER ROSES

These vigorous roses will soon clothe a sunny wall or fence, or clamber through a tree. They only flower once but the mass of clustered, sweetly scented flowers more than makes up for this.

Rosa 'Albertine'
Height – to 5 m/15 ft, spread up to 4 m/12 ft

An old and vigorous rambler with prickly red-green stems, mid-green leaves and rusty-orange buds that turn into very sweetly scented, light salmon pink, cup-shaped flowers in mid-summer.

Rosa filipes 'Kiftsgate'
Height up to 10 m/33 ft, spread up to 6 m/20 ft

Huge clusters of small, open, creamy white, fragrant flowers cover this exceptionally rampant rambler in summer.

Rosa 'Paul's Himalayan Musk'
Height and spread up to 10 m/33 ft

Large clusters of double, pale-pink, rosette-shaped, pleasantly fragrant flowers cover the trailing shoots of this climber in summer.

▲ *Rosa filipes 'Kiftsgate'.*　　▼ *Rosa 'Albertine'.*

CHAPTER 8

PLANTS FOR COLOUR AND DECORATIVE DETAIL

Part of a garden's charm is the way it changes through the seasons. New plants come into flower and take centre stage, creating a different colour scheme from those that are on their way out, and adding new shapes.

Long-season flowers provide continuing colour. Bulbs fill in the spaces, and ground-cover plants introduce more colour and hide patches of bare soil. Annuals and bedding plants provide instant colour for containers and areas of the garden where it is needed. Scented leaves and flowers play a vital role in the enjoyment of the garden, while other specially chosen plants create a natural, integrated look for the pond. Herbs and vegetables not only provide fresh produce but, if chosen carefully, can introduce both colour and decorative leaf shapes too.

In this chapter plants chosen cover all these categories, with tips on sowing seeds, planting, pruning and how to prolong flowering.

Bulbs for all seasons 164–165
Colourful climbers 166–167
Winter colour 168–169
Long-season flowers 170–171
Temporary colour 172–173
Ground cover 174–175
Plants for scent 176–177
Water plants 178–179
Herbs and decorative vegetables 180–181

BULBS FOR ALL SEASONS

Planting bulbs in grass

Many bulbs create colour and a very natural effect if they are planted in grass. Where bulbs are planted, leave mowing the grass until the foliage has died back completely after flowering.

Slice through the grass with a spade or edging iron around the area to be planted. Then use the spade to slice beneath the turf and fold it back for planting.

Scatter the bulbs randomly for the most natural effect, having forked over the soil first to loosen and added some slow-release fertilizer. Just press small bulbs into the loosened surface. Plant larger bulbs with a trowel to a depth twice that of the bulb's size.

(continued opposite)

Not only do bulbs produce wonderful colour and exotic flower shapes but some species flower at times of the year when few other plants are in bloom, then die back to allow shrubs, trees and annuals to take pride of place. Not all have to be grown in beds: for example, crocuses or daffodils can be planted in grass, and the larger lilies look very effective grown in a container and placed in a prominent position when the flowers come into bloom. They can later be moved to take a back seat as the leaves die back. Plant bulbs to a depth twice as deep as the bulb itself.

Allium 'Purple Sensation'
Height up to 1 m/3 ft, spread 8 cm/3 in • Plant 5–10 cm/ 2–4 in deep • Full sun • Fertile, well-drained soil
  A relative of the onion, *Allium* 'Purple Sensation' has a globe-shaped head made up of 50 or more star-shaped, deep violet flowers on a tall stem in summer.

Anemone blanda
Height and spread up to 15 cm/ 6 in • Plant 8–10 cm/3–4 in deep • Full sun – partial shade • Light, sandy, well-drained soil
  Solitary daisy-like flowers, in deep blue, pink or white depending on variety, appear in spring above the decorative and deeply cut green leaves. These ground-hugging plants quickly spread and multiply to form large clumps.

Crocus vernus, Dutch crocus
Height 10–12 cm/4–5 in, spread 5 cm/2 in • Plant 8–10 cm/ 3–4 in deep • Full sun • Gritty, poor to moderately fertile, well-drained soil
  This crocus species, of which there are numerous cultivars, looks most at home grown in grass, where it will flower from early to late spring. The flowers are about 3–6 cm/1.25–2.5 in long and come in white and shades of purple and lilac, sometimes decoratively streaked as in *Crocus vernus* 'Pickwick'. There are numerous other varieties of crocus to choose from, including *Crocus tommasinianus* f. *albus*.

Crocus 'Remembrance'.

Cyclamen repandum
Height 10–12 cm/4–5 in, spread 5 cm/2 in • Plant 8–10cm/ 3–4in deep • Full sun • Gritty, poor to moderately fertile, well-drained soil
  This cyclamen, with rich red flowers that appear in mid- to late spring, also has pretty, dark green leaves marbled with a pale grey-green. For autumn colour there is *Cyclamen hederifolium* 'Album', which has pure white flowers.

Cyclamen repandum.

Fritillaria imperialis, Crown imperial
Height up to 1.5 m/5 ft, spread 25–30 cm/10–12 in • Plant 8–10 cm/3–4 in deep • Full sun • Fertile, well-drained soil
  This very decorative, tall, lily-like plant flowers in spring. Stems and leaves grow rapidly. The bud opens to produce a cluster of around 5–7 downward-hanging, bell-shaped flowers that can be deep red, orange or yellow.

Fritillaria meleagris, Snake's head fritillary
Height up to 30 cm/12 in, spread 5–8 cm/2–3 in • Full sun to light shade • Fertile, damp, well-drained soil
  The small, delicate, bell-shaped flowers of this plant appear in spring in white or a pinkish purple marked with a subtle snake-skin pattern. These fritillaries grow well in grass.

Fritillaria persica
Height 1 m/3 ft, spread 10 cm/ 4 in • Plant 8–10 cm/ 3–4 in deep • Full sun and a hot site • Fertile, well-drained soil
  Up to 30 green-brown to deep purple, bell-shaped flowers make up the long flowering spike on each stem in early spring.

Galanthus 'S. Arnott', Snowdrop
Height 20 cm/8 in, spread 8 cm/3 in • Plant 3.5 cm/ 1.5 in deep • Full sun • Fertile, well-drained soil
  The large, white, honey-scented, hanging flowers of this vigorous and tall snowdrop appear in very early spring.

Fritillaria imperialis,
Crown imperial.

among long, grey-green leaves.
The central inner tepals of the
flowers are edged with green.

Iris reticulata
Height 10–15 cm/4–6 in, spread
6–8 cm/2.5–3 in • Full sun – light,
dappled shade • Moderately
fertile, well-drained soil, from
slightly acid to slightly alkaline
  This pretty iris has blue-purple,
fragrant flowers with a yellow
central ridge in late winter to
early spring. Iris reticulata
'Cantab' has pale blue flowers
with an orange-yellow central
mark; I. reticulata 'J.S Dijt' has
deep purple-red flowers with an
orange-yellow streak.

Lilium regale, Regale lily
Height up to 2 m/6 ft, spread
5–8 cm/2–3 in • Full sun –
light shade • Well-drained soil;
unlike most lilies, L. regale can
tolerate lime
  The fragrant flowers of the
regale lily open in mid-summer
revealing petals streaked white
and pink on the outer side and
white on the inside, with yellow
stamens and a yellow-flushed
throat.

Muscari neglectum,
Grape hyacinth
Height 10–20 cm/4–8 in, spread
5 cm/2 in • Plant 10 cm/4 in
deep • Full sun • Moderately
fertile, moist, well-drained soil
  Fragrant cones of blue-black
flowers with almost closed,
white mouths appear in spring.

Narcissus 'Spellbinder'
Height to 50 cm/20 in; N. bulbocodium is 10–15 cm/4–6 in
• Full sun and a sheltered site
• Moist, well-drained soil; plant
N. bulbocodium in acid soil, to
one and a half times its depth
  This daffodil has bright yellow
flowers up to 11.5 cm/4.5 in
across. The trumpet-shaped
centre fades to white, with whitish
green at the mouth. The hoop-
petticoat daffodil, Narcissus
bulbocodium is a wild hybrid.

Scilla sibirica 'Spring
Beauty', Siberian squill
Height 20 cm/8 in Plant
8–10cm/ 3–4in deep • Full sun
– partial shade • Moderately

AUTUMN-FLOWERING
SPECIES

Colchicum speciosum
'Album', White autumn
crocus
Height up to 18 cm/7 in, spread
10cm/4in • Plant 8–10 cm/
3–4 in deep • Full sun • Fertile,
damp, well-drained soil
  This autumn crocus has
large, pure white, goblet-
shaped flowers which have
bright yellow anthers. The flowers, which appear in autumn
before the leaves, have good
resistance to bad weather.

Eucomis bicolor,
Pineapple Lily
Height 30–60 cm/12–24 in,
spread 20 cm/8 in • Plant
15 cm/6 in deep • Full sun
• Fertile, well-drained soil
  This plant is borderline
hardy, so avoid growing it in
frost-prone areas, or grow in
pots and move indoors. In late

Colchicum speciosum 'Album'.

Lilium regale.

fertile, well-drained soil
  The bell-shaped, deep blue
flowers are produced in spring
at the same time as the leaves.

Nerine bowderii.

summer tall, maroon-flecked
stems hold up pineapple-like
multi-flower heads of pale
green which are edged and
striped at the neck with purple.

Nerene bowderii
Height up to 45 cm/18 in,
spread 8 cm/3 in • Plant
with tip exposed • Full sun
• Well drained soil
  Fine-petalled, star-shaped,
scented pink flowers appear
late in the year. There may be
up to seven or more on one
stem. Nerine flexuosa 'Alba'
has white flowers that are
sometimes flushed faintly
pink. In cold areas, mulch the
plants well in winter.

(continued from opposite)

Fold the grass flaps back over
the planted area, firming them
carefully with your hand so
that the grass remains level.

For large bulbs use a bulb
planter to make individual
holes. Remove the core of
soil, position the bulb, crumble
some soil over the bulb and
press the plug back into the
planting hole.

COLOURFUL CLIMBERS

Planting a climber

Fix the support for the climber to grow up first, then dig a hole large enough to take the root ball comfortably. Position this at least 45 cm/ 18 in away from a wall or fence, where the roots will be able to obtain water.

Fork over the soil in the base of the hole and add plenty of well rotted manure or garden compost. Position the plant so that it leans towards the wall. Use a stick to check that the soil lines are level on the plant and the surrounding soil.

(continued opposite)

Climbers with a showy display of flowers bring a brilliant splash of colour to walls, fences, archways, pergolas and arbours. Many can be grown over a tree or around a pillar to create extra interest or add a focal point, while, trained to cover trellis, they can do a wonderful job in hiding an eyesore. Many of the climbers described below also bring fragrance to the garden.

Akebia quinata, Chocolate vine
Height up to 10 m/30 ft • Sun – partial shade • Fertile, moist, well-drained soil
   This twining semi-evergreen climber from eastern Asia has leaves that turn softly purple in winter. The fascinating open cup-shaped flowers are an unusual purple-brown with a spicy fragrance and fall in short, pendulous streamers in early spring, to be followed by 10 cm/ 4 in-long sausage-shaped purple fruit. A warm spring and a long, hot summer are needed for a good supply of fruit.

Campsis radicans, Trumpet creeper
Height up to 10 m/33 ft • Full sun (will tolerate more shade in warm climates); • Moderately fertile, moist, well-drained soil
   A deciduous climber hanging onto the wall surface with aerial roots, the trumpet vine is clothed in clusters of brilliant orange, slim trumpet-shaped flowers from

Rosa 'Constance Spry'.

late summer to early autumn. For golden flowers choose *Campsis radicans* f. *flava* 'Yellow Trumpet'. In frost-prone areas grow the plant against a warm wall.

Cobaea scandens, Cathedral bell/Cup and saucer plant
Height up to 10–20 m/33–65 ft • Sheltered site in full sun • Moderately fertile, moist, well-drained soil
   The large green buds, wonderfully teacup-like, frilly-edged mauve and white flowers make this a very decorative climber. Although this is a perennial you will probably need to treat it as an annual in frost-prone areas and start it from seed each year. The large, single, slightly scented flowers appear from late summer to early autumn.

Ipomoea lobata, Spanish flag
Height 1–2 m/3–6 ft • Full sun • Moderately fertile, well-drained soil
   This is another perennial climber that is usually grown as an annual. The narrow, scarlet flowers, which change to orange and then white, appear on erect, one-sided spikes from summer through to autumn.

Jasminum nudiflorum, Winter jasmine
Height 3 m/10 ft • Full sun – partial shade • Fertile, well-drained soil
   This arching deciduous shrub adds colour to the winter and early spring months with a mass of small, open, sunny yellow flowers.

Cobaea scandens, Cathedral bell

Passiflora caerulea, Passion flower
Height 10 m/33 ft • Sun – partial shade • Fertile, moist, well-drained soil
   Deeply divided green leaves cover this fast-growing climber, which in summer has saucer-shaped white flowers tinged

Climbing roses, 'Meg' (front), and 'Albertine' (background).

Passiflora caerulea, Passion flower.

Solanum crispum, Potato vine.

(continued from opposite)

Tease out some of the roots from the root ball, then replace the soil in the hole. Firm well to ensure that there are no air pockets around the roots. Water thoroughly.

with pink, with purple streaks and a ring of purple-blue filaments with nail-shaped stamens, said to portray Christ's crown of thorns – hence the common name. Flowers are sometimes followed by orange, lemon-shaped fruits. Grow the plant against a sheltered wall.

Rosa, climbing, Climbing roses

Height up to 3 m/10 ft • Most roses prefer full sun • Moderately fertile, moist, well-drained soil

'Climbing Ena Harkness' has huge, hybrid tea roses of a deep velvety, wine red, and is very fragrant. Many modern climbing roses are repeat flowering unlike the one stunning display of that rambler roses (see page 161 for rambler roses). All these roses flower from summer through to autumn. Handel is a double rose in creamy white, edged with crimson pink and slightly fragrant. Height and spread of 2.5 m/8 ft. 'Zephirine Drouhin' has carmine-pink double flowers and a height of 3 m/10 ft, and 'Golden Showers' has open, double, fra-grant, butter-yellow flowers and a height of 3 m/10 ft.

Solanum crispum Chilean potato vine

Height up to 6 m/20 ft • Full sun• Fairly fertile, moist, well-drained, neutral to slightly alkaline soil

A scrambling climber with terminal festoons of purple-blue

flowers, each with a bright yellow centre. Grow against a warm wall for protection from frost.

Trachelospermum jasmi-noides, Confederate jasmine/Star jasmine

Height 9 m/30 ft • Full sun - partial shade • Fertile, well-drained soil

Pure white flowers with frilled edges, the shape of old-fash-ioned children's windmills, appear on this twining, ever-green climber in mid- to late summer. It has another benefit too, as the dark green leaves turn a rich bronze-red in winter. Grow this plant against a warm wall to give some protection from frost.

Untie stems from any supports the plant arrived with and train the stems to the wall supports, taking them out horizontally as well as vertically to spread them well.

CLEMATIS

Sun – partial shade • Fertile, moist, well-drained soil

The showy, colourful flowers of clematis make this one of the most popular climbers. There is a huge choice, from those with large, open, single or double flowers to those with small bell- or tulip-shaped blooms. The wide range allows you to pick clematis that flower from early spring through to autumn and those listed are good examples. In spring the tiny, brilliant blue, open bell-shaped flowers of *Clematis alpina* with their crisp white centres, are in evidence, soon to be followed by the huge, pale pink, deeper pink-

Clematis 'Percy Picton'.

streaked flowers of *C.* 'Nelly Moser'. In mid-summer the brilliant burgundy pink flowers edged with a deeper red of *C.* 'Ville de Lyon' are on show, and these are followed by the deep purple-blue open flowers of *C.* 'Jackmannii'. Finally, late summer to early autumn brings the tiny, yellow, bell-shaped, scented flowers of *C. rehderiana*. Plant clematis with their roots shaded, away from early morning sun.

Clematis alpina.

WINTER COLOUR

Pruning dogwood

Dogwood needs to be pruned annually in spring, or at least every other year, so it produces the bright red young stems which provide winter colour.

Prune in early spring before the leaves appear. Cut back each stem to an outward-facing bud about 5 cm/2 in from the stump of hard wood at the centre.

(continued opposite)

It is in the winter months that we especially appreciate plants that flower or have leaves or stems that provide colour, for this is usually a less than hospitable time of the year. These plants are not as difficult to track down as could be imagined. Many winter flowers are also scented, providing an added bonus when they are cut and brought into the house.

Berberis thunbergii f. atropurpurea, Berberis
Height up to 1 m/3 ft, spread up to 2.5 m/8 ft • Sun – partial shade • Well-drained soil

A dense shrub, excellent for a hedge, this deciduous berberis has dark purple-red leaves that turn a bright red in autumn. Pale yellow flowers appear in spring, and these are followed by glossy red autumn and winter berries.

Berberis thunbergii f. atropurpurea.

Chaenomeles japonica, Japanese quince/Japonica
Height up to 1 m/3 ft, spread up to 2 m/6 ft • Sun – partial shade • Moderately fertile, well-drained soil, including alkaline

A spreading, thorny shrub that can be trained against a wall. In early spring japonica is covered with small, brilliant orange to red flowers. These are followed in late summer by yellow, edible, aromatic fruits that often stay on the bush all winter.

Chimonanthus praecox, Wintersweet
Height up to 4 m/12 ft, spread

up to 3 m/10 ft • Sheltered position in full sun • Fertile, well-drained soil

The pendent, fragrant, yellow winter flowers of this deciduous shrub appear along the bare stems long before the large and glossy mid-green leaves open. The variety Chimonanthus praecox 'Luteus' has lemon-yellow flowers; C. praecox 'Grandiflorus' has deeper yellow flowers with red centres.

Cornus alba, 'Sibirica', Dogwood
Height and spread up to 3 m/10 ft. • Sun – partial shade • Fertile, well-drained, neutral to acid soil

This deciduous upright shrub is grown for its bright red winter stems. To encourage colourful stems it is important to prune at least every second year in spring. Autumn colour is provided by the leaves, which turn red. (See also Cornus stolonifera and C. alba, page 148.)

Cotoneaster 'Cornubia', Cotoneaster
Height and spread up to 6 m/20 ft • Sun – partial shade • Moderately fertile, well-drained soil

Cornus alba 'Sibirica', Dogwood.

Chaenomeles x superba 'Ernst Finken'.

This arching semi-evergreen shrub provides interest around the year. Clusters of small white flowers appear on branch ends in summer, and these are followed by red autumn berries. Finally the green leaves turn a rich bronze in winter.

Daphne laureola, Spurge laurel
Height 1 m/3 ft, spread up to 1.5 m/5 ft; D. bholua has height 2–4 m/6–12 ft, spread up to 1.5 m/5 ft • Sun–partial shade • Moderately fertile, well-drained, preferably slightly alkaline soil

Most of the daphnes produce clusters of intensely fragrant winter flowers. Daphne laureola is a bushy evergreen shrub which has scented yellow to pale green flowers in late winter to early spring, and the related D. bholua produces its fragrant white to purplish pink flowers in late winter. In both species the flowers are followed by blackish-purple fruit.

(continued from opposite)

Daphne bholua
'Jaqueline Postill'.

Lonicera fragrantissima, Winter honeysuckle

Daphne laureola, Spurge laurel.

Hamamelis x intermedia, 'Diane', Witch hazel
Height and spread up to 4 m/ 12 ft • Full sun – partial shade • Acid to neutral soil

The dark red, fragrant winter flowers and orange-red autumn foliage make 'Diane' a must for winter colour. The earlier flowering 'Jelena' has yellow-orange flowers that appear on the bare stems in winter. 'Pallida' has clusters of large yellow flowers. (See also page 149.)

Helleborus niger, Christmas rose
Height and spread up to 45 cm/ 18 in • Dappled shade • Heavy, neutral to alkaline soil

In winter, from amongst the large, serrated, 7–8 fingered leaves, stems rise to produce saucer- shaped white or green-ish cream flowers.

Prunus subhirtella,
'Autumnalis', Autumn cherry.

Lonicera fragrantissima, Winter honeysuckle
Height up to 2 m/6 ft, spread up to 3 m/10 ft • Sun – partial shade • Fertile, moist, well-drained soil

Grow this honeysuckle against a protective wall if you want it to provide you with a good supply of small but very fragrant creamy white flowers. These appear in late winter or early spring.

Mahonia x media 'Charity'
Height up to 5 m/16 ft, spread up to 4 m/12 ft • Full or partial shade • Moderately fertile, moist, well-drained soil

Ideal for a shady situation, this tall and striking evergreen shrub is another winter-flower-ing plant with sweetly scented flowers. The tiny yellow flowers come in clusters of upright, then spreading, streamers forming sunny festoons above the sharply toothed green leaves.

Prunus subhirtella 'Autumnalis', Higan cherry/Rosebud or Autumn cherry
Height and spread up to 8 m/ 25 ft • Sun – partial shade • Moderately fertile, moist, well-drained soil

This decorative, spreading deciduous tree produces white flowers tinged with pink on its bare branches continuously from autumn until spring.

Viburnum tinus 'Eve Price'
Height and spread up to 3 m/ 10 ft • Sun to partial shade • Moderately fertile, moist but well-drained soil

This dense and bushy ever-green shrub displays pink buds which open into tiny white flowers arranged in hydrangea-like heads. Flowers continue over a long period in late winter and early spring.

Hamamelis x intermedia 'Diane'.

The pruning looks frighteningly severe when it is completed as the shrub will be only about 30 cm/12 in high. However, it will not be long before new shoots appear.

LONG-SEASON FLOWERS

Tips for prolonging flowering

Where space is at a premium flowers that last, or are produced over a long period, are especially valuable as they provide almost constant colour without taking up a lot of space to do so.

Dead-heading Removing the heads of flowers as they die considerably prolongs the flowering period as they are unable to set seed and need to produce more new flowers for survival.

Feeding Feed roses annually in spring or early summer. Follow the manufacturer's instructions and sprinkle the fertilizer around the edge of the plant, avoiding the leaves. On dry soil, water the fertilizer in well.

(continued opposite)

Campanula, Campanula
Sun – partial shade • Moist, well-drained soil

Apart from the spreading and clump-forming campanulas there are also trailing and upright species. *C. glomerata* 'Superba', the clustered bell-flower, needs fertile soil and grows to 60 cm/24 in, with large, spherical heads of deep purple-violet flowers. *C. garganica* 'W.H. Paine' is a spreading vari-ety only 5 cm/2 in high, with lavender-blue, white-centred flowers. *C. carpatica* 'Bressingham White' is pure white and clump-forming, grow-ing to 15 cm/6 in with a spread of 60 cm/24 in. The trailing white or pale blue *C. isophylla* is ideal for hanging baskets and window boxes, and *C. persicifolia*, with its delicate, single, harebell-like flowers in white and blue, forms clumps 90 cm/36 in high with a spread of 30 cm/12 in.

Eryngium giganteum, Sea holly
Height up to 90 cm/36 in, spread 30 cm/12 in • Full sun • Poor to moderately fertile, dry, well-drained soil

The tall, mound-shaped heads of masses of tiny, silvery, metallic-blue flowers rise from silver-grey bracts to create a

Fremontodendron californica.

prickly but very decorative effect. Valuable for dried flower arrangements, in which case the stems should be picked just before the flowers open fully.

Fremontodendron califor-nicum, Flannel bush
Height 6 m/20 ft, spread 4 m/12 ft • Full sun, with shelter from wind • Poor to moderately fertile, well-drained neutral to alkaline soil

An evergreen shrub with showy, saucer-shaped, yellow flowers up to 6 cm/2.5 in across, right through the sum-mer from late spring to early autumn. Grow the plant against a sunny, sheltered wall.

Campanula persicifolia.

Omphalodes cappadocica 'Cherry Ingram', Navelwort
Height 15 cm/6 in, spread 40 cm/16 in • Partial shade – a • Moderately fertile, moist soil

This shade-loving, evergreen ground-cover plant has bright azure-blue flowers through spring and summer. It is similar in colour and shape to forget-me-not but each flower has a white central eye.

Osteospermum, Osteospermum/African daisy
Height 15 cm/6 in, spread 90 cm/36 in ('Nairobi Purple'); height and spread 60 cm/24 in ('Whirligig') • Full sun, warm, sheltered site • Light, moder-ately fertile, well-drained soil

These ground-covering plants have large daisy-like flowers from late spring through to autumn. Those of 'Nairobi Purple' are striped pink and purple, flushed white on the reverse. 'Whirligig' has most unusual white flowers with

Rosa 'The Fairy'.

crimped and spoon-shaped petals with blue centres and blue on the reverse.

Pelargonium, Pelargonium/Geranium
Height and spread various • Full sun in a warm, sheltered site; regal pelargoniums prefer more shady conditions than other types • Light, moderately fertile, well-drained soil

These well-loved, long-flowering plants have flowers in a wide range of sizes and in every shade of pink, apricot and red, as well as white and purple. 'Apple Blossom Rosebud' is pink and white and is of the traditional 'geranium' type known as zonal. 'Attar of Roses' is a scented-leaved pelargonium with clusters of mauve flowers. 'L'Elegante' is ivy-leaved with clusters of white flowers and silver-green leaves, and 'Leslie Judd' is a large-flowered regal pelargonium with apricot flowers, feathered in wine-red. Pelargoniums are not frost-hardy.

Penstemon, Penstemon
Height 60 cm/24 in, spread 45 cm/18 in ('White Bedder'); height 50 cm/20 in, spread 45 cm/18 in ('Stapleford Gem') • Full sun – partial shade • Fertile, well-drained soil

The tubular, bell-shaped flowers of penstemon come in pink,

red, mauve, yellow, and white and appear from mid-summer through to mid-autumn. 'White Bedder' has white flowers becoming pink-tinged. 'Stapleford Gem' has streaked pink and purple flowers with white throats decorated with purple streaks. Protect from frost with dry winter mulch.

Phuopsis stylosa
Height 15 cm/6 in, spread 50 cm/20 in • Sun – partial shade • Gritty, moist, well-drained soil

A low creeping and mat-forming perennial with star-shaped leaves and spherical heads of tiny pink flowers produced throughout most of the summer.

Phygelius 'Africa Queen'
Height and spread 1.5 m/5 ft • Full sun • Fertile, moist, well-drained soil

This plant's long, slim, pale red tubular flowers have yellow mouths and appear like streamers from tall stems throughout the summer and often into autumn. They need protection from frost.

Romneya coulteri, Tree poppy
Height 1.2–2 m/4–6 ft • Full sun • Fertile, moist, well-drained soil

The poppy-like, scented flowers of this perennial are white with bold sunny yellow centres and they will flower through most of summer. Grow the tree poppy against a warm, sunny wall in areas prone to frost.

Rosa species, Roses
• Full sun, with shelter from wind • Fertile, well-drained soil

Repeat-flowering roses often continue with a display from early summer into mid-autumn. The spreading rose 'The Fairy' is a ground-cover shrub rose with masses of scented pale pink flowers. It grows to 75 cm/30 in with a spread of 1.2 m/4 ft. R. x odorata 'Mutabilis' will climb if it is supported, and has single flowers of light yellow turning to copper-pink and

then to deep pink, with height 1.2 m/4 ft, and spread 1 m/3 ft. As a climber it grows to 3 m/10 ft with a spread of 2 m/6 ft. R. 'Little White Pet' is a low-growing shrub rose with pink buds and rosette-shaped creamy white flowers. It grows to 45 cm/18 in with a spread of 35 cm/22 in.

Salvia, Salvia
• Full sun – light, dappled shade • S. guaranitica needs light, moderately-fertile, moist, well-drained soil. S. uliginosa needs moist soil.

The 1.5 m/5 ft-tall spikes of tubular flowers of S. guaranitica 'Blue Enigma' are of a deep purple-blue and each flower head is up to 5 cm/2 in long. S. uliginosa is a moisture-loving plant with sky-blue flowers, that grows to 2 m/6 ft.

Scabiosa caucasica 'Miss Willmott', Pincushion flower/Scabious
Height 90 cm/36 in, spread 60 cm/24 in • Full sun • Moderately-fertile, well-drained, neutral to alkaline soil.

Attractive to bees and butterflies, this is a large, white, open-flowered scabious that flowers in mid- and late summer. Other S. caucasica varieties have lavender or pale blue flowers.

(continued from opposite)

Mulching To suppress weeds and conserve moisture, apply a layer at least 5 cm/2 in thick of an attractive organic material such as chipped bark. Apply when the soil is wet.

Pelargonium quercifolium, Oak-leaved geranium.

TEMPORARY COLOUR

Sowing annuals where they are to flower

First prepare the ground by raking it to break down any large lumps of earth so that the seeds have fine soil in which to germinate.

Mark out the area where they are to grow using sand or grit. Use a hoe to take out shallow drills at a spacing appropriate to the type of seed. To prevent the planting looking too formal, alternate the direction of the drills.

(continued opposite)

Annuals and bedding plants allow you to provide a burst of colour in any part of the garden when it happens to look dull, and at almost any time of the year. They also create more splashes of bright colour when grown in hanging baskets, window boxes and tubs. Most of the plants listed below are easy to grow from seed and very economical to produce.

Ageratum houstonianum, Ageratum
Height and spread 15–20 cm/ 6–8 in • Full sun • Fertile, moist, well-drained soil
    For a patch of bright lavender-blue these compact, mound-forming bedding plants are ideal, with their flowers borne from mid-summer until late autumn, or the first frosts. Pink and white forms of ageratums are also available.

Begonia hybrids, Begonia
Height up to 60 cm/24 in, spread 45 cm/18 in • Partial shade • Fertile, well-drained, neutral to slightly acid soil
    Tuberous begonias with their mix of small female flowers and larger, more showy male flowers provide colour for more shaded parts of the garden in summer. Tubers can be lifted in the autumn and dried ready for planting again the next spring. Trailing varieties are also available. 'Anniversary' has large, wavy-edged, multi-petalled, golden yellow flowers. 'Apricot Delight' is similar but with apricot flowers, while 'Roy Hartley' has pink flowers. 'Bridal Cascade' is a pendent begonia with white flowers, which grows to only 10cm/4in high but has the same spread as the others.

Cosmos bipinnatus 'Sea shells', Cosmea/Cosmos
Height up to 1.5 m/5 ft, spread up to 45 cm/18 in • Full sun • Moderately fertile, moist, well-drained soil
    The unusual flowers of this cosmos rise above the feathery leaves in pink, crimson or white throughout the summer until the first frosts. Each of the many

Begonia 'Non-stop Orange'.

petals is rolled into a delicate cone, which makes the colour appear shaded on the inside.

Lavatera trimestris, Lavatera
Height up to 1.2 m/4 ft, spread up to 45 cm/18 in • Full sun, with shelter from cold winds • Light, moderately fertile, well-drained soil

This annual has open, funnel-shaped, showy flowers in soft pale pink, strong pink or white. Some varieties, such as Lavatera trimestris 'Pink Beauty', which is pale pink, are decoratively streaked, in this case with purple.

Myosotis sylvatica, Forget-me-not
Height 12–30cm/5–12in • Full sun – partial shade • Moderately fertile to poor, moist, well-drained soil
    The small, saucer-shaped, bright-blue flowers, each with a yellow eye, appear in dense clusters to herald the start of summer. Myosotis sylvatica 'Snowball' has white flowers and M. sylvatica 'Victoria Rose' has pink flowers.

Petunia Surfinia Series, Trailing petunia
Height 23–40 cm/9–16 in, spread 30–90 cm/12–36 in

Tropaeolum majus 'Alaska', Nasturtium.

Tagetes patula in yellow and gold.

Verbena 'Aveyron'.

• Full sun, with shelter from wind • Light, well-drained soil
This large, trailing petunia is ideal for hanging baskets and window boxes. The showy, trumpet-shaped flowers of these many-branching petunias appear throughout summer if you deadhead them regularly. Flowers come in a wide range of colours – in shades of pink, magenta, white, lavender and blue.

Platycodon grandiflorus, Balloon flower
Height 60 cm/24 in, spread 30 cm/12 in • Full sun – partial shade • Deep but light, fertile, moist, well-drained soil
Balloon-shaped buds open in late summer to display bell-like flowers of purple-blue, veined with a darker blue. Platycodon grandiflorus f. albus has blue-veined white flowers; P. grandiflorus 'Perlmutterschale' has pale pink flowers.

Tagetes 'Lemon Gem', Signet marigold
Height up to 23 cm/9 in, spread 30 cm/12 in • Full sun – partial shade • Deep but light, fertile, moist, well-drained soil
From spring to early autumn signet marigolds open their single sunny yellow or orange heads above the fern-like, feathery leaves. 'Lemon Gem' has five-petalled lemon heads. These plants are ideal for pots or to edge a border. French marigolds, Tagetes patula has a strong scent which helps to keep aphids at bay.

Tropaeolum majus, Nasturtium
• Full sun • Moderately fertile, moist, well-drained soil
Easy to grow from seed, nasturtiums may be trailing, climbing or bushy. T. majus 'Peach Melba' is a dwarf, bushy annual with semi-double pale creamy yellow flowers that have orange-red centres; it grows to 23–30 cm/9–12 in with a spread of up to 45 cm/18 in. The 'Alaska' series are similar but have leaves that are green, marbled white. T. peregrinum, canary creeper, is a climber which produces smaller, deeply divided bright yellow petals that are fringe-edged. It grows to 2.5–4 m/8–12 ft.

Verbena x hybrida, Verbena
Height up to 45 cm/18 in, spread 30–50 cm/12–20 in

• Full sun • Moderately fertile, moist, well-drained soil
Ideal for the edge of a border, the brightly coloured, sometimes scented flowers of these verbenas come in white, pink, red, yellow or purple and appear in summer and autumn. Other varieties suit hanging baskets.

Viola x wittrockiana, Pansy
Height 16–23 cm/6–9 in, spread 23–30 cm/9–12 in • Full sun – partial shade • Fertile, moist, well-drained soil
These pansies come in plain blue, white, yellow, orange, pink, red and purple, as well as bi-coloured and centrally streaked. Flowering occurs mainly in spring and summer but smaller-flowered cultivars are also available which provide winter and early spring colour.

Viola (purple garden hybrid).

(continued from opposite)

Sow the seeds as evenly as possible, label each section, then gently rake the soil level to cover the seeds.

Water well and continue to do this whenever the weather is dry and until all the seedlings have germinated. Thinning out the seedlings where necessary will allow the young plants to bush out.

GROUND COVER

Planting in spaces in paving

Low-growing plants, whether mat, clump-forming or spreading, are the best method of providing a decorative edge for a border. Planted in cracks and spaces, they soften a low wall or an area of paving. A very attractive alternative to a mulch as, once established, the low spread of leaves keeps weeds at bay and helps to conserve moisture in the soil.

If there are no ready-made spaces chisel out a few to a depth of at least 5 cm/2 in. Add loam-based compost, leaving space to plant.

If using small seedlings trickle more compost around the roots as you plant them, then firm them in gently to remove any pockets of air around the roots.

Ajuga reptans, Bugle
Height 15 cm/6 in, spread 60–90 cm/24–36 in • Partial shade • Any moist soil
This spreading, evergreen perennial with its deep purple foliage creates colour not only when it is flowering. In spring to early summer deep blue flowers appear in whorls up the stems. According to variety leaves may be silvery, with a wine-red tinge, as in 'Burgundy Glow', marked with cream and pink, as in 'Multicolor' or splashed with cream, as in 'Variegata'.

Alchemilla mollis, Lady's mantle
Height 60 cm/24 in, spread 75 cm/30 in • Sun – partial shade • Any moist and fertile soil
This perennial plant is most commonly grown for its attractive foliage. The silky-haired, round, scalloped leaves have a serrated edge and young leaves are concertina-like before they open. They look their best after rain when the water droplets remain to decorate the surface. A haze of multi-headed flowers of a pale yellowish-green cover the plant

Armeria maritime, Thrift.

from summer to early autumn.

Armeria maritima, Sea pink/ Thrift
Height 20 cm/8 in, spread 30 cm/12 in • Full sun • Poor, fertile, well-drained soil
Slim, grass-like green leaves form tufted hummocks from which, in early summer, rise stiff stems topped with bright pink, globe-shaped flower heads. Show sea pinks off by growing them at the front of a sunny border or planted in a rock garden or trough.

Alchemilla mollis, Lady's mantle.

Asarum europaeum, Wild ginger
Height 60 cm/24 in, spread 75 cm/30 in • Partial – full shade • Moderately fertile, moist, well-drained, neutral to acid soil
A creeping, evergreen perennial, which enjoys shade and produces almost heart-shaped and strongly veined, dark glossy green leaves. Concealed beneath the leaves unobtrusive, small bell-shaped, greenish-purple flowers appear in late spring.

Bergenia 'Bressingham White', Bergenia
Height 30–45 cm/12–18 in, spread 45–60 cm/18–24 in • Full sun – partial shade • Fertile, moist, well-drained soil
The leathery cabbage-like leaves of bergenias take on a range of colours in winter, par-ticularly if grown in an exposed position and in poor soil. Flower heads of pink, red or purple are most common but 'Bressingham White' has white flowers in mid-and late spring.

(continued opposite)

Cotoneaster horizontalis

Sedum selskianum.

(continued from opposite)

Chamaemelum nobile 'Treneague', Chamomile

Height 10 cm/4 in, spread 45 cm/18 in • Full sun and an open site • Light, sandy, well-drained soil

The plants of this chamomile, with their feathery leaves, need to be placed close together when they create a lawn-like effect that is suitable for lightly used paths and grassy seats. 'Treneague', unlike other chamomiles, does not flower but its foliage is strongly scented.

Cotoneaster horizontalis, Cotoneaster

Height up to 1 m/3 ft, spread 1.5 m/5 ft • Full sun • Moderately fertile, well-drained soil

A spreading and low-growing cotoneaster, with small dark green leaves that turn red in autumn. Pink-tinged white flowers appear in late spring, followed by bright red berries loved by birds.

Pulmonaria angustifolia, Lungwort

Galium odoratum, Sweet woodruff

Height 45 cm/18 in, spread indefinite • Sun – partial shade • Any moist and fertile soil

A member of the bedstraw family, woodruff was once strewn over floors to sweeten the home. Sweet woodruff has star-shaped, white, scented flowers that appear from late spring through to mid-summer and are very attractive to bees.

Hedera helix, Ivy

Spread up to 10 m/33 ft • Sun – light shade (tolerates full shade) • Tolerates most soils but prefers moist, well-drained, alkaline soil

The variegated forms of the common ivy brighten shady parts of the garden. They can also trail to provide good ground cover. *Hedera helix* 'Angularis Aurea' has lemon-yellow edged and speckled leaves and *H. helix* 'Adam' has larger two-green marbled leaves edged in white.

Lysimachia nummularia 'Aurea', Creeping Jenny

Height 5 cm/2 in, spread 23–45 cm /9–18 in • Sun – partial shade • Fertile, moist, well-drained soil

A fast-growing and spreading evergreen perennial with small, golden lime-green leaves that are rounded. In summer it produces cheerful upturned, cup-shaped, bright yellow flowers.

Pulmonaria, Lungwort/ Soldiers and sailors

Height 30–35 cm/12–14 in, spread 45 cm/18 in • Full – partial shade • Fertile, moist soil

A low-growing perennial with green leaves spotted and splashed with white. Bell-shaped flowers in mixed blue and pink open in early spring on 'Lewis Palmer', while 'Beth's Pink' has deep coral pink flowers and 'Sissinghurst White' has white flowers.

Sedum selskianum, Stonecrop

Height 10 cm/4 in, spread 60 cm/ 24 in • Sun – light shade • Moderately fertile, well-drained, neutral to slightly alkaline soil

A mat-forming evergreen perennial, ideal for the rock garden with branching stems and spoon-shaped, tooth-edged mid-green leaves that are fleshy and succulent-like. In summer clusters of star-shaped bright yellow flowers appear.

If using seeds, sprinkle the seeds over compost, then cover with a little more compost.

Using a spray, water carefully to avoid washing away any compost. Water regularly in the same way until the plants are well established.

PLANTS FOR SCENT

Using scented plants to best effect

Fragrance is to many of us one of the most important ingredients of a flowering plant. To grow sweet-smelling varieties close to a gate or doorway or around a window gives pleasure to both visitors and those inside the house, while scented climbers transform sitting in an arbour or under a pergola into a sensual as well as a relaxing experience.

Near doorways and windows
Scented plants growing around a door or window will perfume the house and the garden.

Chimonanthus praecox **'Grandiflorus', Wintersweet**
Height up to 4 m/12 ft, spread up to 3 m/10 ft • Full sun • Fertile, well-drained soil
   A deciduous shrub that covers its bare branches in winter with pendent bright yellow flowers that are very fragrant.

Choisya ternata, **Mexican orange blossom**
Height and spread up to 2.5 m/8 ft • Full sun • Fertile, well-drained soil
   A compact, evergreen shrub with large, finger-like, green leaves, Mexican orange blossom has hydrangea-like heads of small white flowers in late spring with a scent similar to that of orange blossom. A second flowering often occurs in late summer to early autumn.

Daphne odora, **Daphne**
Height/spread up to 1.5 m/5 ft • Sun/partial shade • Moderately fertile, well-drained, slightly alkaline to slightly acid soil

Lilium candidum, Madonna lily.

Like most daphnes this species is a bushy shrub that bears fragrant deep purple-pink and white flowers in clusters in winter to early spring. These are followed by round red fruit. The very hardy evergreen variety *Daphne odora* 'Aureomarginata' has creamy edged leaves and deep purple-pink flowers with white interiors. Mulch daphnes to keep their roots cool.

Sweet rocket/Dame's violet
Height up to 90 cm/36 in, spread up to 45 cm/18 in • Sun – partial shade • Fertile, moist, well-drained neutral to alkaline soil
   In late spring to mid-summer this hardy but short-lived perennial plant supports large heads of small pale pink, purple or white flowers that are very fragrant in the evening. Sweet rocket self-seeds and is attractive to bees and butterflies.

Lilium candidum, **Madonna lily**
Height 1–2 m/3–6 ft • Sun – partial shade • Fertile, moist, well-drained neutral to alkaline soil (most lilies need neutral to acid soil) • Plant this lily just below ground level
   In mid-summer set atop long stems the very fragrant white trumpet-shaped flowers of the madonna lily open to show bright yellow anthers. *L.* 'Journey's End' is another fragrant, but slightly shorter, lily

Choisya ternata, Mexican orange blossom.

In pots on patios
Pots of scented plants make sitting on the patio even more relaxing.

Hesperis matronalis, Sweet rocket.

Osmanthus delavayi.

hat has large turkscap flowers which are a deep pink with maroon spots and white.

Mahonia aquifolium, Oregon grape

Height 1 m/3 ft, spread 1.5 m/ 5 ft • Sun – partial shade • Moderately fertile, moist, well-drained soil

This low-growing but bushy mahonia has densely clustered heads of small, bright yellow flowers which scent the spring air. The bright green leaflets often turn red-purple in winter.

Nicotiana alata, Tobacco plant

Height up to 1.5 m/5 ft, spread 30 cm/12 in • Sun – partial shade • Fertile, moist, well-drained soil

Little betters the evening fragrance of these tobacco plants with their funnel-shaped white flowers. A group of these plants grown in a container will scent both the house and outdoor sitting area when placed beside an open window. There are also many varieties in reds, pinks, creams and yellow.

Osmanthus delavayi, Osmanthus

Height 2–6 m/6–20 ft, spread 4 m/12 ft • Sun – partial shade, shelter from wind • Fertile, well-drained soil

In mid- and late spring clusters of white tubular flowers give off their heady orange-scented fragrance on this bushy shrub.

Paeonia lactiflora hybrids, Peonies

Height 75 cm/30 in, spread 1 m/3 ft Sun – partial shade Moist, fertile, well-drained soil

These peonies have a flowery fragrance which scents the air around the plants in late spring and early summer. 'Duchesse de Nemours' is creamy white and 'Sarah Bernhardt' pink. Grow the plants where early morning sun will not shine on them and cause damage in periods of late frost.

Sarcococca hookeriana var. humbles, Sweet box

Height 60 cm/24 in, spread 1 m/3 ft • Deep – partial shade • Moderately fertile, moist, well-drained soil

This dwarf, evergreen shrub has clusters of fragrant, pink-tinged white flowers in winter, and can be grown as an ornamental low hedge.

Viburnum x burkwoodii, Viburnum

Height up to 2.5 m/8 ft, spread 3–4 m/10–12 ft • Sun – partial shade • Deep, moist, well-drained soil

Mahonia aquifolium, Holly-leaved barberry

This viburnum has very fragrant, pinky white, waxy, tubular flowers opening from deep pink buds in mid- to late spring. In mild areas the leaves are evergreen. Grow it where the flowers will not be in early morning sun, which causes damage if there is frost.

SCENTED CLIMBERS

Lathyrus odoratus, Sweet pea

Height 2 m/6 ft • Full sun – lightly – dappled shade • Fertile, well-drained soil

This annual climber, with clinging tendrils, produces scented, pea-type flowers through from early summer to early autumn. The more you pick them the longer flowers will appear. This old-fashioned, scented sweet pea has dark blue-red petals and purple wings but many cultivars have developed to produce flowers in a large range of co-ordinated colours, such as deep to salmon pink, lavender to mid-blue, scarlet, and white.

Lonicera periclymenum 'Graham Thomas', Honeysuckle

Height up to 7 m/22 ft • Partial shade • Fertile, moist, well-drained soil

Lonicera periclymenum 'Graham Thomas'

A scented climber that grows well in partial shade, and is twining and vigorous. It produces white buds often flushed with red that open into white flowers which gradually turn to cream and then yellow. The scent is at its best in the evenings. Flowers are followed by small, cylindrical, bright red berries.

Rosa 'Climbing Blue Moon'

Height up to 3 m/10 ft • Full sun – light shade • Moderately fertile, moist, well-drained soil

An unusual and very fragrant climbing bush rose that has lilac-mauve, double, heavily scented flowers from summer right through to the autumn.

WATER PLANTS

Keeping the water clear

Oxygenators help to keep pond water clear by absorbing the underwater food supply and so starving out the algae.

Lagarosiphon, Curly water thyme
• Full sun • Grow underwater in baskets in loamy soil
   A vigorous oxygentor with curly, whorl-like, spiral leaves. It is easily removed if it becomes too prolific. Simply pull out older stems.

Myriophyllum aquaticum, Water milfoil
• Full sun • Grow underwater in baskets at a depth of 1 m/ 3 ft
   This is an attractive water plant, with its bright green feathery foliage. Bright yellow flowers appear in spikes rising up from the submerged parts of the plant.

Myriophyllum aquaticum, 'Parrot's feather', Water milfoil.

For the best effect ponds require both plants that survive in deep water with leaves and flowers floating on the water surface on long stems, and marginal plants that grow in shallow water to break up the hard edges of a garden pond. Plants that grow close to a pond also need to enjoy the local damp conditions. Apart from the pleasing effect of visually, attractive plants, some plants are required for the practical job they do in creating a balanced pond with clear water. Water lilies, by shading the water with their large leaves, help to keep down the algae that create green water, as do oxygenating plants which absorb the food supply otherwise available to algae. Creatures such as water snails are a very valuable addition as they rasp away at the algae as well as gobbling up decomposing plant material. If blanket weed algae occurs remove this by hand.

For the bottom of the pond

Aponogeton distachyos, Water hawthorn/Cape pondweed
Spread up to 1.2 m/4 ft
• Grow in soil on the bottom of the pond or in baskets at 30–90 cm/12–36 in deep
   The oblong green leaves of water hawthorn float on the water surface to be joined in spring and autumn by spikes of striking white flowers with dark, almost black anthers. The flowers are faintly scented.

Eichhornia crassipes, Water hyacinth
Height and spread 45 cm/18 in
• Full sun
   A floating plant, with decorative purple-green roots that hang beneath the surface. In summer tall spikes of pale blue flowers with yellow markings appear. In areas prone to frost lift plants and overwinter them in loamy soil in a shallow bowl kept in a light position. Return to the pond when frost is past.

Marginal plants for shallow water

Caltha palustris 'Flore Pleno', Marsh marigold/ Kingcup
Height up to 23 cm/9 in, spread 30 cm/12 in • Full sun

• Water's edge or bog; prefers very shallow water but will grow in water up to 23 cm/9 in deep
   The waxy, bright yellow spring flowers of kingcups are well-known to most country people who pass by streamsides and boggy areas. Caltha palustris 'Flore Pleno' has double yellow flowers, while C. p. var. alba has single-headed white flowers with bright yellow centres. Restrict roots by growing in aquatic baskets.

Iris pseudacorus, Yellow flag
Height 1–1.5 m/3.5 ft • Sun – partial shade • Moist to wet, deep, humus-rich acid soil
   A plant of bogs and shallow water, yellow flag has long, ribbed, strap-like leaves and

Aponogeton distachyos, Water hawthorn.

Caltha palustris 'Flore Pleno', double-flowered Marsh marigold.

Astilbe 'Sprite'.

tall stems of bright yellow flowers, typically iris in shape. Each is decorated with violet or brown markings. The flowers appear in summer, a number flowering in turn on each stem.

Mentha aquatica, Watermint

Height 15–90 cm/6–36 in, spread 1 m/3 ft or more • Full sun • Poor, moist soil, submerged to a depth of 15 cm/6 in

A stream-side plant that grows happily in the shallow water of a pond margin. The green, hairy leaves have the typical strong scent of other mint species. Tubular lilac flowers are produced in dense spherical heads in summer.

For the edge of the pond or a bog garden

Aruncus dioicus 'Kneiffii', Goat's beard

Height up to 1.2 m/4 ft, spread 45 cm/18 in • Full – partial shade • Moist, fertile soil

Tall streamers of white feathery flowers top the arching stems of this waterside plant in early and mid-summer. The fine leaves are fern-like.

Iris pseudacorus, Yellow flag.

Astilbe 'Sprite', Astilbe

Height 50 cm/20 in, spread 1 m/3 ft, 'Purpulanze' and 'Irlicht' are taller • Sun – partial shade • Moist, humus-rich soil or boggy conditions

Ideal for the pond edge, this plant requires fairly damp conditions and is very decorative with

NYMPHEA, WATER LILY

A 'must' with almost everyone who has a pond are water lilies, with their exotic, floating heads and large, saucer-shaped leaves. They come in a wide range of sizes and colours with spreads to suit most ponds, even tiny tub ponds.

Nymphea 'Albida' has pure white flowers with a bright yellow centre, and has a spread of 1–1.2 m/3–4 ft.

Nymphea 'Escarboule' has flowers of a beautiful vermilion-red with lighter coloured outer petals and yellow-orange and pink stamens. It also has a spread of 1–1.2 m/3–4 ft.

bright green, divided leaves, and streamers of fluffy pink flowers in summer. 'Purpulanze' has taller spikes of deep purple-pink flowers and 'Irlicht' has plumes of white flowers.

Dormero peltata, Umbrella plant

Height up to 2 m/6 ft, spread 1 m/3 ft • Sun – partial shade • Moist, well-drained soil

A large-leaved waterside plant, the umbrella plant shows its early clusters of white to deep pink flowers before the large umbrella-like leaves unfurl.

Nymphea tetragona 'Helvolva' is a good choice for a tiny pond, with its pale yellow flowers with star-shaped petals and deeper yellow centre. Its spread is 25–40 cm/10–16 in.

Nymphea 'Escarboule'.

Planting a water lily

A washing-up bowl makes an ideal container – alternatively use a special planting basket Fill the bowl with poor soil or a special aquatic compost and plant the lily in the centre.

Add oxygenating plants around the edge if you use a bowl, just pushing the ends into the soil. Alternatively plant in separate containers.

Cover the surface of the soil with gravel. This helps both to anchor the plants and to keep the soil in place.

Lower the container into the pond. If the leaf stems are not long enough stand it on bricks and remove the bricks as the stems grow longer.

HERBS AND DECORATIVE VEGETABLES

Making a herb wheel

First mark out a circle. Use string pulled taut from a central stake to mark the shape. Then excavate the circle to a depth of about 15 cm/6 in.

Around the edge of the circle lay bricks at an angle to create a dogtooth effect. You may need to adjust the diameter of the circle slightly for a close fit. Compact the earth around each brick, checking the height with a spirit level.

Add lines of bricks to form 'spokes' to the wheel. It is not essential that bricks meet exactly at the centre as you can use a plant, ornament or herb in a pot to disguise this.

(continued opposite)

There is always space for herbs and vegetables in the smallest garden and nothing compares with the pleasure and taste of food freshly picked. Decorative food plants earn a space amongst the garden flowers in the time-honoured way that was used in the English cottage garden. Many herbs and vegetables are also suitable for growing in containers against a sunny wall. A wheel-shaped herb bed is a decorative alternative.

Decorative vegetables

Beta vulgaris, Swiss chard
Height 23 cm/9 in, spread 45 cm/18 in • Sun – partial shade • Rich, light, moisture-retaining soil

Easy to grow and very decorative, this member of the spinach family has arching, crinkled leaves with white, pink or bright red ribs and sometimes the leaves themselves are also a deep wine-red, as in Beta vulgaris 'Feurio'. Swiss chard is drought tolerant and can be cropped over a long period.

Brassica olerocea var. *gongylodes,* Kohl rabi
Height 1 m/3 ft, spread 60–70 cm/24–30 in • Sun – partial shade • Fertile, well-drained soil

A fast-growing vegetable with a flavour like turnip, kohl rabi produces a tennis ball-sized bulb part way up the stem and this is the part to eat. The leaves may be purple with deeper purple veins or green with purple veins.

Brassica rapa chinensis, Pak choi.

Rhubarb chard.

Brassica rapa, Pak choi
Height 23 cm/9 in, spread 38 cm/18 in • Sun – partial shade • Fertile, well-drained soil

An oriental vegetable, pak choi has stiff, upright, outward-curling, bright green leaves with white veins, and broad white leafstalks that are widest where they overlap at the base.

Brassica rapa var. *nipposinica,* Mizuna
Height 23 cm/9 in, spread 38 cm/15 in • Sun – partial shade • Fertile, well-drained soil

A very decorative Japanese vegetable with strongly dissected dark green leaves that have white leafstalks. Both parts are edible. Mizuna does best in the cooler months of the year and if sown in late summer and early autumn will be available for use in the winter.

Cucurbita pepo, Courgette
Height 1 m/36 in, spread 75 cm/30 in • Sun • Rich, moisture-retentive soil

These miniature marrows, simply marrows picked while still young, fill a sunny space with their large, ornate, serrated leaves and bold bright-yellow flowers. They can also be grown in large containers. Picked regularly the fruit will supply a demand over several months.

Lactuca sativa, Lettuce
Height 15 cm/6 in, spread 23 cm/9 in • Sun – partial shade • Rich, light, moisture-retaining soil

Lettuces with ornamental leaves can form a decorative low-growing border at the front of a bed. Red-leaved cos lettuces such as 'Little Leprechaun' can be interspersed with green-leaved varieties such as 'Little Gem'. Alternatively use the loose-headed 'salad bowl' lettuces in the same way, mixing green 'Lollo' and red 'Lollo Rossa' or red and green oak-leaved lettuces. With the loose-headed type, leaves can be cut, and the plant will continue to grow, soon to provide new leaves which are often more strongly coloured than the first.

Phaseolus species, Climbing beans
Height up to 2.5 m/8 ft • Sun, with protection from strong wind • Rich, very fertile soil

Climbing runner beans are ideal for the small garden, as they take up little ground space and can also look decorative on a trellis, wigwam or pergola. Phaseolus coccineus 'Painted Lady' has bi-coloured flowers of red and white. French beans, Phaseolus vulgaris, also come in varieties that climb. 'Purple

Podded' has deep purple pods, which turn green when cooked.

Pisum sativum, mangetout or sugar pea
Height up to 1.28 m/6 ft • Sun, with protection from strong wind • Rich, very fertile soil
These small, sweet-tasting peas that are picked when young and eaten along with their pods come in climbing as well as bush varieties.

Herbs

Allium schoenoprasum, Chives
Height 30–60 cm/12–24 in, spread 5 cm/2 in • Sun – light shade • Fertile, moist, well-drained soil
Lightly tasting of onion, chives are traditionally used in cooking and salads and as an edging herb in decorative herb gardens. Remove the stalks of the pretty purple-pink spherical flower heads if you want to continue cutting back the leaves for culinary purposes or allow some to flower for decorative effect. *Allium tuberosum*, Chinese chives, have star-shaped, fragrant white flowers. All parts of chives – leaves, buds and flowers – are edible.

Foeniculum vulgare, Fennel
Height up to 2 m/6 ft, spread 45 cm/18 in • Full sun • Fertile, moist, well-drained soil
The tall stems and large feathery leaves of this aromatic herb ensure that it is a beautiful

Allium schoenoprasum, Chives.

Foeniculum vulgare, Fennel.

plant to grow in any sunny part of the garden. The leaves are used in cooking or added to salad, and provide an attractive background in any natural-looking garden flower arrangement.

Levisticum officinale, Lovage
Height up to 2 m/6 ft, spread 1 m/3 ft • Sun • Deep, moderately fertile, moist, well-drained soil, but tolerant of most soils
A tall, decorative, divided-leaved perennial which dies back in the autumn to re-emerge each spring. The mildly celery-tasting leaves will spice up an ordinary salad.

Rosmarinus officinalis, Rosemary
Height and spread up to 1.5 m/5 ft • Full sun • Poor to moderately fertile, well-drained soil

Thymus x citriodorus, Lemon-scented thyme.

Rosmarinus officinalis, Rosemary.

An evergreen shrub with fine, needle-like, very aromatic leaves and small, two-lipped, funnel-shaped, purple-blue or white flowers in spring to early summer. Apart from the use of the leaves as a culinary herb, rosemary can also be grown to make an attractive low, informal hedge.

Thymus vulgaris, Garden thyme
Height 15–30 cm/6–12 in, spread 40 cm/16 in • Full sun • Well-drained neutral to alkaline soil
This low-growing aromatic evergreen shrub likes well-drained soil and is an ideal plant to grow in cracks in paving on the patio or in a path. Bees cluster to enjoy the whorls of summer pink-purple or white flowers. A wide range of other thymes is readily available.

(continued from opposite)

Top up the soil between the spokes with a loam-based potting compost or good garden compost. Plant up the spaces with the herbs of your choice, planting several plants of each species in a group.

Use a decorative mulch of cocoa shells, stone chippings or ornamental bark to cover the soil and finish off the bed.

Planting between the spokes of a wooden carriage wheel makes an attractive, small-scale alternative to a brick-built herb wheel and is ideal in a country setting.

CHAPTER 9

PLANTS FOR PROBLEM AREAS

Almost every garden has problem areas where few plants thrive. These may consist of shaded patches where the soil never dries out, or, conversely, shady places where the soil is always much too dry, such as under a tree or large shrub, next to the house or close to a hedge, wall or fence. Equally, few plants can survive in sun-baked areas, which go with dry conditions, while in exposed areas harsh, cold winds can burn leaves, break stems and damage flowers.

Luckily there are plants which can survive each of these problems and some of the best are described in the following pages. Something can also be done to improve the situation. Soil can always be made more fertile (see pages 102–105), shade can be provided from strong sunlight, and shelter from wind.

Plants for shade 184 –185
Plants for full sun 186 –187
Plants for wind and poor soil 188 –189

PLANTS FOR SHADE

Most plants find it difficult to flourish in the extremes of very moist or very dry shade. You can offer some aid to plants in these inhospitable conditions if you dig in lots of bulky organic matter, which helps to improve the soil's structure, retaining water and nutrients within the soil while improving drainage. On dry soil, after watering well, add mulch, which will help to stop the soil drying out so quickly in the future. Choose plants which are most able to cope with the conditions.

Ferns

Many ferns are ideal for damp, shady conditions and their arching, verdant leaves create beautiful effects. Some suitable species are *Asplenium nidus*, Bird's nest fern and *A. scolopendrium*, Hart's tongue fern. Both are evergreen and very decorative with their long, lance-shaped leaves.

In a shady corner ferns can be grown by a pond, to be reflected in the water. Moss will gather and add more shades of green.

Plants for moist shade

Dicentra formosa, Bleeding heart
Height 45 cm/18 in, spread 60–90 cm/24–36 in • Partial shade • Moist, humus-rich, neutral to slightly alkaline soil

In late spring and early summer arching stems of beautifully spaced pendent flowers appear above the fern-like green leaves. The unusual, almost heart-shaped flowers are pink fading to white.

Epimedium pinnatum ssp. colchicum Barrenwort/ Bishop's mitre
Height 30–40 cm/12–16 in, spread 4 m/12 ft • Partial shade • Humus-rich, moist,well-drained-soil

With its evergreen, hairy leaves barrenwort makes an excellent ground-cover plant for

Epimedium pinnatum ssp. colchicum, Barrenwort.

Dicentra formosa, Bleeding heart.

areas of shade under trees and shrubs. In spring spikes of yellow, open, four-petalled flowers with pretty brown flecked spurs are produced.

Mimulus luteus, Yellow monkey flower/ Monkey musk
Height 30 cm/12 in, spread 60 cm/24 in • Sun – light, dappled shade • Fertile, humus-rich, very moist soil

The ornate trumpet-shaped flowers of this spreading perennial appear in late spring to summer and are yellow, spotted with purple-red on the petals and within the throat. Other species come in red, apricot, pale and deep pink.

Symphytum, Comfrey
Height up to 1.5 m/5 ft, spread up to 2 m/6 ft • Sun – partial shade • Moderately fertile, moist soil

Comfrey provides excellent ground cover in a shady area, with its large, coarse and hairy green leaves. In late spring to

summer small groups of drooping purple violet, pink or creamy yellow flowers add extra interest.

Tellima grandiflora, Fringe cups
Height up to 75 cm/30 in, spread 30 cm/12 in • Partial shade • Moist, humus-rich soil

On this shade-loving plant pretty serrated leaves are topped from late spring to early summer by tall stems of tiny, greenish white to white trumpet-shaped flowers.

Uvularia grandiflora, Merrybells
Height 75 cm/30 in, spread 30 cm/12 in • Partial – deep shade • Fertile, moist, well-drained-soil

Hanging, bell-shaped, yellow flowers appear in mid- to late spring amongst the drooping, green, sword-shaped leaves of this unusual shade-loving plant.

Symphytum grandiflorum, a small, neat, spreading comfrey.

Plants for dry shade

Alchemilla alpina, Alpine lady's mantle

Height 8–12 cm/3–5 in, spread 50 cm/20 in • Sun – partial shade • Humus-rich soil

This mat-forming ground-cover plant has very divided, finger-like leaves with silvery-haired undersides. Tiny yellow-green flowers appear in summer.

Bergenia cordifolia, Bergenia

Height up to 60 cm/24 in, spread 75 cm/30 in • Sun – partial shade • Humus-rich soil

The strongly veined, large, tough, rounded heart-shaped deep-green leaves of bergenia are tinted purple in winter. In late winter to early spring pale rose to deep pink flowers appear on long red stalks.

Digitalis purpurea, Foxglove

Height 1–2 m/3–6 ft, spread 60 cm/24 in • Partial shade • Humus-rich soil

The tall spikes of purple,

Bergenia cordifolia.

Digitalis purpurea, Foxglove.

pink or white foxglove flowers are produced in early summer. The flowers are hooded and trumpet-shaped, and beautifully maroon- or purple-spotted inside. Foxgloves often reseed themselves. You can grow them annually from seed.

Euphorbia amygdaloides var. robbiae, Mrs Robb's bonnet

Height 60 cm/24 in • Light, dappled shade • Moist, humus-rich soil

A spreading plant with dark green spoon-shaped leaves with red undersides. These are topped in late spring to early summer by large torches of small lime-yellow flowers.

Geranium phaeum, Mourning widow

Height 75 cm/30 in, spread 15 cm/6 in • Sun – partial shade • Well-drained, neutral to slightly acid soil

Unusual white-centred flowers in dark purple-black, deep maroon, violet-blue, light mauve or white appear in summer on this member of the cranesbill family.

Iris foetidissima, Stinking iris

Height 30–90 cm/12–36 in, spread 3 m/10 ft • Full sun –

partial shade • Well-drained soil

A beardless iris with tough, sword-shaped dark green leaves that have an unpleasant smell if crushed. Insignificant pale purple flowers, touched with yellow, appear in early summer, and these are followed in autumn by seed capsules that split open to reveal bright orange-red seeds.

Geranium phaeum

Vinca major ssp. hirsuta.

Vinca major, Periwinkle

Height 45 cm/18 in, spread indefinite • Sun – partial shade • Any but very dry soil

The open white, deep mauve or blue flowers of the evergreen periwinkle appear in spring and can continue right through until autumn. Vinca major 'Variegata' has white-edged green leaves that add light to a shady spot.

Iris foetidissima, Stinking iris.

PLANTS FOR FULL SUN

Planting a rock garden

Before you start, place the plants in their pots in position among the rocks and check you are happy with the effect. Move them around if you are not satisfied. Water plants well.

Knock each plant out of its pot as you plant it. Invert the pot, while holding your hand over the root ball. If necessary tap the edge of the pot on a rock to loosen it.

(continued opposite)

An exposed site in full sun often goes with light soil that drains quickly. Some plants can survive these conditions, but most wilt. To increase the choice of suitable plaints, improve the soil by regularly digging in lots of bulky organic matter such as well-rotted manure and compost. Mulch with a thick layer of ornamental bark or compost and grow ground cover plants to help to retain moisture within the soil. Never mulch soil that is already dry as this will make matters worse. Water well first.

Cistus hybrids, Rock rose
Height and spread 1.5 m/5 ft (C. x cyprius); C x purpureus and C. x skanbergii both have height 1 m/3 ft • Full sun • Poor to moderately fertile, well-drained soil

The open summer flowers of rock roses, with their paper-thin petals, come in a range of pinks or white with bright yellow centres and striking contrast markings. C. x cyprius has white flowers with deep purple marks, one on each petal, towards the centres, while C. x purpureus has dark pink flowers with maroon marks and C. x skanbergii has pale pink flowers.

Dianthus hybrids, Garden pinks
Height 25–45 cm/10–18 in, spread 30–40 cm/12–16 in • Full sun • Well-drained, neutral to alkaline soil

Pinks look decorative bordering a sunny bed or trailing over the edge of a container. They are renowned for their silver foliage and clove-scented, often bi-coloured flowers. 'Alice' is very striking with white, semi-double flowers and a large splash of dark crimson. 'Doris' is pale pink with a dark pink centre, and 'Musgrave's Pink' is an old-fashioned pink with single white flowers which have a green eye.

Diascia species/Diascia
Height 15–25 cm/6–10 in, spread 50 cm/20 in • Full sun • Fertile, moist, well-drained soil

Ideal for a sunny bank or a rock garden, diascias have a

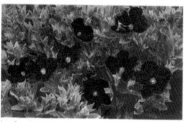

long flowering season from summer to autumn and pretty trumpet-shaped flowers. *Diascia* 'Blackthorn Apricot' has clusters of apricot-coloured flowers, while *D. rigescens* has tall spikes of deep pink flowers.

Euphorbia polychroma, Euphorbia
Height 40 cm/16 in, spread 60 cm/24 in • Full sun • Light, well-drained soil

This clump-forming perennial

Cistus 'Sunset'.

is topped by a mass of short-stemmed and tight-headed lemon-yellow flower-like bracts from mid-spring to mid-summer.

Gaura lindheimeri 'The Bride'
Height up to 1.5 m/5 ft, spread 90 cm/36 in • Full sun • Fertile, moist well-drained soil.

Pinks in a sunny border.

Diascia barberae.

From late spring to early autumn the butterfly-like white flowers of this pretty plant open at dawn from pale pink buds, changing later to pink again.

Inula helenium, Elecampane
Height 1–2 m/3–6 ft, spread 1 m/3 ft • Full sun • Deep, fertile, moist, well-drained soil
This tall perennial becomes a mass of striking bright yellow daisy-like flowers with very fine petals in mid- and late summer.

Iris sibirica
Height 50–120 cm/20–48 in • Full sun • Well-drained, moist, neutral to slightly acid soil
The deep purple-blue flowers of this iris, which appear in early summer, have white markings and darker veining. The foliage, which grows up in spring is an attractive mass of slim, grass-like leaves.

Knautia macedonica
Height 60–75 cm/24–30 in, spread 45 cm/18 in • Full sun • Moderately fertile, well-drained soil, preferably alkaline
In mid- to late summer the dark crimson-scarlet flowers of this vigorous perennial appear, to last over a long period. *Knautia arvensis* has lilac-blue flowers.

Lavandula species, Lavender
Height and spread 30–50 cm/

12–20 in (L. x intermedia); L. latifolia has height 1 m/3 ft, spread 1.2 m/4 ft • Full sun • Moderately fertile, well-drained soil
Lovers of sunshine, lavenders with their mauve, fragrant flowers and silver-grey foliage form an ornamental edge or low hedge for an open border. *L. x intermedia* has spikes of light blue to violet flowers, while the taller *L. latifolia* has mauve-blue flowers.

Leycesteria formosa, Pheasant's eye
Height and spread 2 m/6 ft • Full sun – partial shade • Moderately fertile, well-drained soil
The deep wine-red bracts interspersed with tiny white bell-shaped flowers appear from summer to early autumn on this deciduous shrub. They later decoratively amongst the pointed green leaves and the flowers are later followed by purple-red berries.

Sanguisorba minor, Salad burnet
Height and spread about 15–20 cm/ 6–8 in • Full sun – partial shade • Moderately fertile, moist, well-drained soil
A wild plant grown in gardens for its tiny deeply-toothed leaves with a hint of cucumber that provide a tasty addition to a salad. In summer it has pretty red bobble-like flowers.

Santolina chamaecyparisus, Cotton lavender
Height 50 cm/20 in, spread

Santolina chamaecyparisus, Cotton lavender.

1 m/3 ft • Full sun • Poor to moderately fertile, well-drained soil
This attractive plant has fine-leaved silver foliage and pretty button-shaped bright yellow flowers. These appear in mid- and late summer, making this a delightful plant to grow in a rock garden, as ground cover or edging, and even as a low hedge.

Verbascum chaixii 'Album', Nettle-leafed mullein
Height 90 cm/36 in, spread 45 cm/18 in • Full sun • Poor, well-drained, alkaline soil
Tall spires of creamy white flowers with decorative deep mauve centres appear in mid- to late summer. A relation of the bright yellow wild mullein, this is a plant to show off in a herbaceous border or a wild or woodland garden.

Lavenders enjoy the baking conditions of a sunny patio.

(continued from opposite)

Use a narrow-bladed trowel to make a hole a little larger than the root ball. Trickle some gritty soil around the roots, making sure that the crown of the plant is not buried too deeply.

Firm well, then trickle coarse grit around the plant, keeping it off the leaves. Firm and level the grit with your hands to create a neat finish.

PLANTS FOR WIND AND POOR SOIL

Creating artificial windbreaks

When wind hits a solid object such as a wall or fence it goes over or around it, often causing severe turbulence a short distance from it on the leeward side. This can be very damaging to plants. Planting a hedge is the solution.

Hedges and screens of tall shrubs and trees make the most efficient windbreaks, because they reduce the velocity of the wind while causing less turbulence than a solid windbreak such as a wall or fence.

Moulded plastic windbreak nets give some protection to plants for up to ten years, or even longer. They are a very useful temporary addition to help while more natural windbreaks such as hedges and other living screens are becoming established.

Few plants can cope well with cold winds and poor soil. The plants listed here, some of them used in coastal conditions, will do better than most others in these situations, but they grow better in less exposed conditions and in more fertile, well-drained soil. By following the tips to cut down wind turbulence, described on page 122 and in the left column, and by improving the soil condition, a wider range of plants can be grown.

Agapanthus, Agapanthus
Height 60 cm–1.2 m/2–4 ft, spread 60–45 cm/18 in • Full sun • Preferably fertile, moist but well-drained, soil

These eye-catching plants have huge globes of closely packed deep blue, bell-shaped flowers that top each tall stem in mid- to late summer. The long, dark green, strap-like leaves appear in early spring and arch decoratively outwards.

Allium, Allium species.

Allium, Allium species
Height up to 1.5–2 m/5–6 ft, spread 5 cm/6 in (A. giganteum); A. 'Globemaster' has height up to 75 cm/30 in, spread 20 cm/8 in; A. caeruleum has height up to 60 cm/24 in, spread 2.5 cm/1 in • Full sun • Preferably fertile, well-drained soil

Ping-pong balls of colourful, tiny flowers rise on tall stems on these decorative members of the onion family. *Allium giganteum* has strong pink-purple flowers in summer, A. 'Globemaster' has deep purple blue summer flowers and A. caeruleum has silvery blue

flowers which appear in early summer.

Alstroemeria, Alstroemeria
Height 50 cm–1 m/20 in–3 ft, spread up to 60 cm/24 in • Full sun – partial shade • Preferably fertile, moist but well-drained soil

In summer the trumpet-shaped flowers of alstroemerias appear in colours of pink, red, apricot and yellow, each with its own decorative tiger-like throat markings. *Alstroemeria hookeri* has soft creamy apricot flowers with yellow and brown markings and brown stamens, and A. pelegrina has magenta pink petals, white at the throat, also with the characteristic yellow and brown flecks. A. aurantiaca is bright orange or red, streaked in dark red.

Cortaderia sellowana 'Sunningdale Silver', Pampas grass
Height up to 3 m/10 ft, spread up to 2.5 m/8 ft • Full sun • Fertile, well-drained soil

Alstroemeria aurantiaca.

Agapanthus campanulatus.

This is a plant for a prominent position. With its tall silver-white plumes towering above the long, grass-like leaves it makes a striking display in late summer.

Crambe maritima, Sea kale
Height up to 75 cm/30 in, spread up to 60 cm/24 in • Full sun • Preferably fertile, well-drained soil

The thick and leafy stems, which are forced for use as a vegetable, bear fragrant flower heads in early summer. These are made up of masses of tiny white flowers.

Griselinia littoralis
Height up to 8 m/25 ft, spread up to 5 m/15 ft • Full sun • Light, fertile, dry, well-drained soil

A bold, evergreen shrub that is grown for its glossy, bright apple-green leaves. In 'Dixon's Cream' the leaves are strongly marked with creamy yellow centres.

Cortaderia sellowana, Pampas grass.

Kniphofia, Red hot poker

Height 1.2 m/4 ft, spread up to 75 cm/30 in (K. 'Atlanta'); K. 'Bees' Sunset' and K. 'Erecta' have height 90 cm/36 in, spread up to 60 cm/24 in • Full sun – partial shade • Prefers fertile, moist, well-drained soil

A striking plant when in flower, Kniphofia 'Atlanta' has yellow, red-topped poker heads of tiny pendent, tubular flowers in late spring and early summer. K. 'Bees' Sunset' flowers later in the year, during summer, and

produces brilliant yellow-gold heads, while K. 'Erecta' has flaming orange heads in late summer and early autumn. These appear in tall, slim cones that widen at the top.

Potentilla fruticosa, Potentilla

Height 1 m/3 ft, spread up to 1.5 m/5 ft (Potentilla fruticosa 'Elizabeth' and P. fruticosa 'Farrer's White'); P. fruticosa 'Princess' has height 60 cm/24 in, spread up to 1 m/3 ft • Full sun • Poor to moderately fertile, well-drained soil

The dainty, rose-like, single, open flowers of these potentillas come in shades of pink, red, yellow, and white and flowers appear over a long period from late spring to early autumn. Potentilla fruticosa 'Elizabeth' has lemon-yellow flowers, P. fruticosa 'Farrer's White' has white flowers and P. fruticosa 'Princess', which is slightly smaller, has pink flowers with yellow centres.

Stipa calamagrostis

Height up to 1 m/3 ft, spread up to 1.2 m/4 ft • Full sun

• Prefers medium to light, moderately fertile, well-drained soil

This densely tufted grass with arching blue-green leaves has silvery, purple-tinted, feathery flowers from early summer to autumn. The flower stems form decorative additions to flower arrangements.

Tamarix ramosissima 'Pink Cascade', Tamarisk

Height and spread up to 5 m/15 ft • Full sun • Well-drained soil near coast, moister soil inland; also needs some protection from cold winds inland

An ideal shrub or small tree to grow as a windbreak or hedge in coastal areas.

Potentilla fruticosa.

Tamarisk 'Pink Cascade' has bottle-brush spikes of pretty, feathery, deep-pink flowers in the late summer and early autumn.

Zantedeschia aethiopica, Arum lily

Height 90 cm/36 in, spread 60 cm/24 in • Full sun • Prefers humus-rich, moist soil

The large, pure-white, upstanding trumpet flowers of the arum lily appear above glossy, bright green, arrow-shaped leaves in succession from late spring through to mid-summer.

Kniphofia, Red hot poker.

Zantedeschia aethiopica, Arum lily.

INDEX

Abelia x grandiflora 25, 44
Acanthus spinosus 30
Achillea 'Moonshine' 89, 90
acid soils 108–9
Actinidia kolomikta 160
Adam's needle (Yucca)
 Y. filamentosa 41, 43, 59, 61, 155
 Y. gloriosa 16, 63
Agapanthus 25, 188
alkaline soils 108–9
Allium 164, 188
Alstroemeria 188
Amelanchier canadensis 62
Ampelopsis brevipedunculata 160
Anemone blanda 164
Angelica archangelica 96, 98, 99
annuals 172–3
Antirrhinum 16, 20, 77
aralia, Japanese (Fatsia japonica) 16, 18, 154
arbours 132–3
architectural plants 33, 99, 154–5
Argyranthemum 89
Artemisia 83, 89
arum lily (Zantedeschia aethiopica) 189
autumn crocus (Colchicum speciosum) 165
azaleas 56, 109

bamboo 18, 20, 32, 34, 63, 64, 77, 81, 89, 155
barbecues 142–3
barrenwort (Epimedium pinnatum colchicum) 184
baskets 135
bay tree (Laurus nobilis) 35, 152
beans, climbing 78, 131, 180–1
beech (Fagus sylvatica) 124, 151
Begonia 23, 172
bells of Ireland (Molucella laevis) 63, 77
Berberis 70, 124, 125, 168
Bergenia 20, 29, 41, 63, 174, 185
birch (Betula) 29, 37, 38, 44, 150
bird baths/tables 91, 97, 137, 138
black-eyed Susan (Rudbeckia) 77, 81, 82, 89, 90, 146
blackberry (Rubus laciniatus) 81
blackthorn (Prunus spinosa) 96
bleeding heart (Dicentra formosa) 184
blue fescue grass (Festuca glauca) 41, 42, 154
bog gardens 13, 179

box (Buxus sempervirens) 16, 20, 98, 124, 125, 152
brick 116–17, 118, 119
 edgings 22
 herb arbour 180–1
 paving 56–7
 pergolas 95
 walls 120–1
bridges 129
buckthorn (Rhamnus) 59, 63, 96
buddleia (Buddleia) 44, 70, 89, 109, 156
bugle (Ajuga reptans) 174
bulbs 164–5
bull bay (Magnolia grandiflora) 29, 30, 32, 153
busy lizzies (Impatiens) 41, 42, 63

cabbage palm (Cordyline australis) 32, 59, 154
Camellia 29, 44, 109, 148
Campanula 25, 170
Canary creeper 131
cardoon (Cynara cardunculus) 32, 96, 98
catmint (Nepeta) 70, 81
Ceanothus 25, 29, 37, 44, 51, 53
cedar (Thuja occidentalis) 125
cedar, Japanese (Cryptomeria japonica) 152
cedar of Lebanon (Cedrus libani) 70
Ceratostigma 25, 70, 72
chalk soil 108
Chamaecyparis lawsoniana 124
Chamomile (Chamoemelum nobile) 75
cherry (Prunus) 29, 70, 85, 151, 169
children's gardens 80–3, 138–9
chilean potato vine (Solanum crispum) 167
China aster (Callistephus) 81
chocolate vine (Akebia quinata) 166
Christmas rose (Helleborus niger) 169
Chusan palm (Trachycarpus fortunei) 37, 44, 85
circles, designing gardens with 12
clay soil 102, 103, 104, 109
clearing the site 102
Clematis 95, 109, 131, 167
 C. alpina 167
 C. armandii 20, 22, 36, 37, 63, 95
 C. cirrhosa 37
 C. 'Comtesse de

Bouchaud' 95
 C. florida 'Sieboldii' 41
 C. 'Jackmanii' 51, 167
 C. macropetala 29, 37
 C. 'Nelly Moser' 95, 167
 C. 'The President' 44
 C. rehdenana 167
 C. texensis 37
 C. 'Venosa Violacea' 59
 C. 'Ville de Lyon' 95, 167
 C. viticella 20, 37
 C. 'Vyvyan Pennell' 37
climbing plants 130–3, 160–1, 166–7
cobbles 117 (see also pebbles)
comfrey (Symphytum) 184
compost 106–7
concrete yards 66–9
confederate jasmine (Trachelospermum jasminoides) 37, 44, 167
conifers 29, 124
containers 35, 39, 134–5, 176
 easy-care plants 79
 flowering plants 65
 grouping 53
 planting trees in 152–3
 ponds in 126
 watering 111, 134
Convolvulus 20, 44
coral flower (Heuchera) 25
cornflower (Centaurea cyanus) 41, 42, 43
Cosmos bipinnatus 93, 172
Cotoneaster 51, 52, 125, 168, 175
cottage-garden style 12
cotton lavender (Santolina) 59, 66, 69, 89, 125, 156, 187
courgettes 180
courtyard garden 16–19
cranesbill (Geranium) 39, 86
 G. cinereum ssp. subcaulescens 20
 G. 'Johnson's Blue' 25, 26, 37
 G. macrorrhizum 20
 G. nodosum 95
 G. x oxonianum 94
 G. phaeum 185
 G. pratense 16
 G. psilostemon 16, 18
 G. pyrenoicum 20
 G. renardii 37
 G. sanguineum var. striatum 93
creeping jenny (Lysimachia nummularia) 175
Crocosmia 'Lucifer' 94
crocus, Dutch (Crocus vernus) 164
crown imperial (Fritillaria imperialis) 164

cup-and-saucer plant (Cobaea scandens) 133, 166
curry plant (Helichrysum italicum serotinum) 156
cuttings, heel 158
Cyclomen repandum 164
Cytisus 63, 64, 77

daisy (Bellis perennis) 93
daisy, African (Osteospermum) 20, 22, 170–1
daisy bush (Olearia transversii) 59
daylily (Hemerocallis) 77
dead-heading 170
deciduous trees 150–1
decking 44–7, 59–61, 78–9, 117
designing a garden 9–13
digging 107
dog rose (Rosa canina) 96
dogwood (Cornus) 16, 44, 54, 148, 154, 168–9
Doronicum carpetanum 77
drainage 13, 103
dry areas 186–7

Eastern redbud (Cercis canadensis) 150
edgings 118, 119
 brick 22
 pebble 56
 ponds 127
 timber 119
elder (Sambucus nigra) 96, 158, 159
elderly, gardens for 88–91
electricity 112–13, 144–5
Escallonia 125, 148
Eucryphia 63, 85, 87
Euonymus alatus 70, 72, 148–9
 E. europoeus 85
 E. fortunei 54, 64, 158
evergreens 35, 124, 152–3
eyesores, disguising 136

false acacia (Robinia pseudoacacia) 51, 52, 85, 86, 151
fan palm (Chamaerops humilis) 32
fences 122–3
fennel (Foeniculum vulgare) 20, 181
ferns 85, 184
fertilizers 104–5, 134, 170
firethorn (Pyracantha) 149
fish 129
flagstones 18
flax (Phormium) P. cookianum ssp. hookeri (mountain flax) 41, 63, 66

P. tenax (New Zealand flax) 29, 32, 34, 37, 59, 89, 155
focal points 12, 136
foliage: gold-leaved plants 158–9
 grey and silver plants 156–7
forget-me-not (Myosotis sylvatica) 172
formal gardens 12
forsythia 124
Fothergilla major 70, 72
fountains 38–9, 113, 126, 128–9
foxglove tree (Paulownia tomentosa) 85, 86
foxgloves (Digitalis) 63, 96, 185
fringe cups (Tellima grandiflora) 184
fritillaries (Fritillaria)
 F. meleagris (snake's head fritillary) 164
 F. persica 164
front gardens 40–3
Fuchsia 23, 38, 125
 F. 'Tom Thumb' 20, 22, 23, 66
furniture 133, 140–1

gates 121
Gaura lindheimeri 186–7
giant feather grass (Stipa gigantea) 155
ginger, wild (Asarum europoeum) 174
globe artichokes (Cynara scolymus) 16
Glyceria maxima 77, 78
gnomes 137
goat's beard (Aruncus dioicus) 179
gold-leaved plants 158–9
Good King Henry (Chenopodium bonus-henricus) 98
grape hyacinth (Muscari neglectum) 165
grasses 42, 46, 78, 189
gravel 116, 117
grey-leaved plants 156–7
ground-cover plants 111, 174–5
ground surfaces 116–17
guelder rose (Viburnum opulus) 96
gum, sweet (Liquidambar styraciflua) 154–5
gum trees (Eucalyptus) 59, 89, 90, 152
Gunnera manicata 85

x Halimiocistus wintonensis 60

hanging baskets 134, 135
hart's tongue fern (Asplenium scolopendrium) 96

awthorn (Crataegus)
  C. laevigata 85, 151
  C. monogyna 96, 125,
    150–1
azel (Corylus avellana)
  96, 99
eather 89, 124–5, 188
edges 99, 124–5, 188
elleborus argutifolius 66
erbs 66, 180–1
olboellia latifolia 77, 78
olly (Ilex aquifolium) 96,
  125, 152, 157, 159
olm oak (Quercus ilex) 153
oneysuckle (Lonicera)
  L. x brownii 51, 54
  L. fragrantissima 51, 52,
    169
  L. hildebrandiana 133
  L. japonica 'Halliana' 89
  L. periclymenum 96,
    133, 177
  L. x tellmanniana 77, 78
hops (Humulus lupulus) 29,
  63, 131, 159
hornbeam (Carpinus
  betulus) 124
horseradish (Armoracia
  rusticana) 156
Hosta 29, 37, 54, 56, 63,
  66, 85, 159
houseleeks (Sempervivum)
  54, 56
Hydrangea 65
  H. arborescens 29
  H. petiolaris 44, 51, 54
    160
hyssop (Hyssopus
  officinalis) 125

Indian bean tree (Catalpa
  bignonioides) 89, 158
informal gardens 12
Indocalamus latifolius 20
Iris 25, 63, 85, 165, 187
  178–9, 185
ivy (Hedera) 125,
  H. canariensis 99
  H. colchica (Persian ivy)
    158, 160
  H. helix 22, 96, 175

Japanese angelica tree 77
Japanese gardens 12
Japanese mock orange
  (Pittosporum)
  P. crassifolium
    'Variegatum' 41
  P. tenuifolium 29, 30, 51,
    52
  P. tobira 29, 31, 32, 37
jasmine (Jasminum) 44, 51,
  63, 89, 133, 160, 163,
  166
Jerusalem sage 89
juniper (Juniperus)
  J. communis 16, 18, 70,
    81

  J. x pfitzeriana 44
  J. scopulorum 41, 152
  J. squamata 44

Kerria japonica 51
Knautia macedonica 187
kohl rabi 180

lady fern (Athyrium
  filix-femina) 63, 66
lady's mantle (Alchemilla)
  A. alpina 185
  A. mollis 66, 68, 96, 174
Lamium 'White Nancy' 29,
  96, 174
laurel (Prunus lusitanica)
  125
  cherry (Prunus
    laurocerasus) 153
  Alexandrian (Danae
    racemosa) 32
  spotted (Aucuba japonica)
    37, 77
Lavatera assurgentiflora 93
  L. trimestris 172
lavender (Lavandula) 93,
  125, 157, 187
  L. angustifolia 41, 53, 72,
    81, 89
  L. 'Hidcote' 66, 83
  L. x intermedia 16
  L. stoechas 51
  L. vera 89
lawns 22–3, 52–3, 81,
  111, 117–18, 138
lemon (Citrus limon) 39
Lenten rose (Helleborus
  orientalis) 85
Leptospermum scoparium
  77
lettuce 81, 82, 180
Leyland cypress
  (Cupressocyparis leylandii)
  124, 125
lighting 19, 43, 112, 113,
  144–5
lilac (Syringa) 109, 151
lilies (Lilium) 109, 134
  L. candidum (Madonna
    lily) 66, 176–7
  L. 'Connecticut King'
    89, 90
  L. regale (regal lily) 165
lilyturf (Ophiopogon
  planiscapus) 32
lime, in soil 104, 108, 109
Livingstone daisy
  (Dorotheanthus) 59, 81
Lobelia 16, 41, 42, 70
long, narrow gardens 18
Lonicera nitida 159
loquat (Eriobotrya japonica)
  32
lovage (Levisticum
  officinale) 181
love-in-the-mist (Nigella
  damascena) 81
low-maintenance garden 76

lungwort (Pulmonaria) 175
  P. saccharsta 29, 31

male fern (Drysopteris
  filix-mas) 70, 81
maples (Acer)
  A. campestre 59, 60
  A. capillipes 54
  A. griseum 85, 87, 150
  A. palmatum 29, 44, 47,
    54, 89, 91
  A. saccharinum 89
marigold, French (Tagetes)
  83, 173
marigold, pot (Calendula) 77
marsh marigold (Caltha
  palustris) 128
Maurandya scandens 20, 22
meadow rue (Thalictrum) 79
meadows 99, 117
measuring: scale plans 10;
  slopes 11
merrybells (Uvularia
  grandiflora) 184
Mexican orange blossom
  (Choisya)
  C. 'Aztec Pearl' 66, 68
  C. ternata 20, 23, 25,
    82, 125, 158, 176
mignonette (Reseda
  odorata) 59
millstone fountains 129
mint (Mentha) 96
  M. aquatica (watermint)
    179
  M. rotundifolia 'Variegata'
    89
mizuna 180
mock orange (Philadelphus)
  52, 89, 93, 149
  P. coronarius 51, 159
monkey flower (Mimulus
  luteus) 184
morning glory (Ipomoea)
  I. indica 133
  I. lobata (Spanish flag)
    166
  I. purpurea 54
  I. tricolor 63
mountain ash (Sorbus
  aucuparia) 29, 30, 70
mulches 104, 105, 111
mullein, nettle-leafed
  (Verbascum chaixii) 187
myrtle (Myrtus communis)
  25, 44, 77

Narcissus 'Spellbinder' 165
narrow gardens 28, 31
nasturtium (Tropaeolum)
  73, 77
  T. majus 66, 70, 72, 73,
    81, 131, 173
  T. speciosum 81
navelwort (Omphalodes
  cappadocica) 170
Nemesia 16, 91
Nemophila maculata 41

Nerine bowdenii 27, 165
  N. filifolia 27
new sites 50–3
nitrogen 105
nutrient deficiencies 104–5

oleaster (Elaeagnus)
  E. angustifolio 156
  E. x ebbingei 25, 37, 44,
    85, 86,
Oregon grape (Mahonia) 177
  M. x media 25, 93, 149,
    169
organic matter 104, 105
Osmanthus decorus 85
  O. delawyi 29, 177
overlooked gardens 62–5
oxeye daisy (Leucanthemum
  vulgare) 99

pak choi 180
pampas grass (Cortaderia)
  66, 82
  C. selloana 81, 188
pansies (Viola) 70
  V. cornuta 41, 66, 69
  V. x wittrockiana 41, 173
passion flower (Passiflora
  caerulea) 44, 46, 166–7
paths 31, 40–1, 118–19
paved town garden 36–9
paving: brick 56–7
  planning 116
  planting in 174–5
peaty soil 103
pebbles 18, 116–7, 129
Pelargonium 38, 70, 77,
  79, 171
Penstemon 16, 19, 171
peony (Paeonia) 37, 93
  P. delavayi 29
  P. lactiflora 177
  P. lutea var. ludlowii 33
pergolas 16–17, 42, 65,
  69, 95, 132–3, 161
periwinkle (Vinca major) 185
Persicaria campanulata 93
perspective 12
Petunia 20, 47, 66, 172–3
pH, soil 108–9
pheasant's eye (Leycesteria
  formosa) 187
Phlox 93
phosphate 108
phosphorus 105
Photinia x fraseri 25, 29, 51,
  153
pine trees, dwarf (Pinus
  mugo) 31, 54, 89
pineapple lily (Eucomis
  bicolor) 165
pinks (Dianthus) 25, 66,
  156, 186
plant frameworks 130–1
plans, scale 10–11
playhouses 139
Polypodium vulgare 54
ponds and pools 13, 30–1,

  62–3, 67–9, 89–90, 99,
  126–7, 145
poppy 59, 61
poppy, California
  (Eschscholtzia) 59, 77
poppy, tree (Romneya) 29,
  59, 61
potassium (potash) 105
potato vine (Solanum
  jasminoides) 41, 58
Potentilla 51, 149, 189
privacy 62–5
privet (Ligustrum)
  L. lucidum 153
  L. ovalifolium 25, 125, 153
  L. vulgare 96
problem areas, plants for
  183–9
pruning: dogwood 168–9
  grey-leaved shrubs 156–7
  rambler roses 160
Pseudosasa japonica 96
pumps 113, 128

quince, Japanese
  (Chaenomeles japonica)
  168

raised beds 23, 30, 68–9,
  108, 120
rambler roses 160–1
rectangular gardens 12
red-hot poker (Kniphofia)
  25, 189
redcurrant (Ribes rubrum) 8
retaining walls 120
Rhodochiton 93
Rhododendron 29, 54, 57,
  63, 64, 109, 149
rock gardens 186–7
rock rose (Cistus) 186
  C. x corbariensis 59
  C. x cyprius 41
  C. x purpureus 16, 18,
    19, 20
  C. x skanbergii 92
roof gardens 44–7
'rooms', designing gardens
  12
rosebay willowherb
  (Epilobium angustifolium)
  96
roses (Rosa) 16, 20, 23, 25,
  37, 51, 59, 66, 70, 73,
  77, 78, 89, 93, 94, 96,
  125, 171, 177
  climbing 133, 167
  fertilizers 170
  pruning 160
  ramblers 161
rosemary (Rosmarinus)
  16, 32, 41, 66, 81, 89,
  125, 181
sage (Salvia) 125, 171
  S. farinacea 70
  S. officinalis 25, 89
salad burnet (Sanguisorba
  minor) 187

sandpits 83, 139
sandy soil 102–4, 108
Saxifraga paniculata
var. baldensis 54
scabious (Scabiosa
caucasica) 171
scale plans 10–11
scented plants 133, 176–7
Schisandra grandiflora 66
Schizophragma integrifolium
16
screens 120–1, 188
sea holly (Eryngium) 25,
26, 41, 170
seating 133, 140–1
sedges (Carex) 46, 59, 60,
81, 158
senecio (Brachyglottis) 156
shadbush (Amelanchier
lamarckii) 66, 81, 82, 150
shady spots 54–7, 184–5
short, wide gardens 24–7
shrubs 148–9
moving 148–9
pruning grey-leaved 156
silk-tassel bush (Garrya
elliptica) 21, 149
silty soil 102, 103, 104
silver-leaved plants 156–7
sink gardens 38
Skimmia japonica 41, 51
slopes: measuring 11
steeply sloping land 70–3
terraces 12, 13, 72
Smilacina racemosa 66
smoke bush (Cotinus
coggygria) 148

snowdrops (Galanthus) 164–5
soft shield fern (Polystichum
setiferum) 32
soft tree fern (Dicksonia
antarctica) 59
soil 102–9
Sophora tetraptera 77
Sorbus commixta 'Embley' 16
S. 'Joseph Rock' 81, 82
sowing annuals 172–3
Spanish broom (Spartium
junceum) 51
Spanish flag (Ipomoea
lobata) 166
split-level gardens 32–5
sprinklers 110
spurge (Euphorbia):
E. amygdaloides var.
robbiae 63, 185
E. characias ssp. wulfenii
77, 85
E. polychroma 166
spurge laurel 168
square gardens 20–3
squill, Siberian 165
stag's horn sumach (Rhus
typhina) 155
stepping-stones 61, 118,
129
steps 73, 83, 86, 118–19
Stipa calamagrostis 189
stock (Matthiola) 205
stone 117, 120–1
stonecrop (Sedum) 34, 54,
175
strawberry tree (Arbutus)
29, 32, 85, 148

sundrops (Oenothera
fruticosa) 59
sunflower (Helianthus
annus) 81, 83, 138
sunny areas 186–7
sweet box 51, 176
sweet peas (Lathyrus
odoratus) 41, 42, 66, 78,
131, 133, 138, 177
sweet rocket (Hesperis
matronalis) 176
swimming pools 92–5

tamarisk (Tamarix
ramosissima) 189
terraces 12, 13, 72
thyme (Thymus) 98
T. x citnodorus 'Aureus'
42, 96
T. 'Doone Valley' 96
T. 'Pink Chintz' 72
T. serpyllum 'Snowdrift' 96
T. vulgaris 96, 181
timber 116
decking 117
edgings 119
furniture 140–1
tobacco plant 63, 177
topiary 98, 152
topsoil 13, 102
town gardens, paved 36–9
Tradescantia 37
training trees 154–5
tree of heaven (Ailanthus
altissima) 29, 30
trees: deciduous 150–1
evergreen 152–3

planting 150–1, 152–3
staking 151
training 154–5
watering 111
trellis 47, 121, 123
trumpet creeper (Campsis
radicans) 166

umbrella plant (Cyperus) 35
umbrella plant (Darmera
peltata) 179
urns 56, 136

vegetables 111, 138, 180–1
veronica (Hebe) 16, 41, 66
Viburnum x bodnantense 89
V. x burkwoodii 177
V. carlcephalum 25
V. davidii 20, 25, 34, 93
V. farreri 44
V. opulus 96
V. plicatum 149
V. tinus 25, 125, 169
views 12, 84–7
vines (Vitis)
V. coignetiae (crimson
glory vine) 63, 65, 70,
72, 81, 82, 161
V. vinifera 'Purpurea' 77
Virginia creeper
(Parthenocissus
quinquefolia) 161

wall fountains 39
wallflowers (Erysimum) 20,
66
walls 120–1

water butts 111
water features 48–9, 91,
126–9, 137
moving water 47, 65,
128–9
ponds 13, 59–61, 78–9,
99, 126–7
raised water features 19,
30–1, 67, 89–90
running water 34–5, 73,
87
stepping stones 61, 129
water lilies (Nymphea) 129
179
N. tetragona 77
water plants 178–9
waterfalls 73, 113, 126,
128, 129
watering 110–11, 134
whitebeam (Sorbus aria) 16
wide gardens 24–7
wigwams 99, 130–1
wildflower meadows 117
wildlife gardens 12, 96–9
willow 99, 125, 151, 157
window boxes 134, 135
windy locations 58–61,
188–9
Wisteria 16, 18, 32, 51,
161
wooden tubs 135
worms, improving soil 104

Yew (Taxus baccata) 54,
124, 125, 153

Zinnia haageana 70

ACKNOWLEDGEMENTS

Key TL=top left; TC=top centre;
TR=top right; CL=centre left;
C=centre; CR=centre right;
BL=bottom left; BC=bottom
centre; BR bottom right

Gay Search's portrait, page 7,
© BBC Books

**Special photography Dr Bob
Gibbons • 01202 675 916**
8–9, 14–15, 16TL, BL,
17TL, TR, BL, BC, 22–3,
30TL, BL, 31TL, TR, 34–5,
38, 39TL, TR, BL, BC, 42TL,
BL, BC, 43TL, TR, 46TL, BL,
47TL, TR, C, 48–9, 52TL,
53TL, TR, BR, 56TL, BL,
60CL, TC, BL, C, 61TL, TC,
TR, 64BL, 65TL, TC, BL, BC,
69BR, 72, 73TL, TR, BL, 75,
78, 79, 82, 83TL, TR, BL,
BR, 94–5, 98–9, 100–01,
106BC, 108BL, 109BR,
110TR, 116CL, BL, 117TC,
BL, 118, 119TL, BL, 120BL,
BR, 122BR, 125TL, 132BR,
134TR, BR, 139TR, 149BC,

150BR, 156BR, 159BR,
161TR, 162–3, 173B, 181BC,
184BL, 186BR, 187B
Peter Wilson 86TL, BL,
87TL, TC, TR, BR
A–Z Botanical Collection Ltd
127TC, Mrs W Monks;
127BL, A Stenning;
129BC, BR, Adrian Thomas
Photography
Agriframes Ltd • 01342 310 000
132TC
Malcolm Birkitt
26TL, 27TL, TR
Brookbrae Ltd • 0181 876 9238
137TC
Capital Garden Products Ltd
• 01580 201 092 137BL
**Croft Studios/Designer:
Caroline Russell-Lacy**
01384 393 389 39CR, 137TL
Garden Answers/EMAP
17CR, 112, 113TR, CR,
BR, 126TR, 129TR, 143
Gloster Furniture Ltd
• 0117 931 5335 4TL,
140TL, BL, 144TR
Jean Goldberry • 01803 712 611

60TL, 61BL, BC, BR, 64TL,
65TR, 68TL, 69TL, TR
**David Goode, Sculptor • 01865
717 966** 137TR
Houses & Interiors Ltd
Victor Watts, 145T
Hozelock • 01844 291 881
110BL, 111TL,BL
**Marley Building Materials
Ltd/Paving • 01675 468**
400 57TL, right hand column:
1–4, 116TC, BR, 19TC
Marston & Langinger Ltd
• 0717 824 8818 4-5, 145CR
Natural Image/Robin Fletcher
64C, 87BL, 109CR, BC, 148R,
151BC, 153TL, 156TR,
157TL, 167TC, 177B, 182–3
Natural Image/Dr Bob Gibbons
2, 7, 26BL, C, 27BL, BC, 30C,
31BL, BCB, 42C, 43BL, BC,
46C, 47BL, 52BL, C, 53BL,
C, 56C, 57BC, 68BL, C, 69BL,
BC, 73BC, 83BC, 86C, 87BC,
109TR, TC, 120TR, 124CR,
125TC, 146–7, 148TR, 149TL,
TC, 150TR, 151TL, TC, 152BR,
153TC, 154TC, BL, 155TL,

TC, B, 157TC, 158BC, 159TC,
160TR, BR, 161BR, 164TC,
BC, 165TL, TC, C, BC, 166TR,
BC, 167TL, C, BC, 168TR,
BC, 169TL, TC, BL, BR,
170BL, 171TL, BR, 173TL, T
C, 174TR, BL, 175TL, TC, B,
176TC, BC, BR, 177TL, TR,
178L, TR, BR, 179TC, BC,
180TC, BC, 181TL, TC, BL,
183R, 184, BC, BR, 185TR,
BC, BR, 186TR, 187TC, 188TR,
CL, BC, 189TL, TR, BR
Natural Image/Dr Liz Gibbons
16C, 124TC, BC, 125BC,
161TL, 170TR, 184TC,
185TL
Natural Image/Peter Wilson
154BR, 159TL, BC, 161CR,
185BL, 187TL, 189BL
**Natural Wood Products Ltd/ The
Jolly Roger House Company**
• 01268 511 512 139BL
Osmo-Gard • 01895 234 899
113TL, 114–15, 121TL, BC,
122TC, 123TL, TC, BL, BC,
131TC, 133C, 138, 140TR,
141BR, 145BR,

Pots & Pitjoi • 01342 714 793
126BC, 134BC
Pedro Prà-Lopez 3, 6, 57 right
hand column: 5, 654BR,
108CR, 113BC, 119BC,
121TC, 128, 129TL, TC, BR,
136, 137BC, BR, 141TL, TR,
152TC, 13B, 157B, 158BR,
166BR, 176TL, BL, 179TL,
181BR, 184TL
Redwood Stone • 01749 677 777
Tim Mercer, 1
Tim Sandell 74–5, 90–1

Some photographs in this book
have previously appeared in The
Practical Gardening Encyclopedia,
© Abbeydale Press, 1996

Garden plan illustrators –
Jean Goldberry, Joanne Hipshon

Every effort has been made to
trace copyright holders. Any
unintentional omissions or
errors will be corrected in future
editions of this book.